Finding the Family:

The Coleman-Webb-Looney-Phillips Family History
Including Associated Kin

2015

By Celia Webb

On the cover: Mack H. Webb, Sr. with Mack H. Webb, Jr. circa 1965.

Finding the Family:

The Coleman-Webb-Looney-Phillips Family History
Including Associated Kin

2015

By Celia Webb

Pilinut Press, Inc.

Finding the Family:

The Coleman-Webb-Looney-Phillips Family History
Including Associated Kin

2015

Copyright 2015, Celia Webb

All rights reserved.
No part of this book may be reproduced, stored in a retrieval system or transmitted by any means, electronic, mechanical, photocopying, recording, or otherwise, without written permission from the author.

Book and cover design by Celia Webb

Pilinut Press, Inc.
www.pilinutpress.com

The Pilinut is the edible seed of the *Canarium ovatum* tree which is native to Southeast Asia. Tasting like sweet almonds, it is eaten for its health benefits including prevention of anemia and for nourishment of the brain and nervous system.

Library of Congress Control Number: 2015956968
Printed in Warrenton, Virginia

ISBN 978-1-944390-00-6

Dedication

To my beloved husband, Mack H. Webb, Jr.
and his warm and loving family who welcomed me
into their lives over thirty years ago.

Table of Contents

Acknowledgements i
Introduction 1
   Organization of this Book 8
Historical Framework 11
DNA Results and Their Meaning 19
   The Y-DNA Results for the Looney Line 19
   The Y-DNA Results for the Phillips Line 21
   The Y-DNA Results for the Webb Line 24
   About Autosomal DNA 26
   What does it mean? 27
The Coleman Line 33
   Rhode Coleman 34
   Frank C. Coleman 44
   Reuben Saunders 53
   Possible Slave Holders 56
      The James Nathaniel Sanders Line 56
The Looney Line 61
   Robert Looney 62
   James Knox Looney and Family 71
   The Slave Holders of the Everett Line 87
      The James Abbington Everett Line 87
      The Turner C. Everett Line 102
      The Henry Kaigler/Kegler Line 105
   Charlotte Everett 107
   Delia Hart 109
   Katherine Looney 111

- Burrell Looney 113
- Robert Emmett Looney 120
  - The Gilbert Line 121
  - The Lillie Bell Booker Line 131
- **Willie Coleman/Webb and Lucy Looney** 141
  - Willie Coleman/Webb 142
    - The Ida Jackson Line 147
  - Lucy Looney 151
    - Solomon "Sol" or "Saul" Phillips 154
- **The Children** 157
  - Pernella Coleman 158
  - Sarah Coleman 158
  - Savanna "Dora" Coleman 160
  - Jesse James Burks 160
  - Harry Gordon Phillips, Sr. 161
  - Virda Thelma Phillips 171
    - The Reed Line 173
    - The Lott Line 184
  - Joseph Garlin "Joe" Webb 187
    - The Wilson Line 191
    - The King Line 193
    - The Grissom Line 195
  - Flora Webb 199
    - The William Lee Perry Line 202
  - Bernice Webb 204
    - The Isaac Briggs Line 205
  - Mack Henry Webb, Sr. 206
    - The Ruth Mae Barnes Lines 213

The Hunter Line 213
The Harper Line 216
The Barnes Line 221
Mary Eliza "Mickey" Webb 224
George Austin William "Bill" Webb 225
Appendix A — Meaning and Origin of Surnames in this Family 228
Appendix B — Selected Bibliography 233
Appendix C — Will & Probate of James Abbington Everett 235
Appendix D — Maps 277
Appendix E — Mortality Information 297
Index 298
Meet the author 312
You can help! 312

Table of Figures

Figure 1 Surname Association Diagram 10
Figure 2 Ethnic Breakout of the Looney, Phillips, and Webb lines 27
Figure 3 Table of 1860 Census Results 30
Figure 4 The fire-damaged remains of the Quitman County, Georgia Marriage Register recording Frank Coleman's marriage to Flora Sanders. 47
Figure 5 Frank C. Coleman's only existing known signature is in the left margin of this extract of Book I-5, Sunflower County Deed Register 51
Figure 6 Robert Looney's signature from his will. 62
Figure 7 Marriage Certificate for James K. Looney and Nellie Everett. 72
Figure 8 James K. Looney's application for marriage to Tomanna Mack in 1903. The application preceeding his shows how the record would appear once a marriage had been completed. 78
Figure 9 World War I Draft Registration for Solomon Phillips 155
Figure 10 Atlantic Slave Trade Routes with relative numbers of slaves traded on particular routedepicted by the size of the arrows. The Bight of Biafra is the probable starting point for the African side of the family based on DNA evidence. 278

Figure 11 Location of Ballygilley, Isle of Mann the birthplace of Robert Looney (b. 1692) from whom the Looney side of the family descends. 279
Figure 12 Mississippi counties of primary interest to this history. 280
Figure 13 Terrain of Chickasaw Bayou, Vicksburg, Mississippi with the location of the Tennessee Regiments. 281
Figure 14 Sites of interest along Route 82 in Mississippi with regard to this history. 283
Figure 15 Location of Frank C. Coleman's Plantation south-east of Shaw, Mississippi. 284
Figure 16 Alabama counties of primary interest to this history. 285
Figure 17 Enlargement of Pike County, Alabama depicting locations of particular interest. 286
Figure 18 Georgia counties of primary interest to this history. 287
Figure 19 Tennessee counties of primary interest to this history. 288
Figure 20 Looney sites of interest in Hawkins County, Tennessee. 289
Figure 21 Selected Points of Interest in Memphis, Tennessee 292
Figure 22 Virginia counties of interest to this history. 294
Figure 23 Robert Looney Homestead at Looney Creek, Botetourt County, Virginia. 295
Figure 24 Average life span based on birth year. Note the large increase between 1930 and 1950 largely based on the discovery and widespread use of antibiotics and immunizations. 297
Figure 25 Causes of Death compared for 1850, 1900, and 2013. Infectious diseases are bolded. 297

Acknowledgements

Family histories are collaborations. Family members generously contribute their memories, share their photographs, family Bible entries, and other ephemera of family life. Without the input of family members, the history is barren, relying solely on official documentation when it can be found.

Fortunately, many family members have been very supportive of the effort to reclaim and celebrate the lives of our ancestors. They have answered my many questions with patience and generosity of spirit.

The Coleman/Webb/Looney/Phillips Family History documents the lives of the nucleus family of Willie Webb and Lucy Looney and their kin. The original family group is a blended family. Both Willie and Lucy had been married before they met each other and brought children into their new family. Both Willie and Lucy came from large families. The result is there are hundreds of people who are connected to the family.

I thank the many family member and friends who have helped in this effort and continue to provide me with support and I look forward to working with many more. Those family members and friends (some of whom have passed) include:

Mack Henry Webb, Sr.	Mack Henry Webb, Jr.
George Austin William Webb	Rev. Jesse James Burks

Ernestine Phillips Battle	Carl Looney
David Phillips	Angela Battle Greer
Laverne Gail Webb	Sandra Webb Dye
Anita Webb	Lucy Webb
Jackie Reed	Cheryl Looney-Johnson
Sheryl Webb-Broughton	Maxine Perry Saunders
Walter Randle	John Phillips, Jr.
Celess Funderburk	Larry W. Johnson
Wayne Modlin	Melissa Barger Thompson

The names of Larry W. Johnson and Wayne Modlin are probably not familiar to the family. These two men are distant cousins on the Looney side who have helped me tremendously with the Looney line prior to James K. Looney. Melissa Barger Thompson is related through the Coleman line. A talented researcher, we share information and strategies as we explore the Coleman line.

A number of librarians, archivists, funeral home personnel, and researchers have also been incredibly helpful, going out of their way to look up information in local repositories, answering questions about the local history, and recommending resources for further exploration. Special thanks to:

Karen Bullard, Troy Public Library, Pike County, Alabama	Gloria Bell, Byas Funeral Home, Indianola, Mississippi
Jennifer Rose, Sunflower County Library, Indianola, Mississippi	Vicki Wood, Tallahatchie County Library, Mississippi
Lawson Holladay, Lawyer, Sunflower County, Mississippi	Laurie Brasher, Researcher, Mississippi
Peggy Cook, Genealogy Society, Hawkins County, Tennessee	Will Wilson, Park Guide, Vicksburg National Military Park, Mississippi
Linda Williams, Morgan County Records Archives, Georgia	Tina Sansone, Researcher, Genealogy Society, Shelby County, Tennessee
William Ashley Vaughan, Researcher, Mississippi	Lee Miller, Researcher, Houston County, Georgia

Introduction

As you read this history of the Coleman-Webb-Looney-Phillips family, it will be helpful to have some understanding of the process and limitations of genealogical research. First of all, it is important to know that I am not a professional genealogist and am only an enthusiastic amateur. My father did much research on his father's line and introduced me to some of the resources and techniques.

My husband, Mack H. Webb, Jr. and I became interested in learning what we could of his family when we realized he knew very little about who his forefathers were. Since then I have worked diligently to uncover what I could and began what I call the Coleman-Webb-Looney-Phillips project. The project started with the blended family of Willie Webb and Lucy Looney as its nucleus and worked out from there. DNA tests on several family members led to some interesting insights and made us even more curious.

James K. Looney is my husband's great-grandfather. It was clear from what records I could find, there was much to be learned. Part of the puzzle of James's history is determining who his father might be. For help in learning as much as possible it would be necessary to find a direct male descendent who would be willing to do a Y-DNA test. Fortunately, family members did volunteer to assist, not just in the Looney line but also the Phillips and Webb lines. As a result, more is now known, as you will see documented here.

Genealogy Challenges

In order to make the most of DNA results, traditional genealogical techniques must be applied. Genealogists search for records to try to piece together a history of a family and interview family members both to learn more family stories and find clues for the challenges in such research.

Challenges abound for anyone tackling such a project. The first challenge is "Was a record created?" For many reasons records might not ever have been created. For example, birth and death records were not required by many states until well into the 1900s.

Another challenge is "Did the record survive?" Many records have burned in courthouse fires, or been damaged in floods, or been thrown away after someone's death.

A third challenge is "Where is the record?" The United States does not have a central repository for all records. States, counties, universities, libraries, archives, funeral homes, cemeteries, and private collections may contain records of interest to a particular line of inquiry. Determining who might hold the record and then obtaining it is part of the challenge.

A fourth challenge is "Can the record be read?" Many records have faded, been torn, splattered with coffee, damaged by flooding, and other such circumstances which may make it difficult to decipher the entire record. In other cases the handwriting (as all of the old records were written by hand usually in cursive, not block print) can be hard to read. Spelling was not standardized until the first quarter of the 1900s, people recorded what they heard; spelling phonetically. Additionally, if you are searching online resources, you then have the added layer of obscurement when someone transcribed the information in order for it to be "searchable".

A fifth challenge is "Is the record available?" The primary barrier here is privacy laws. Many states do not make records public until some long period after the creation of the record. Common time periods range from 50 to 100 years depending on the jurisdiction controlling the record and the type of record. The U.S. Census, which has been conducted every ten years since 1790, is made public 72 years after the census was completed. The latest one available now is the 1940 Census.

A final challenge for individual records is "Is the record accurate?" The accuracy of a record depends on what the person who provided the information knew. Could they remember or did they ever know? Birth dates for people born prior to laws requiring birth certificates are frequently different in each record. People did not celebrate birthdays like they do now. Many people were illiterate and did not keep a written record. Although family bibles are often cited as a place to find birth dates or at least years, a family had to own one, somebody had to be able to write, and the book had to be kept, in order for it to become a source. Many members of this family lived in Mississippi prior to 1940; some family lines have been in Mississippi for as far back as it is possible to trace. Mississippi did not start requiring birth and death certificates until 1912 and compliance was reportedly spotty in the first few years.

Accuracy also depends on the person providing the correct information. Sometimes people deliberately provided misinformation. The reasons were many, but the end result is a record which must be examined carefully and measured against the bulk of information found. And then there is always the possible layer of confusion created by the person who wrote the record. Did they hear what the provider of information said correctly? Did they record the information in the right place on the form? Were they in a hurry and didn't take the time to make sure they got the information right?

Another aspect of genealogy that puts limits on what might be learned is expense. Most records cost something to obtain whether it is $3.50 for making a copy and mailing it to you, the $15 to $50 research fee charged by most repositories for the time it takes their personnel to retrieve the record and get it to you, the cost of hiring a local researcher to pull records from courthouses or local museums or archives, membership in one of the online genealogy database collections, or the hundreds of dollars of DNA testing; it all adds up.

Family members who are willing to share what they know are the best resource for learning more. They can give you what records cannot—stories that help you understand individual family members. Family members can put flesh on the bones of the simple facts contained in the records. It has been extremely helpful to me to "meet" (mostly via telephone conversations and e-mail exchanges) the extended family. I look forward to meeting many more.

It is also important to note that my primary research is on the period of time prior to and including the year 1940. This aligns with the last Census release and also respects the privacy of living family members. For those family members who have passed, I try to recover what I can, so the larger family will know when someone passed and where their grave might be found should someone wish to pay their respects. Keeping biographies of family members also helps retain them in memory and keep them from being forgotten. Additionally, younger family members benefit by knowing how they connect to the family as a whole, who their people are, what they accomplished, where they lived, and what they experienced. Assistance by family members is essential to keep the family history up-to-date and I appreciate the family members who help me in this effort.

Some notes on the availability of records will be helpful for understanding what might be learned. The U.S. Census started in 1790 for the purpose of assessing how many men could be raised to fight. Therefore the first Census only recorded free white men over the age of 21. Every Census has collected different information. Women, children, and slaves were inventoried by number and age group until the 1850 Census. In 1850, women and children were named but no relationships of persons occupying a household were specified. Slaves were recorded in a separate Schedule in both 1850 and 1860 and only listed by age, mulatto or black, if deaf, dumb, or blind, and gender unless over the age of 100 when a name would be recorded.

The Slave Schedules of 1850 and 1860 are probably fairly accurate in terms of distinguishing between mulatto and black because mulatto slaves were worth 3 to 5 times the amount of a slave of similar age and gender. In later Censuses these descriptions of race are much less reliable. The original definition of mulatto is a person of mixed racial heritage with one black parent and one white parent. People may have been recorded under different descriptions depending on the year of the Census and the subjective opinion of the enumerator. Many states particularly in the South enacted "one drop" rules where a person having any amount of African heritage was recorded as black. The Census of 1870 is the first time all people are recorded by name.

The State of Mississippi, where so much of the family lived during the latter part of the 1800s and the first half of the 1900s, is a challenging state for genealogy research. Birth and death certificate requirements did not get passed into law until 1912. Many county records were destroyed by floods of the great Mississippi River and there were a couple of courthouse fires as well. So far, there are very few records which have been digitized and are, therefore, searchable in any other way than making a trip into the County Courthouse or Department of Archives and History. Mississippi privacy laws restrict access to the records to direct relatives or legal representatives with varying time restrictions up to 100 years from the record's creation. Additionally, the requestor needs a fairly accurate idea of when the person was born or died in order to successfully obtain a copy of the appropriate certificate.

Despite all the obstacles, much has been learned about the family's history and more will be uncovered as time goes on.

This summary does not include many images of the original documents found during the research because these documents are very difficult to read when printed in this format. The original documents are much larger than the standard letter-sized page. As a result, when printed they must be reduced and therefore become even harder to read. A few enlargements of particular documents are included to illustrate occasional details in the text. All census material comes from the National Archives and was found through both Ancestry.com and FamilySearch.com. Other material was obtained through county courthouses, funeral homes, cemetery administrative offices, local archives and museums, FindAGrave.com, and the Mississippi Department of Archives and History. Various libraries provided images of the obituaries. Historical perspectives, photographs, maps, and information came from searches on the web, books, city directories, magazine and newspaper articles from the time period, funeral programs, and family interviews. I have collected some family photographs, but have not included them in this work knowing that their reproduction in this format would be extremely poor as their age and condition makes them difficult to reproduce here. Also, there are questions about copyright ownership with many of these photographs.

  This is a work in progress. I continue to research our family and hope to answer more questions as time goes on. Family histories are endlessly engaging and new chapters of family life are being lived as you read these lines. There is always some new aspect to explore and one could spend many, many years happily exploring and searching for those answers. If I waited until the family history was complete, nothing would ever be shared with the larger family. So I am publishing this admittedly incomplete work to give the family as much detail as I have found to date.

Organization of this Book

The scope of this book is large. At least part of this family has been in this country for roughly 300 years. Some members had multiple marriages. There are name changes for reasons beyond marriage. To more fully understand the family's roots, it is necessary to explore slave holding families at least one of which contributed to the family's DNA. Other slave holding families contributed a name and certainly knowing the history of the slave holding family gives us a picture of where our family was and what they were doing. There are families for whom quite a bit has been discovered and others for whom relatively little has emerged. There are families who preceded the union of Willie Webb and Lucy Looney and then there are the families whose children married their offspring.

The book follows major paternal surnames, introducing the surnames that feed into that family line in a loosely chronological way. The lines preceding the Webb-Looney union are covered first, then the family of Willie Webb and Lucy Looney, and then the families which married their children. Slave holding families are included with the person(s) believed held by them.

Some information can be found in several sections. This is to help family historians who are referring to this book who are interested in their particular family line and will probably only read that section pertaining directly to their search. There is also an index of names which will aid those researchers.

It helps to have a mental picture of how the family puzzle fits together. The diagram on page 10 shows how various surnames enter the picture. There are a number of other surnames who touch the family briefly which will get mentioned in the text but are not explored in any depth and not included in this diagram. One might visualize it as an hourglass with a large number of people contributing to create Willie and Lucy and then the subsequent fanning out of people as their children marry and have children of their own. The greyed boxes form major sections of this book with some of the associated families depicted in the diagram being expanded upon in that section.

The personal data of living family members is not included.

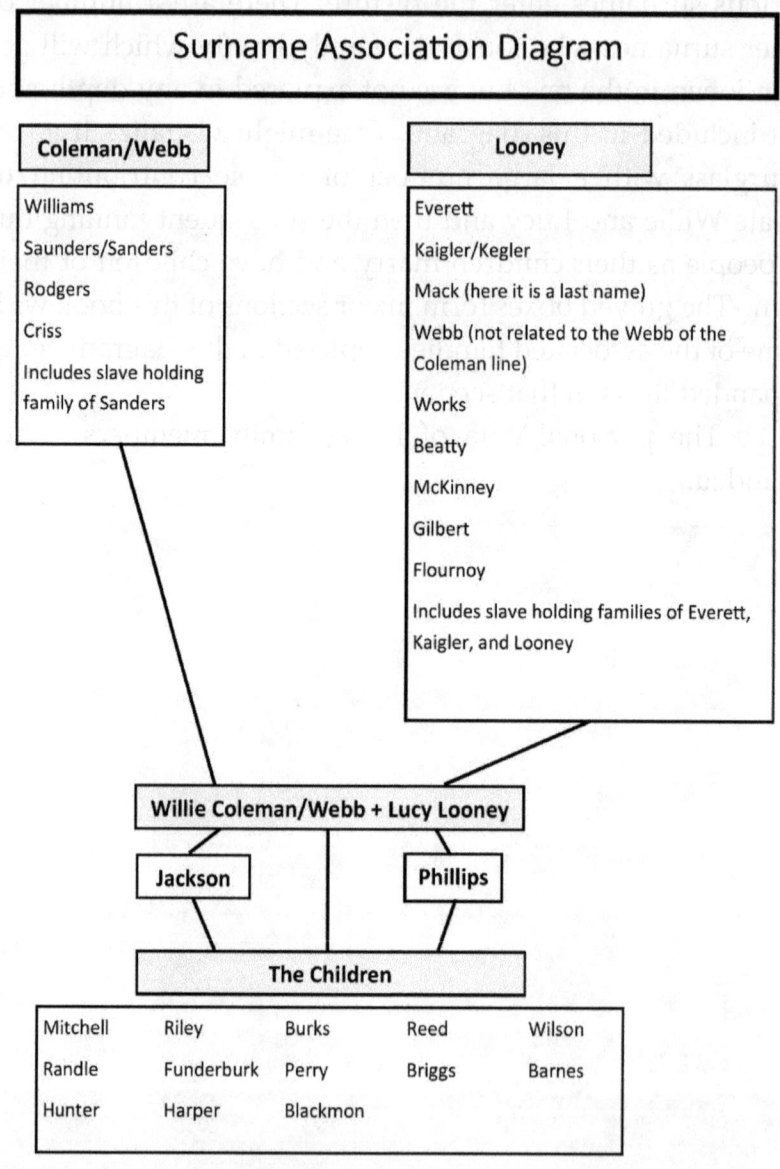

Figure 1 Surname Association Diagram

Historical Framework

The Coleman/Webb/Looney/Phillips project is naturally shaped by historical events. This family has origins in both Europe and Africa. In writing about various family members I include information about life during their lifetime. However, there are some international and national events which influenced the flow of people, their occupational and educational opportunities, and their legal status which it will be helpful to outline here. The following timeline gives a framework for understanding the family history in light of the larger picture of man's history edited to relate to our family.

Year	Event
793-1284	Viking Invasions of British Isles.
1581	First African slaves brought to St. Augustine, Florida.
1603	Emigration from Ireland to Colonial America begins.
1619	Twenty slaves imported to Virginia to work on tobacco plantations.
1636	Colonial America enters the slave trade with a Yankee clipper sailing from Massachusetts.
1641	Massachusetts first state to legalize slavery.

Year	Event
1643	The New England Confederation passes fugitive slave law.
1650	Rhode Island restricts slavery.
1654	Virginia passes law granting blacks the right to hold slaves.
1657	Virginia passes fugitive slave law.
1662	Virginia passes Hereditary Slavery Law decreeing children of black mothers "shall be bond or free according to the condition of the mother".
1663	Maryland legalizes slavery.
1664	New York and New Jersey legalize slavery.
1664	Maryland first colony to take action against marriage between white woman and black males.
1664	Maryland first colony to mandate lifelong servitude for all black slaves. New York, New Jersey, the Carolinas, and Virginia all pass similar laws.
1666	Maryland passes fugitive slave law.

Year	Event
1668	New Jersey passes fugitive slave law.
1670	Virginia passes law preventing free blacks and Indians from holding Christian (i.e. white) slaves.
1676	Bacon's Rebellion in Virginia.
1680	Virginia passes law forbidding blacks and slaves from bearing arms, prevents blacks from gathering in large number, and mandates harsh punishments for slaves who assault Christians or attempt to escape.
1682	Virginia declares all imported black slaves are slaves for life.
1694	South Carolina starts rice plantations and the importation of slaves rises dramatically.
1695–1829	English Crown enacts severe Penal Codes; the cause of some migration to the Americas.
1776-1783	Revolutionary War.
2 Jan 1788	Georgia ratifies the Constitution and becomes a State.
25 Jun 1788	Virginia ratifies the Constitution and becomes a State.

Year	Event
1789-1833	Land grants awarded to veterans of the Revolutionary War. Nine states also provided land grants in their western regions shaping the futures of Kentucky, Ohio, Indiana, Maine, and Tennessee. The states providing veterans with bounty land included: Connecticut, Georgia, Maryland, Massachusetts, New York, North Carolina, Pennsylvania, South Carolina, and Virginia.
1794	U.S. prohibits the outfitting of ships for the purpose of carrying slaves.
1 Jun 1796	Tennessee ratifies the Constitution and becomes a State.
1800	U.S. enacts stiff penalties on American citizens participating in the slave trade between two foreign countries.
1 Mar 1803	Ohio admitted to the union and becomes a State.
1807	Britain, the principal slave trading nation, bans the Atlantic slave trade.
1807	U.S. bans the trading of slaves effective 1 Jan 1808.
1807	Peak year of importation of slaves to the U.S. totaling 28,892 people.

Year	Event
1812-1815	War of 1812 between the U.S. and Britain.
1815-1858	Land grants awarded to veterans of the War of 1812 leading to the settling of Arkansas, Illinois, Michigan and Missouri.
10 Dec 1817	Mississippi admitted to the union and becomes a State.
1817	Illegal slave trade peaks with 1420 slave brought to the U.S.
14 Dec 1819	Alabama admitted to the union and becomes a State.
1820	U.S. deems slave trading an act of piracy punishable by death.
26 May 1830	Indian Removal Act signed into law to move all Native Americans living east of the Mississippi to the west.
27 Sep 1830	Choctaw Indians sign the Treaty of Dancing Rabbit Creek which grants the U.S. government their lands in Mississippi including the area which becomes Sunflower, Leflore, and Bolivar Counties.
1831	The Trail of Tears begins with the removal of the Choctaw.

Year	Event
1832	Chickasaw Indians sign Treaty of Pontotoc Creek ceding land including the northern most counties in Mississippi to the U.S. government in exchange for land and roughly $3million which went unpaid for 30 years.
1836	Portugal, the second largest slave trading nation, bans the trading of slaves.
20 Jan 1837	Michigan admitted to the union and becomes a State.
3 Mar 1845	Florida admitted to the union and becomes a State.
9 Sep 1850	California admitted to the union and becomes a State.
1860	Last group of slaves brought illegally to the U.S. totaling 110 people.
1861	Start of the Civil War.
1862	Battle of Vicksburg, Mississippi
1865	Civil War ends.
1865	Emancipation declared effective 15 December 1865.
1865-1877	Reconstruction.
9 Jul 1868	14th Amendment to U.S. Constitution ratified granting citizenship to former slaves.

Year	Event
1914	Start of World War I.
5 Jun 1917	Draft Registration in U.S. for men born between 6 Jun 1886 and 5 Jun 1896.
5 Jun 1918	Draft Registration in U.S. for men who turned 21 since last registration.
24 Aug 1918	Draft Registration in U.S. for men who turned 21 since 5 Jun 1918.
12 Sep 1918	Draft Registration in U.S. for men born between 11 Sep 1872 and 12 Sep 1900. In total the Draft Registration for WWI results in the registration of approximately 24 million men born between 1872 and 1900 about 98% of men born in that period.
1 Sep 1939	Start of World War II.
16 Sep 1940	Selective Service Act signed into law. In total from Nov 1940 to Oct 1946 over 10 million men registered. Men born between 17 Feb 1877 and 31 Jul 1900 may have registered for both world wars.
7 Dec 1941	Attack on Pearl Harbor.
8 Dec 1941	U.S. enters WWII.

Year	Event
1945	World War II ends.
1940-1970	The Great Migration is the largest mass internal movement of people. It outranks the migration of any other ethnic group. Some historians divide it into two periods. The first being between 1910 and 1930 when 1.5 million people move. A lull followed during the Depression years. Our family members participated in the Second Great Migration when 5 million African-Americans move out of southern States to northern industrial cities and western states.
Nov 2000	Alabama becomes the last state to overturn a law banning interracial marriage.

DNA Results and Their Meaning

The following information reflects DNA test results for three family lines within our family. These results include Y-DNA results and autosomal results. The first results to be examined are the Y-DNA test results. It is important to note that DNA testing conducted for the purpose of genealogical research does not look at the same set of markers as DNA testing conducted for paternity reasons. The results of these tests are not sufficient to conclude paternity by a specific individual; instead, the results identify a family line; further genealogy work must be done to identify individuals who may have been the father. Y-DNA tests were conducted for the Looney-Lee Ann Webb line (which includes Cecil, Asa, Robert Emmett, Willie Bell, and so on), the Webb line and the Phillips line. The Y-DNA is passed directly from father to son.

The Y-DNA Results for the Looney Line

We will look at the results of the Looney line first. All male relatives descended in a direct male line from James Knox Looney would have the same Y-DNA. All relatives, male and female, who have James Knox Looney in their line will have part of his DNA and share his ancestors.

The haplogroup for the Looney Y-DNA is I-M253. I-M253 is a Northern European group which shows up most often in the Scandinavian countries, England, Ireland, and in other places invaded by the Vikings.

The matches confirm that James Knox Looney is from a Looney line which originated in the Isle of Mann which is located between Ireland and Great Britain. People from the Isle of Mann are referred to as Manx. You may run across this term as you read more about this line.

I am working now with the matches identified and their family historians to see how much of the line we can verify. We already know for sure that it is the Robert Looney (b.1692 Ballagilley Farm or Kirk Lonan, Maughould County, Isle of Mann d. 14 Sep 1769 Reed Creek, Augusta, VA) and Elizabeth Llewillyn (Llewellyn) (b. 1696 d. 20 Aug 1747 Augusta, VA) line. This line has large numbers of children at every level so it may take some time to verify the exact line subsequent to the most distant known ancestors. Hopefully a match will come up that is very close to our direct descendant of the Looney male line results and we will be able to settle the matter.

Based on other DNA results, it is likely that James Knox Looney was of mixed racial heritage with a white father and possibly a mulatto mother. James Knox Looney lists his mother with various birthplaces. If it were possible to trace her lineage back, it is likely her line would have entered the country through South Carolina or Virginia given the time period when her ancestors would have arrived.

I am continuing to work with the data, other genealogists, and the matches found in the database to see what other insights might be discerned. I am quite hopeful that we will have a line identified for James Knox Looney. Because he was a child born into slavery, we may never find a written record of his birth or an acknowledgement of his existence by his father. Nevertheless, the family stories about his father and the DNA of the direct male descendants in the family carry narrow down the field significantly. I had already identified a likely candidate prior to this test and the results keep this candidate as a possibility requiring further research. Working with several other Looney genealogists has turned up another possible candidate. I am now trying to do as much verification as is possible given the records and history available. We will be comparing the results with others in the Looney surname project. In particular, there are two participants who showed as the "most likely to share a common ancestor within the last 4 generations". Neither of these men have been able to trace back their Looney ancestors far enough to find the shared ancestor with the James Knox Looney, so part of the work is to see if anything further can be done in establishing their lines.

The Y-DNA Results for the Phillips Line

According to 23andMe, a DNA testing service:

"Most of your relatives will actually fall outside of your haplogroup, because your haplogroup only tells you about direct paternal or maternal ancestors. Typically, the DNA mutations that define a haplogroup occurred thousands of years ago, so many pairs of people who share a haplogroup are not closely related. .... Matches are labeled as "distant cousins" when the degree of relationship is difficult to estimate, due to the small amount of DNA shared. For every degree of separation in a relationship, the average percent DNA shared drops by half, so that the percent DNA shared remaining is quite small when you get to distant cousins. The vast majority of relatives found by DNA Relatives share a common ancestor within the last five to ten generations. A few may be more distantly related."

The Y-DNA test results for the Phillips line show the haplogroup E-M2 which is a line out of the west coast of Africa often associated with Cameroon and Nigeria. Interestingly there were only four matches in the database at this time. Those four matches were distant and place the connecting person in the American Colonial period or even further back. None of the matches bear the surname Phillips. The Phillips line has an admixture of European and Central Asian larger than the 12.5% inherited through the Lucy Looney/James K. Looney line. The remaining 4.5% most probably came from Lucy's first husband, Solomon Phillips, who was recorded as mulatto in the 1920 Census, and not through the Reed line which thus far has no indicators of being mixed race prior to marrying into the Phillips line.

During the Colonial Period, it was possible for people to intermingle. There are recorded cases of African men fathering children with white women out of wedlock. This is of particular interest because these children were most often given the surname of the mother and treated with the mother's status. This intermingling occurred most frequently between the slave and indentured servant classes. According to the historian and foremost expert on "free Negroes of the colonial period", Paul Heinegg, as paraphrased by Henry Louis Gates, Jr. in "Finding Your Roots":

"There are only 250 court records of white women bearing the children of black men, Negro slaves, on record in all of American colonial history. This means that less than 1 percent of the black people in colonial Virginia could be mulattoes descended from white women."

As an example, there was a case in Virginia involving an indentured servant named Mary Phillips. Mary Phillips (born circa 1670) was the servant of Mr. Thomas Banks in Northumberland County, Virginia. On 16 July 1690 she confessed in Northumberland County court that she had a child by her master's "negro" named William Smyth. This child was probably the "mulatto" William Phillips (b. 16 Mar 1690) bound over on 19 July 1710 as apprentice to Thomas Banks' wife, Elizabeth, until the age of 24. Mary had another "mulatto" son named Thomas (b. 16 Jan 1693/4) who, on 15 August 1694, she bound over as an apprentice to Thomas Downing until the age of thirty years by indenture recorded in Northumberland County [Orders 1678-98, pt. 2, 668; 1699-1713, pt. 2, 511, 684]. The quotes indicate the descriptions used in the records.

Fornication and bearing children out of wedlock carried heavy penalties which were doubled when the crime was committed with a black person. The mother's term of servitude was extended by four years and she may well have been lashed. In another such case, Elizabeth Banks (b. 1665) found guilty in 1683; "thirty-nine lashes on the bare back well laid on" formed part of the punishment. The child would be bound over to a term of indenture of 30 years.

William and Thomas Phillips are considered possible fathers for 8 children born as free mulattoes who lived in various counties of Virginia and North Carolina. Records for this period are sparse and tracing these families forward through time may not be possible. It is recorded that in at least one of these households of the 8 children was a white woman. I mention it as a further example of the continuing mix of races at this time in history.

The matches for the Phillips line show a connection to the Melungeon people of Applachia. It is likely that the Melungeon people started with people who were racially mixed. The Melungeons claimed to be descended from the Portuguese and Indians. DNA shows a different story. As C. S. Everette states in the article "Melungeon History and Myth" published in 1999 in the Appalachain Journal, Volume 26, number 4 page 369:

> "Readers need to be aware of the fact that throughout much of the 19th century and well into the early 20th. "Portuguese" like the frequently heard "Cherokee Indian Princess," was nothing other than a euphemism for African-American heritage. In fact that is precisely the way "Portuguese" has been understood by generations of black Americans. "Portuguese" and "Indian" were contrived defensive mechanisms employed by both light- and dark-pigmented individuals of partial African Heritage to hide or disguise racial identity in an oppressive social climate where skin color essentially determined one's legal status."

One of David's Y-DNA matches is a direct descendent of Valentine Collins, one of a group of Melungeons who first settled in Hawkins County, Tennessee before spreading throughout West Virginia, Tennessee, Kentucky, and Illinois. Hawkins County at the time was part of the frontier and sparsely inhabited.

The Y-DNA Results for the Webb Line

The Webb direct male line haplogroup is also E-M2 with the subclade (a smaller division of a haplogroup) of L485. Only one distant match showed up in the database and the match was not to Phillips line even though both the Phillips line and the Webb line share an E-M2 haplogroup. The individuals tested in the Phillips and Webb lines are autosomal matches as the nephew and uncle they are; which makes sense as we know them to be related through Lucy Looney as opposed to a direct male line. That is an example of how far back the haplogroup designations reach. This branch of lineage was born in West Africa about 25,000 years ago when the land was fertile. With the drying of the Sahara, these ancestors migrated south into sub-Saharan Africa. This marker was spread in part due to the migrations of the Bantu speakers throughout Africa in the past 2,500 years.

The Webb line shows a mix of Scandinavian and Southern European in his European percentage in his autosomal results. It turns out that such a mixture is not unknown in England and Ireland; both being seafaring nations and invaded repeatedly by the Vikings, Romans, and French and trading with nations around the Mediterranean. British royalty married Spanish royalty and many other Britons followed suit. So this result is in keeping with the finding that the Looney line originated at the Isle of Mann.

About Autosomal DNA

The following test results are from an autosomal DNA test which is separate from the Y-DNA test results explained above. Y-DNA test gives specific information on the Looney direct male descendant line while the autosomal test gives insight into both parents' lines. The autosomal test results give a breakout of the origins of people in the pedigree of the person tested. Here is the ethnic breakout for the Looney, Phillips, and Webb lines. Comparison of the lines is useful for identifying which admixtures are present in the separate lineage lines. Knowing these results gives clues as to the different genetic make-up of the ancestors line and help define search criteria.

Autosomal DNA is DNA from one of our chromosomes located in the cell nucleus. It generally excludes the sex chromosomes. Humans have 22 pairs of autosomal chromosomes and one pair of sex chromosomes. You inherited your autosomal DNA from both of your parents, all four grandparents, all eight great-grandparents, etc. Results from this test generally include matches from all of your lines.

You get about half of your autosomal DNA from each parent. Siblings will have an ethnic markers breakout that is basically the same. Small variances may occur but are not statistically significant. Your children in turn received about half of their autosomal DNA from each of their parents. Each time autosomal DNA passes from parent to child, it is partly mixed. This is called "recombination". The randomness of recombination means that after 5 to 6 generations you may have much less autosomal DNA from one line than another.

Random recombination means that while autosomal DNA and genetic matching are powerful tools, beyond 3rd cousins it is possible to have a cousin who does not show up as a match to you. Therefore, genetic matching proves relationships, but failure to match does not always disprove them.

Ethnic Breakout	Looney	Phillips	Webb
African	**60%**	**82%**	**77%**
West Africa	53%	74%	71%
East Central Africa	5%	6%	5%
South Central Africa	2%	2%	1%
European	**39%**	**17%**	**23%**
British Isles or West/Central Europe	24%	17%	
Scandinavia			13%
Southern Europe	15%		10%
Native American	**1%**		
Central Asian		**1%**	

Figure 2 Ethnic Breakout of the Looney, Phillips, and Webb lines.

What does it mean?

According to Wikipedia's article titled "Genealogical DNA Test" approximately 30% of African-Americans have a European Y-chromosome haplogroup. About 58% of

African-Americans have the equivalent of one great-grandparent (12.5% of their chromosomes) of European ancestry. Only 5% have Native American ancestry. About 75% of African-Americans are from regions in West Africa.

There are two possibilities for the 1% returns.

>**Possibility 1.** The result is within the margin of error of 15% of the test and could mean there is no Native American in the Looney lineage or Central Asian in Phillips lineage. As an example, my father received a test result of 2% Native American. However, all of his line arrived in this country in the late 1870's. His line has been well researched and documented and includes no Native Americans at all.

>**Possibility 2.** There is a distant Native American or Central Asian ancestor in some or one of the family lines leading into the individuals who were tested in the Looney and Phillips lines. By comparing the three samples, we know there is no Native American or Central Asian in James Knox Looney or his ancestors specifically. Careful selection of other family members for DNA testing may lead to results which could provide even greater clarity on which family line, if any, contains Native American heritage.

The percentage indicates the possible number of generations between the tested person and the ancestor who would have been Native American or Central Asian. With each generation the percentage cuts in half. So if someone's father is full-blooded Native American and the other parent is full-blooded European, then that person will be 50% Native American and 50% European. To get to the 1% return (which is rounded from 0.781%) you have to go back 7 generations to a great-great-great-great-great grandparent. At this generational level, there are normally 128 people in your direct line. (There can be a smaller number if cousins married along the way.) If you use the standard 20- to 25-year calculation for generations, we would be looking for a Native American born around 1775 or so. In the Looney case we know that James Knox Looney fathered the children in the line tested late in life, so that adds, perhaps, another 30 years to the distance adjusting the date to around 1745.

With regard to the European ancestry of 39%, the Looney-Lee Ann line can be confident that roughly 12.5% comes from James Knox Looney. That means other contributors to their DNA had European markers. Tests of other relatives would be needed to determine which lines also include Europeans and to determine in which generation they might be found. For instance, autosomal tests of some of the 1st cousins from the James Knox Looney and Lee Ann Webb line might help define the answer. A test of a half-brother where they exist might be useful as well since it might tell us more about the mother's line.

You may be interested in the article at this link about understanding autosomal test results with regard to low percentage origin categories.

http://www.dnaexplain.com/publications/pdfs/autosomaldnatesting5-20-09.pdf

With regard to the African results, West Africa is the most common set of markers in African-Americans. The largest numbers of slaves brought to America came from the West African coast. There was a small number brought in from the East Coast of Africa on Yankee clippers during a period when all the concessions on the West Coast were controlled by England and Portugal. The Cambridge University Press Database shows 361,100 or 3.8% of all slaves transported to the New World were taken to colonial North America and later the United States. More than 40% of the slaves taken out of Africa went to Brazil.

Despite relatively small numbers of slaves being imported to the States, by 1825 there were about 1,750,000 slaves. More than 80% of them had been born in America. Legal importation stopped 1 January 1808. By 1860, the number of slaves had increased to 3,953,761 or 12.7% of the total U.S. population. The reason the figure became so large when no slaves had been imported for more than two generations is because U.S. law allowed chattel slavery where people are treated as personal property (chattel) and the offspring of slaves were also legally bound as slaves.

Total - 1860 CENSUS	
Total Population	31,183,582
Free Persons of African Descent	476,748
Total Free Population	27,233,198
Total Number of Slaves	3,953,761
Slaves as % of Population	12.7%
Total Persons of African Descent	4,427,132
Free Persons of African Descent as % of total population of African descent	10.8%
Total Number of Families	5,155,608
Total Number of Slaveholders	393,975
% of Families Owning Slaves	7.6%

Figure 3 Table of 1860 Census Results

Another practice which shaped slavery procedures in America was called "entailing". First adopted by Barbados, Virginia passed a law in 1705 which allowed planters to treat slaves as real estate attaching them to the land to maintain viable working units in probate settlements. The person who inherited the land also inherited the means to work the land. This practice meant the slave could not be sold and had to be passed to the son who inherited. They could, however, be removed to other tracts their current master owned. Usually, not all family slaves were entailed, and these might be freely sold or bequeathed. While a man might give one or two slave children whom he owned outright to a daughter or grandchild, he usually willed almost all the slaves, entailed or not, to one or more of his sons. This practice was abolished after the American Revolution, but it remained a common inheritance scheme to leave the majority of slaves to the person who inherited the land.

Chattel slavery is just one form of slavery. The other forms are lower caste which freezes everyone in the society to their place for their lifetime, bonded labor where a person serves for a period of time to pay off a loan, forced labor when a person works against his will under the threat of violence or punishment, and forced marriage where a person (usually the female) is forced by violence, threats, and intimidation to engage in sexual acts and domestic duties without any personal control.

The largest number of slaves were exported from the Bight of Benin (bight means gulf or bay) formerly known as the Slave Coast. The second largest exporting region was the Bight of Biafra with over 1.5 million slaves shipped (13.7% of the total shipped). Major trading ports of Bight of Biafra included Calabar and Bonny, both located in present day Nigeria, and the Port of Bimbia located in present day Cameroon. DNA results show this is the region were the Webb family and the Phillips male line originated, specifically from Cameroon. This may well be true for other parts of the family.

The majority of slaves traded from the Cameroon coast came from inland invasions as well as from the neighboring Bataga, Bassa, and Bulu. Four groups accounted for 62 percent of the people carried out of the River and from Bimbia during the trading period: the Tikari, Douala-Bimbia, Banyangi and Bakossi, and Bamileke. The Bamileke Chiefs and Kings were the major suppliers of slaves that left the coasts of Cameroon during the Atlantic slave trade.

Nine ports in the United States participated in the slave trade although at different times and for different lengths of time. Those ports were: Boston, Massachusetts; Newport, Rhode Island; New York, New York (~27,000 slaves through these northern ports); Annapolis, Maryland; Tidewater Region of Virginia (~128,000 slaves through these Chesapeake ports); Charleston and St. Helena Island, South Carolina; Savannah, Georgia (~210,000 slaves through these ports); Biloxi, Mississippi, and New Orleans, Louisiana (~22,000 slaves through these Gulf ports).

The Coleman Line

Rhode Coleman

The earliest recorded Coleman in our family line is a woman named Martha Coleman who was born in 1810 in Georgia. She had at least two sons; Rhode and Milton. From the birth information of Rhode's children, Rhode moved to Pike County Alabama between 1854 and 1857 which is probably when the Martha and Milton moved there too.

Pike County was organized on 17 December 1821 and is one of the oldest counties in Alabama. The territory which contained what became Pike County Alabama was taken from the Creek Indians under the terms of the Treaty of Fort Jackson signed on 9 August 1814. In the mid-1830's there were a number of clashes with groups of Indians as they were removed and resettled from nearby parts of Alabama under the Treaty of Cusseta. Although Pike County was not directly part of this round of removals, there was concern that the Creeks would attempt to join the Seminoles in Florida and thus attempt to travel along the Pea River which flows along the eastern side of the county. In 1838 a site was chosen for the new county seat of Troy. It was an oak-covered hill overlooking the cane breaks. There was an Indian trail which traversed the hill in a north-south direction. This old Indian trail became military road number 6 to transport troops and supplies from Fort Barrancas in Florida to Fort Mitchell in Alabama. The road had to be cut from the wilderness. To mark the route, three blazes were cut into trees along the roadway. Roads thus marked were often referred to as "Three Chopped Ways". The road through Troy was called Three Notch Road and the moniker stuck. Three Notch Road is important to our family history because family no doubt arrived in the county along this road and parts of the family lived and are buried along this road as well.

The only information we have on Martha is her entry in the 1870 Census. Most likely, she died before the 1880 Census was conducted. Martha and Milton lived next door to Rhode and his family in 1870. Rhode Coleman was born in Georgia between 1827 and 1833. According to the Census of 1900 Rhode, his wife, Harriet (b. 1835 Georgia) and both sets of their parents were all born in Georgia. The names of the parents are not recorded in that census and we may never discover all their names. However, it is likely they were born in the first decade of the 1800's. The importation of slaves was outlawed by an act of Congress effective 1 January 1808.

According to the Slaveholders Census of 1860, 8,950 souls were held as slaves in Pike County Alabama where the Coleman and Sanders families lived. In 1870 Rhode and his family, Milton, and Martha were all living near Troy. Troy was then and is now the largest town in Pike County.

Rhode and Harriet had 11 children. Two children died before 1900. One of these was Rhode's namesake son. The other has yet to be found in any record. Here are the ten known children.

1. John Coleman (b. 1852 Georgia m. Nancy Folmar 29 Oct 1870)
2. Julia Coleman (b.1854 Georgia, m. Charles Maynor 3 May 1874 Pike, Alabama, d. 18 Aug 1930 Dothan, Houston, Alabama, buried Hartford, Alabama)
3. Robert Coleman (b. 1857-1859, Alabama)
4. Frank C. Coleman (b. Jan 1860 Pike, Alabama, m. 3 times First: Flora Sanders 18 Sep 1881,

Quitman County, Georgia; Second: Flutie "Lizzie" Rodgers 15 Mar 1898, Sunflower County, Mississippi, Third: Emma Virginia Criss 26 May 1910, Sunflower County, Mississippi, d. around 1949, Mississippi)

5. Mary J. Coleman. (b. Sep 1862 Pike, Alabama m. 3 times First: Joe Parks 1 Aug 1880, Pike, Alabama, Second: John Stringer, 1888, Pike, Alabama,Third: Given Siler, Pike, Alabama d. 17 Sep 1935 Troy, Pike, Alabama, buried Mount Zion Cemetery, Pike, Alabama)
6. Martha Coleman (b. 1864 Pike, Alabama)
7. Lizzie Coleman (b. 1868 Pike, Alabama m. Thomas Howe (or possibly the surname is Howard) 30 Dec 1886 Pike, Alabama)
8. Rhode Coleman (b. 1870 Pike Alabama, d. 17 Jul 1886 Dixons, Pike, Alabama, buried Wesley Chapel Methodist Church Cemetery, Dunn, Pike, Alabama)
9. Arter "Art" Coleman (b. 1872-1874 m. Harriet Green circa 1897 Pike, Alabama, d. 19 Mar 1953 Troy, Pike, Alabama)
10. Joe Coleman (b. 1876 Pike, Alabama d. 3 Dec 1920 Birmingham, Jefferson, Alabama)

Rhode may also be the father of three others as he is listed on their Death Certificates although there were no other references to that effect discovered as yet.

1. Anna Coleman (b. circa 1874 Alabama to Celia Hall (1842-1922), m. 2 times First: Unknown Seymore circa 1886, Second: Findley McMillan, d. 17 Dec 1926 Troy, Pike, Alabama)

2. Tobe Coleman (b. 1 Mar 1872 Pike, Alabama to Ella Walker, d. 6 Aug 1968 Troy, Pike, Alabama)
3. James C. Coleman (b. 12 Mar 1876 Troy, Pike, Alabama to Eloise, d. 28 Oct 1947 Detroit, Wayne, Michigan)

The first record for Rhode after the Civil War is an entry in the Alabama State Census of 1866 when he is listed as having a household of 4 males and 4 females. The enumerator actually made an addition error and lists the household as having a total of 7 people but there are actually 8 entered into the columns. The tally of eight and the genders and ages is consistent with their household through the birth of their child Martha.

Then in 1867 he appears on the Alabama Voter Registration Records Database: County: Pike, Precinct: 3 Election District: 7 where his first name listed as Rade. Rhode's first name is often misspelled; some of the variations found include Road, Rode, and even Rowe.

In 1870 Rhode and family live in the Cross Roads area of Pike County. This was part of Beat 4 and was served by the Troy Post Office. He was farming as a share cropper. He did not own land or have a personal property of significant enough value to be listed on the Census. The nearby farms are relatively small operations; it does not look like there were any large plantations in this vicinity. He was most probably working 40 to 80 acres of land. Typically one man might work 40 acres, but with the help of teenage sons, he might be working as much as 80 acres. His oldest son, John married Nancy Folmar on 29 October 1870. He would have been the first one in the family to enjoy the privilege of a legally and religiously recognized marriage. Before Emancipation, slaves were not permitted to marry since they were considered property and as such could not fulfill the vow of "'til death do us part". Slaves could be sold at any time to settle a debt, raise money for some new purchase, or be used in partial trade for another slave perhaps with a skill like blacksmithing. Additionally, marriages are considered legal contracts and only free persons can participate in a contract. "Jumping the broomstick", a marriage tradition which actually has roots in Europe, not Africa, was a way for couples to publicly declare their commitment to the relationship.

By 1880 Rhode had shifted his family to the Dixons area of Pike County to farm there. This area is south of Troy. He was assisted by his sons, Frank C. and Rhode, and daughters, Mary J. and Martha. His brother Milton lived next door with family, wife Sina (b. 1840 Georgia), and children, Fannie (b. 1861 Alabama), Alph (this might be short for Alfred) (b. 1865 Alabama), Lafayette (b. 1877 Alabama), and Georgia A. (b. 1879). Since Milton was single in the 1870 Census and living with his mother, it is likely that Fannie and Alph are step-children even though they are not annotated that way in the Census. It is not uncommon to find entries where the precise relationship is not correctly specified. Rhode's son, Robert, lived a couple of houses down the road boarding with a farmer named Jack Brown and his family. Robert worked with Jack Brown on his farm.

Interestingly on 31 July 1880, Rhode put his mark to a bond along with Isam Parks for *"the penal sum of two hundred dollars; for the payment of which, well and truly made, we bind ourselves, and each and every of our Heirs, Executors, and Administrators, jointly and severally, firmly by these presents."* It was not uncommon at the time for such a bond to be signed in testimony of the truth of the information recorded in the marriage license application. The purpose of the bond was for the marriage of his daughter Mary J. to Joe Parks. Fred Ardis, M. G. (meaning Minister of the Gospel) solemnized the marriage on 1 August 1880 at "Mrs. Dalton's". Mrs. Dalton was the wife of the white farmer living next door. The wedding was held at her home. Mr. Dalton was Perry W. Dalton. According to an article by J. J. Collins on Geneva County History, Perry W. Dalton moved to Pike County from Georgia with his wife's family, the Jordans, before the Civil War. The article says *"As a young man he was the overseer of slaves on the Jep Hill Plantation, until he was called into the services of the army of the Confederate States of America. He served under Colonel Swanson in the 61st Alabama Infantry."* Three of his children moved to Geneva County which is why he was mentioned in the article. Perry W. Dalton is listed in the 1860 Census in Pike County but he probably was not an overseer for Jeptha "Jep" Hill who was an 18-year-old white grocery clerk at the time. In 1872, Jep's father died and it looks likely that it was Jep who inherited the farm. In 1880, Jep Hill and Perry Dalton lived close to one another and Rhode Coleman and his family and Reuben Sanders and his family lived right there as well. Jep and Perry owned their farms; Reuben and Rhode were listed as Farm laborers. It seems highly likely that they were working for Jep and/or Perry.

  The Daltons had a large family and it would not be surprising to learn that Harriet Coleman delivered at least some of the children. Obviously the families were close enough for the Dalton's to host the wedding of Mary to Joe Parks.

Tragically on 17 July 1886 Rhode Coleman the son who was only 16 years old died of a "stone bruise". An explanation of this medical diagnosis from the late 1800's has yet to be found, but it may be something as straight forward as Rhode fell and hit his head on a stone. He was a farm laborer. He is buried in an unmarked grave at the Wesley Chapel Methodist Church Cemetery, Dunn, Pike County, Alabama. Dunn is just to the northeast of Troy. It is a small, single intersection, farming community even today. Wesley Chapel is a simple, well kept, white clapboard building. There is no bell tower or steeple. The building is situated next to its adjoining cemetery on Route 15/29 or 3 Notch Road as it is known as this road makes its way through town. If you are traveling east from Troy, you would turn left, cross the railroad track, and park in the shade of the single tree in the church yard. The church is no longer active but the church and graveyard have been preserved and is maintained. There is a current effort to place markers for those known to be buried there who had been unmarked.

Rhode farmed cotton and all the children helped. In addition to housekeeping duties, Harriet also served as a midwife assisting in the births of both white and African-American children. Her name appears frequently in the Pike County Register of Births during the late 1800's.

Rhode's son, Arter Coleman, who lived in Pike County throughout his life, married Harriet Green at her father's (Lewis Green) home on the 24 December 1896. Noted on their marriage record was *"Man of age. Personal consent of father of woman."* Their marriage was officiated by Reverend Elick Terry. They had 8 children:

1. Lizzie Coleman (b. Oct 1897)

2. Dixie Coleman (b. 9 Nov 1900 Pike, Alabama d. 29 Oct 1994 Hamilton, Butler, Ohio)
3. an infant son (b. 15 Nov 1904 Pike, Alabama d. 27 Nov 1904 Pike, Alabama)
4. Mary Coleman (b. 12 Apr 1906 Pike, Alabama m. Simmons d. 21 Apr 1981 Hamilton, Butler, Ohio)
5. Walter Coleman (12 May 1908 Pike, Alabama d. 9 Oct 1990 Fairfield, Butler, Ohio buried 15 Oct 1990 Greenwood Cemetery, Hamilton, Ohio)
6. Charles Coleman (b. 11 May 1910 Troy, Pike, Alabama d. 29 Oct 1975 Hamilton, Butler, Ohio)
7. James Coleman (b. 1913)
8. Annie Coleman (b. 1915).

Arter lived most of his adult life in Troy and worked as a carpenter. His sons, Walter and James, daughters, Dixie and Mary, and grandson James Arthur Simmons (b. 27 Jan 1926 Pike, Alabama d. 19 Apr 1995 Oxford, Butler, Ohio) moved to Hamilton County, Ohio around 1946 to work in the steel mills in the vicinity of Cincinnati.

In 1900 Rhode and Harriet lived with their daughter Mary and her family in Troy. The family lived on North 3 Notch Street which is in the downtown district of Troy. It is one of the two main north-south streets and is Routes 29 and 15 through the town. It is now mostly commercial. For the first time, Harriet's occupation is listed as midwife, although from the Register of Births, we know she had been a midwife since at least the 1870's. The Register also shows she assisted both black and white women during their travail.

In 1900 less than 5% of women gave birth in hospitals. By this time many middle and upper-class women had a physician in attendance during the birthing process. Poor women and foreign-born women had midwives attend to the births of their children. The early Colonists brought midwife traditions from Europe. When Africans were brought to this country, West African midwives brought their traditions with them. Before the Civil War every plantation had at least one midwife. After Emancipation, African-American midwives continued to care for both black and white poor women in most rural areas of the South, where they were referred to as "granny midwives". By the end of the 1950's, African-American midwives had nearly disappeared.

Pike County did not have any training program or licensing requirement for midwives during the period that Harriet served. She most probably learned from an older midwife. Skills were often passed on from one generation to the next in the form of what might be called an apprenticeship. Later, when we learn about Lucy Looney, the other midwife in the family, we will see a different set of circumstances. Midwifery continued in the South for much longer than in other parts of the country. However, puerperal (childbed) fever was at epidemic proportions during the 1800s. It was the single most common cause of maternal mortality accounting for half of all deaths related to childbirth and second only to tuberculosis in killing women of child-bearing age. It was primarily spread by physicians and midwives who did not wash their hands prior to assisting in a birth. The discovery of bacteria which caused illness by Louis Pasteur in the 1850's through the 1860's led to changes in hygiene practices and medical treatment.

In the early 1900's, doctors began to press for control over births, treating birth as a pathological process rather than a natural one, and there was a precipitous decline in the number of midwives in this country. An effort to bring professional knowledge to the arena began in 1925 with the introduction of nurse midwifes in Kentucky as part of the Frontier Nursing Service. Nurse midwives remained a very small group with fewer than 70 in practice by the early 1960's. Now the idea of midwives attending "normal" births is once again gaining some momentum.

Rhode was working as a Day Laborer in 1900. Mary worked as a Laundress. Her husband, John Stringer, was working as a Laborer in the Timber industry. Mary had delivered four children, three of whom were alive when the enumerator visited. Leona (b. Jul 1880, Pike, AL) who was 19 at the time was most probably Mary's daughter from her first husband, Joe Parks, worked as a Farm Laborer. She is recorded as a Stringer in this Census although her name at birth was probably Parks. Rebecca (b. Mar 1887 Pike, AL) and Sular (b. Dec 1888 Pike, AL) were both working as servants despite being 13 and 11 years old. Remember child labor and mandatory education laws were still in the future at this point.

By 1910, Rhode and Harriet are again in a separate household at 289 Tait Street (now spelled Tate). Their house would have been between Lilac Lane and Segars Street. Tate Street is a cross street to South 3 Notch Street. This is a little further down Notch Street from where they had lived in 1900. 3 Notch Street changes from South to North at Madison Street which is the next intersection as one travels north along Notch Street from Tate Street. The housing stock in this area was rebuilt in the 1970's and nothing remains of the housing which would have existed when Rhode and Harriet lived here. Rhode was still working; doing odd jobs.

On 19 May 1913, Rhode died of paralysis while still living in Troy. His attending physician was Dr. William Bryan Sanders, a nephew of James Nathaniel Sanders who will be covered shortly. His age at time of death is cited as 86 which would put his year of birth at 1827. This is, not surprisingly, inconsistent with earlier records. Since no birth certificates were issued during the time period he was born, it was not uncommon for birth information to be approximate. The Dealer in Coffins who filled out the Death Certificate was F. S. Wood, a widower who was a Furniture Merchant. F. S. Wood and Dr. William Bryan Sanders both lived on College Street just a few doors apart.

Frank C. Coleman

Frank Coleman was born into slavery in Pike County, Alabama in January of 1860. Frank was the third child of ten children raised by Rhode and Harriet Coleman (the eleventh child having died young).

Frank was educated and could read and write. During the era of Reconstruction, the Freedman's Bureau opened 1000 schools across the South for black children. Schooling was a high priority for Freedmen and enrollment was high and enthusiastically supported. The Bureau spent over $5 million dollars setting up these schools. In 1870 roughly 23% of African-American heads of household could read and write compared to 80.9% of white heads of households. By 1900 the percentage had increased to 38.2% compared to 86.9% of whites. This disparity existed for a number of reasons including the need for all family members in African-American rural households to work from an early age in order for the family to survive and the lack of equal educational opportunities. Despite the efforts of the Freedman's Bureau, there were many more children who needed a school within walking distance and the time to attend. It was not until 1918 all states in the Union at the time required children to complete elementary school. The states in the Deep South were among the last states to adopt such a provision. Alaska adopted a compulsory education law in 1929 but was not admitted as the 49th state of the U.S. until 3 January 1959. Nevertheless, for those who could and did attend school, they gained an advantage by being able to read and sign contracts and legal documents among other things.

Frank married Flora, the daughter of neighbors Reuben and Emily Saunders, on 18 September 1881 in Quitman County, Georgia where they had probably moved to find work. The marriage date is about 6 weeks after the birth date given for their eldest child. It could be that the dates are accurate, but given that no birth certificates were issued at this time, it could also be that their eldest child was actually born in 1882 rather than 1881. They had eight children including:
1. Willie Coleman (b. 5 Aug 1881 Pike, Alabama m. 3 times d. 6 Apr 1968 Indianola, Sunflower, Mississippi buried 14 Apr 1968, St. Rest Cemetery, Indianola, Sunflower, Mississippi – Willie will be discussed in more detail later.)
2. Ella Coleman (b. 1883 Pike, Alabama m. Daniel Branch)
3. Emily Coleman (b. 1885 Pike, Alabama)

4. Sarah Coleman (b. 1886 Sunflower County, Mississippi m. Joe Jackson 6 Feb 1911 Sunflower County, Mississippi)
5. Pernella Emma Coleman (b. Jan 1889 Sunflower County, Mississippi m. Isaac Crenshaw (b. 1887 Tennessee; at least one child Willa or Willie (records differ on spelling) Mae Crenshaw b. 1905); lived in Memphis, Tennessee in the 1920's and 30's; Isaac was a laborer at a Feed Plant and later worked for Memphis Power and Light as a carpenter; during that time the family lived just off Castex d. 24 May 1942 Chicago, Cook, Illinois buried 29 May 1942 Burr Oak Cemetery, Alsip, Cook, Illinois)
6. Walter Coleman (b. Nov 1890 Sunflower County, Mississippi b. Pearl surname unknown (b. 1893 Mississippi); at least 5 children: occupation: farmer)
7. Julia Coleman (b. 1894 Sunflower County, Mississippi)
8. Rhode Coleman (b. 15 Jan 1896 Shaw, Sunflower, Mississippi m. at least 2 times Inell Wanetta Gant 7 Nov 1917 Sunflower, Mississippi and then Flossie Thomas 20 Jan 1940 Shaw, Sunflower, Mississippi d. Aug 1976 Shaw, Bolivar, Mississippi)

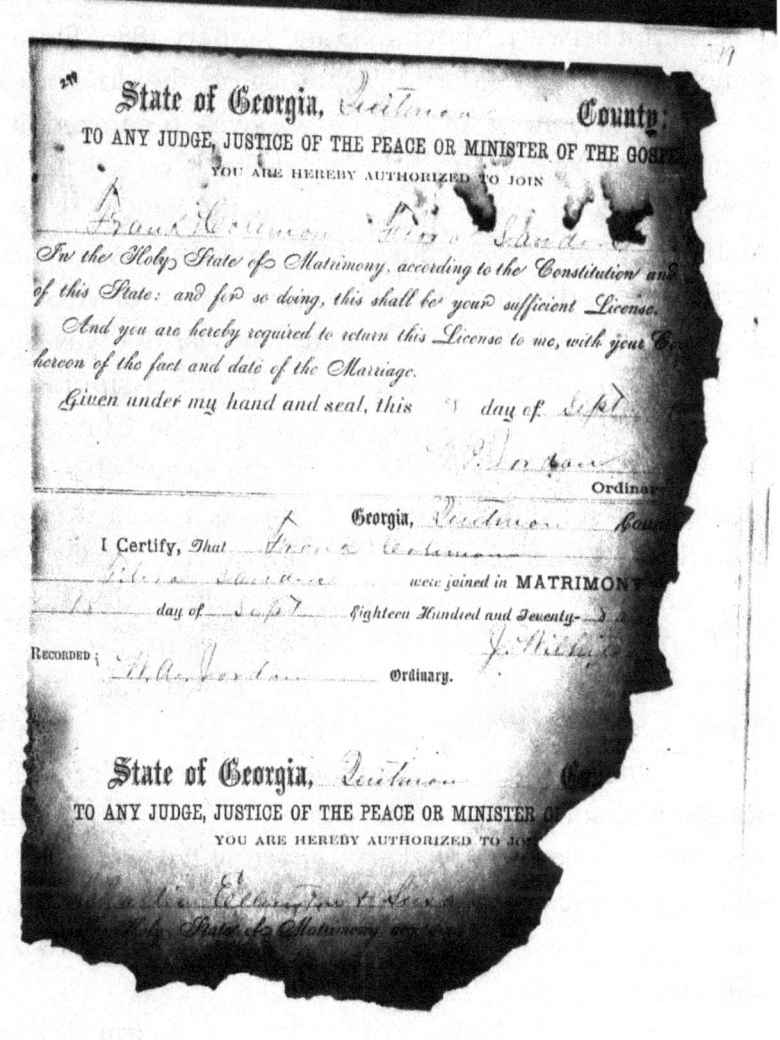

Figure 4 The fire-damaged remains of the Quitman County, Georgia Marriage Register recording Frank Coleman's marriage to Flora Sanders.

Frank and Flora moved to Sunflower County, Mississippi between March 1885 and January 1886. Flora died sometime after 15 January 1896 and before the close of 1898.

The Territory of Mississippi was organized as an incorporated territory of the United States on 7 April 1798. The Territory of Mississippi included the land that became Alabama. On 10 December 1817, the final extent of the territory was admitted to the Union as the state of Mississippi.

On 28 May 1830 the Indian Removal Act was signed. It called for all Indians living east of the Mississippi River to be moved to reservations in the west. The Choctaw and Chickasaw peoples, who inhabited the region that became Mississippi, moved west to areas in Oklahoma during the years 1831 to 1836. Other tribes were moved into Oklahoma and Kansas. A total of 19,554 Choctaws plus white citizens of the Choctaw Nation and 500 black slaves lived east of the Mississippi before the removal treaty. Notice that the Native Americans held slaves. Some African-Americans even held slaves; some freed men bought their family members. Others bought and sold slaves in the same way as slave holders of any racial background. The Chickasaw nation had 4,914 Native Americans and 1,156 black slaves east of the Mississippi. Their relocations took place between 1837 and 1847.

Many of the Native Americans died in transit to their new locations. This was the "Trail of Tears". Of the Choctaws, the estimates are 12,500 people emigrated and 2,000 to 4,000+ died along the way, mostly of cholera. Of the Chickasaws, about 500 to 800 people died mostly due to dysentery and small pox. Overall, some 10,000 Native Americans died during the removal.

During the Civil War, the Indian tribes sided with the Confederacy. Their treaty was renegotiated in 1866 requiring the Indians to emancipate their slaves in addition to losing some of the lands they had at that time.

What became Sunflower County was largely Chickasaw land prior to the removal, although the Indians did not have the concept of land ownership the white population did and Choctaws also used this area. Sunflower County was established on 15 February 1844 and encompassed most of what is now Sunflower and Leflore Counties. It was named in honor of the Sunflower River flowing through the middle of the county which gets its name from the sunflowers adorning its banks. Leflore was set up in 1871. In 1882 the county seat was established in the town then named Eureka and now named Indianola. After the Civil War, many African-Americans migrated to Sunflower. From a population of 3,243 African-Americans in 1870, the number swelled to 12,070 by 1900, making up 75% of the residents in Sunflower County. By 1920, the African-American population had almost tripled over the level in 1900. The county population as a whole peaked in 1930 at 66,364 and is presently less than half that total.

Running east-west through the county is Route 82. This modern road follows a centuries-old Native American trail which connected the areas which have become Greenville, Mississippi and Montgomery, Alabama. It is the route many settlers to this area followed. Many of our family's ancestors obviously followed this pathway into Mississippi as we find them recorded not far off this route through Carroll, Leflore, and Sunflower Counties. The major family lines of Everett, Kaigler, Coleman/Webb and the families into which they married, all likely followed this route.

On 14 November 1896 Frank Coleman entered into a Contract for Deed to buy a 40-acre tract of land for $400 with Mr. Burroughs of Chicago, IL. The deed was transferred in January, 1904. The legal description of the property is Northwest Quarter of the Northwest Quarter Section 27, Township 20 North, Range 5 West, Sunflower County, Mississippi. The land is located at the intersection of Hodges and Winston Road. It is nestled in a hook of the Porter Bayou and is not far from Shaw, Mississippi which lies just over the border of Sunflower County with Bolivar County.

Mississippi was one of the states surveyed and divided with a grid system. While the early colonies were surveyed and divided based on natural terrain features, later lands are gridded. Roads built after initial settlement frequently followed property boundaries resulting in straight stretches punctuated by perpendicular crossroads. In the early years of Sunflower County (and most counties probably followed a similar scheme), land owners were required to maintain a wagon-wide road on land bordering their property. In the swampy regions of Mississippi as in the sandy desert regions of California, some of these roads were corduroy roads. Corduroy roads consist of logs or planks laid perpendicular to the direction of the road. While rough, these roads kept wagon wheels from sinking in the mire or sand, making an area passable.

Frank married a woman named Flutie "Lizzie" Rodgers on 14 March 1898. On 26 May 1910, he married again, this time to Emma Virginia Criss. The marriage was solemnized by Reverend W. S. Shipman in Bolivar County which is the county on the western border of Sunflower County. Frank stayed married to Emma for the rest of his life.

Frank also purchased another 40-acre tract adjoining the first property on 10 November 1903 for $350. It is Northwest Quarter Section 28. This land was sold to Thomas Halliday on 1 April 1918 for $2,800. The buyer gave Mr. Coleman a deed of trust for $1,800 recorded in Book I-5, page 385 of the Sunflower County Deed Register. When the deed was paid off F.C. Coleman canceled the deed in the margin of the book so his signature appears there. No document found thus far spells out his middle name.

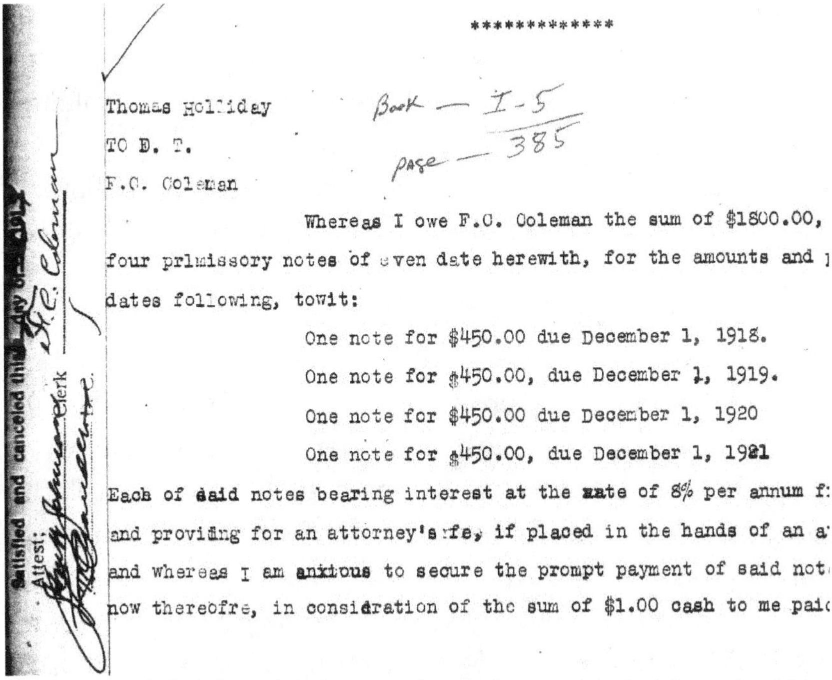

****

Thomas Holliday

TO D. T.

F.C. Coleman

Book — I-5
page — 385

Whereas I owe F.C. Coleman the sum of $1800.00, four prlmissory notes of even date herewith, for the amounts and dates following, towit:

One note for $450.00 due December 1, 1918.

One note for $450.00, due December 1, 1919.

One note for $450.00 due December 1, 1920

One note for $450.00, due December 1, 1921

Each of said notes bearing interest at the rate of 8% per annum f: and providing for an attorney's fe, if placed in the hands of an a and whereas I am anxious to secure the prompt payment of said not now thereofre, in consideration of the sum of $1.00 cash to me paid

Satisfied and canceled this ___ day of ___ 191_
F.C. Coleman
Attest: ___ Clerk

Figure 5 *Frank C. Coleman's only existing known signature is in the left margin of this extract of Book I-5, Sunflower County Deed Register.*

In the early 1900's Frank borrowed money using his 80 acres as collateral from the Delta Penny Savings Bank of

Indianola, MS. The bank was founded by Wayne Wellington Cox and his wife, Minnie, on 29 October 1904. On one such loan on 9 January 1914, for the amount of $568.82, all 80 acres plus one black mule named "Mag", one dark bay mule named "Bill", and one two-horse wagon were put up as collateral. Additionally all farming implements and crops raised or produced in 1914 were part of the collateral. The loan was payable on 2 January 1915. Probably the loans were for crop production purposes.

Throughout the plantation's history, Frank raised cotton, had an extensive kitchen garden, and kept chickens, hogs, and a milk cow. On 5 June 1917, Rhode Coleman (Frank's youngest son) registered for the World War I Draft. On his draft registration form, he lists the Frank Coleman Plantation as his place of employment.

Later, Frank borrowed from the Federal Land Bank of New Orleans. On 12 October 1936 F.C. Coleman and his wife, Emma, deeded the property to Mrs. L.B. Ely for $25 cash and Mrs. Ely's assumption of the debt owed to the Federal Land Bank plus all taxes and special assessments against the land due now or in subsequent years. Roughly half of all farmers in the United States lost their farms during the Great Depression. Frank was fortunate to be able to sell his property and clear his debt instead of having the bank foreclose on the property.

According to family sources, Frank died in 1949.

The land is now is agricultural production with no structures on it. In 2006 the 80 acres, which had once belonged to Frank, were owned by Vincent Muzzi.

Reuben Saunders

Reuben Sanders was born around 1834 in Georgia. His name is recorded with a variety of spelling including both Saunders and Sanders for his surname and Ruben, Reubin, Reuben for his first name. He and a woman named Emily (b. 1834 Georgia) started a family about 1853 in Alabama. This would be before marriage was allowed between slaves. The couple may have had 12 children including:

1. Dick Sanders (b. 1853 Pike, Alabama)
2. Henry Sanders (b. 1856 Pike, Alabama)
3. Susan Sanders (b. 1857 Pike, Alabama)
4. An infant daughter (b. Aug 1859 Pike, Alabama d. Feb 1860 Pike, Alabama of Cold, ill for 3 months; listed on 1860 Mortality Schedule as Property of J. N. Sanders immediately following the entry for James Nathaniel Sanders first wife who also died within that year. It is at the moment only a postulated relationship between the Reuben Sanders family and the J. N. Sanders family so it is possible that this child is not a daughter of Reubin's)
5. William Sanders (b. 1860/61 Pike, Alabama)
6. Joseph "Joe" Sanders (b. 1863 Pike, Alabama)
7. Fannie Sanders (b. 1864 Pike, Alabama)
8. Flora Sanders (b. 1865 Pike, Alabama m. Frank C. Coleman 18 Sep 1881 Quitman County, Georgia d. est. 1896 Sunflower County, Mississippi)
9. Mack Sanders (b. est 1866/67 Pike, Alabama)
10. Warren Sanders (b. 1870 Pike, Alabama)

11. Fox Sanders (b. 1873 Pike, Alabama)
12. Guss Sanders (his name was spelled with a double "s" in the Census, but may have more usually been spelled with a single "s")(b. 1876 Pike, Alabama)

In the 1866 Alabama State Census he is listed as Ruben Sanders. Then in 1867 he appears in the Alabama Voter Registration Records Database: County: Pike, Precinct: 1 Election District: 7.

In 1870 Reuben Sanders and family are recorded in the Census twice. On 1 July Reuben (listed as Rubin) is recorded next to James Nathaniel Sanders. He is noted again on 6 July in Troy itself.

In 1880 two of Reuben's sons, Joe age 16 and Mack age 13, were living with and working on James Nathaniel Sanders' farm. Reuben had probably hired out these two sons to obtain more cash for the family. "Hiring out" was a common practice in large families where there were enough children to help the father sharecrop the land where the family lived. Mostly it was male family members who were hired out. If at all economically possible, females were kept within the protection of the family. Nevertheless, economic necessity might dictate that a daughter be hired out either to work as a field hand or a domestic servant.

Reuben, Emily, and their other children were living in Beat 7, Dixons right next to Jeptha P. Hill, the man referenced in the Rhode Coleman section as having been mentioned as the owner of a farm where Perry W. Dalton was credited as the overseer in one historical article. Reuben's sons Henry, William, and Warren (10 years old at the time) are all working the farm. His daughters Susan and Flora are helping their mother keep house. Only their youngest children Fox and Guss (7 and 4 respectively at the time) are not listed with an occupation.

Additionally in the same vicinity is a household headed by Austin Sanders. Austin Sanders was born either in March 1835 or 1843 (the two Censuses in which he is found provide very different birth years) in Georgia. In 1867 he appeared in the Voter Registration Records in Randolph County, Georgia. Randolph County was established on 20 December 1828. The original county contained land which subsequently was allotted to five other counties. The county was named for John Randolph, a Virginia planter and controversial politician. At the time of its formation, there was still contention between the Native Americans and the white settlers. In fact, part of the Creek Indian War of 1836 was fought in Randolph County.

After the Civil War, the Howard Normal School opened its doors to African-American students. A Normal School was a school opened to train high school graduates to be teachers. Its purpose was to set teaching standards or norms and hence its name. Richard R. Wright became its first black headmaster for a term of 4 years. Then in 1880 Fletcher Hamilton Henderson, Sr. began a long tenure as the headmaster. He served until 1942. His son, the band leader, Fletcher Henderson (b. 1897 d. 1952) is one of Randolph's most famous residents.

In 1880, Austin had moved to Pike County Alabama and was living near Reuben. In his household are his wife Lila, his mother recorded here as "Mariar" (this name is probably Maria or Marianne) Sledge (b. about 1823 Georgia), and his sisters Manerva Sanders (b. 1860 Georgia) and Mary

Sanders (b. 1865 Georgia). In 1870 Maria Sledge and her daughter Manerva lived in Upson County, Georgia – the same county where the possible slave holders of Reuben lived before moving to Pike County. Additionally, Maria Sledge has the same last name as James Nathaniel Sanders first wife. Most likely, Maria was "owned" by the Sledge family. Amos Sledge and his son Peyton T. Sledge appear to be likely candidates for the slave holding family in Upson County. More research is underway to see if there is a link between Nancy Jane Sledge, who married James Nathaniel Sanders, and Amos Sledge who might have been her father.

It is very likely there is a family link between Reuben, Maria, Austin, Manerva, and Mary, although proving what that link might be will be quite difficult. With the end of slavery, African-American families tried to reconnect with family members who had been sold or moved away prior to Emancipation. Sometimes this process took a number of years as newly freed people did not have the resources to travel large distances or even know where to travel to at first as they searched to find other family members. It could be that what is recorded in the 1880 Census is evidence of the successful conclusion of this process of reconnection.

Possible Slave Holders

The James Nathaniel Sanders Line

James Nathaniel Sanders was born on 5 June 1822 in Jones County, Georgia to James Isaac Sanders and his wife, Elizabeth Naomi Cadenhead Sanders. They had married in

Jones County on 28 December 1819. James Isaac used his middle name throughout his life. Isaac was farming in the Capt. Phillips District of Jones County when his first son was born.

By 1830 the family had moved to Upson County, Georgia and stayed there until 1853. Upson County was established on 15 December 1824 from parts of Pike and Crawford Counties in Georgia. The county is named after Stephen Upson, a lawyer and legislator in the early years of Georgia. The county seat is Thomaston. The Sanders family were among the county's first inhabitants. Early settlers came from eastern Georgia counties and North and South Carolina primarily as a result of land lotteries. After clearing the land, settlers farmed cotton. The first cotton mill in the county was built in 1833 and textile manufacturing began in 1835. This continued as a major industry here until early this century. Thomaston Mills moved its operation to Mexico in 2001 and Martha Mills ceased operating in 2006.

James met and married his first wife, Nancy Jane Sledge (b. 1823 Georgia) on 21 December 1843. James and his wife, Nancy, had three sons Amas (or Amos) (b. 1844), Isaac M. (b.1849), and Thomas S. (b. 1852).

In 1850, Isaac is listed on the Slave Schedule as holding 8 persons and his son, James, holds a 14-year-old female. Prior to the move to Pike County, Alabama, James scouted out farmland in both Alabama and Texas. The well-watered rich farmland of Alabama won out. James purchased 900 acres located along Blindjack Road near a road intersection and helped found the small community of Hephzibah. He built a sturdy house of logs on the crest of the ridge overlooking a valley. Meanwhile, Isaac moved into the town of Troy. He was a Deacon at the Beulah Primitive Baptist Church which included both black and white congregants. This Church was also referred to as "Hard Shell" Baptists and were known for not having Sunday School or supporting missionaries.

James lost both his mother Naomi and his wife Nancy in 1859. His mother died on the 6th of March. After two years of illness, Nancy died in October of consumption (tuberculosis). In 1860, he and his sons continued to farm. He then had a total of 9 slaves. He might have had ten if a 7-month-old baby girl had not died in February of 1860 before the Census was taken. This infant is recorded on the 1860 Mortality Schedule right below the entry for Nancy as "Property of J.N. Sanders". It is unlikely we will ever learn her name. That child may have been one of Reuben and Emily's children.

Isaac died in 8 November 1866. His son James was appointed as Administrator to his estate which was divided among his heirs: Mary (his second wife), children Alexander, John R., James N., Amanda Sanders Bragg, and his grandchildren by his daughter, Sarah Sanders Reddock (Martha Wells, Isaac, Naomah Winn, Eliza Wells, John Thomas, Franklin, and Fannie), and son, Martin Sanders (Joel, Naomah, and John), both of whom had died previously.

Farming 900 acres requires more than one active worker. Slaves had provided the necessary labor before Emancipation, now workers had to be hired. And interestingly, in 1880, James had two of Reuben's sons boarding with him and helping him work the farm. Joe was 16 and Mack was 13 at the time.

James died on 6 November 1890 in Goshen, Pike County, Alabama. He died without a will and his property was divided equally amongst his family. He had a respectable estate. There was the farm, by then 940 acres, 1 horse, 49 hogs, 5 mules (Emma, Sally, James, Joe ,and Pete), 1 milk cow and calf, 30 bales of cotton, 2000 bushels of cotton seed, 100 bushels of potatoes, 7½ bushels of rye, 800 bushels of corn, 6 bushels of ground peas, fodder, 1 buggy, 3 farm wagons, 2 sets of harnesses, 6 sets of plow gear, 1 set farming tools, 1 set blacksmith tools, 1 set carpenter tools, 1 iron safe, 1 double barrel shot gun, and more. He had $1,400 on hand. The sale of his "perishable effects" brought $3,060.53 and were purchased primarily by family members and near neighbors.

In 1948 the small hamlet of Hephzibah consisted of about six houses, a Baptist Church, a country store, a "Negro" school, and a two-teacher elementary school for whites. Local historian, John P. Johnston, explains that in 1916 Pike County had 66 schools for whites and 45 schools for blacks. In the 1920's Pike County gained at least one "Rosenwald" school. The Rosenwald foundation funded the building of some 5,000 schools throughout the South to serve the African-American community.

The Looney Line

Robert Looney

Figure 6 *Robert Looney's signature from his will.*

Y-DNA test results and matches lead back to Robert Looney (b. Feb 1692 Ballygilley Farm, Maughold County, Isle of Mann, Ireland d. 17 Sep 1769 Reed Creek, Augusta County, Virginia; will proved 13 Nov 1770) as the most distant recorded ancestor on the Looney line. There is a direct male line running from James Knox Looney back to this white Irish man. Any blood descendent of James K. Looney will also be a descendant of this man. Additionally, all descendants of Robert Looney will be related to any blood descendant of James K. Looney. Robert Looney's line is prolific and there are literally thousands of people living in the United States today who are his descendants.

The DNA evidence points to a more distant Viking male ancestor whose name we will probably never know, but has the lineage marker name of M253. The Vikings invaded the British Isles repeatedly for a nearly 500 year period. Often the raids were short incursions of looting, burning, killing, and raping. At other times settlements were established and maintained. Viking blood runs through the veins of millions of Europeans as the Vikings were an adventurous lot who roamed far and wide—to the East working down Russian riverways as far south as Turkey, through northern Europe, and to the west reaching Iceland, Greenland, and even the North American mainland.

Robert married Elizabeth Llewillyn around 1720 while still on the Isle of Mann. They emigrated from Ireland to North America around 1731, landing in Philadelphia where they lived for a short time along with their older children including at least 7 sons. Philadelphia was the fastest growing city in the colonies at the time and had a population of 11,500 in 1730. On 12 November 1735 Robert received a land patent for 294 acres on the south bank of the Upper Potomac River near "Samuel Owen's plantation". This is probably not far from Hagerstown, Maryland where tradition has it that some of the Looney children attended school. The couple continued to be fruitful and added more children to their family. There are at least 14 sons and an unknown number of daughters—only a few daughters show up in any records, but researchers postulate there were more than the known few.

The Baylor's Book of Surveys at the Frederick County Courthouse shows that Robert Looney had a survey on "Lunies" Creek in April 1740. The family probably moved south down the Shenandoah Valley into Virginia as part of the Quaker settlement in 1739 or 1740. Robert obtained a grant of 250 acres on the James River and "Lunies" Creek. On 30 July 1742 another 400 acres on "Lunies" Creek was added. The house and barn were built on the south side of the James and west side of the creek. The James River at this point was often not fordable so the Looneys operated a ferry.

Robert and his sons also hunted, grazed cattle and horses, and ran a mill, a plant nursery, and an orchard. They supplied troops in service on the frontier for years. Robert and his sons were pioneers; developing the land, fighting Indians, and establishing small communities in the farthest reaches of Colonial America.

Perhaps part of the type of spirit it takes to be a pioneer, also leads to discord amongst family and neighbors.

In any case, Robert and a number of his offspring were involved in legal disputes of one sort or another quite frequently and, therefore, left behind a rich record of their lives.

The DNA matches are not specific enough at this point to spell out the line linking James Knox Looney to this ancestor. However, we have a couple of other clues to work with that give us two possible lines. There may be more possibilities which further research may uncover, but at the moment, there are only two men who appear to be possible candidates for fathering James Knox Looney.

One clue to his parentage is his name—not the last name in this case, which of course, we now know was a concrete clue—but the middle name. Knox is normally a last name. It was a custom in some families during this time in history to use the mother's maiden name as the middle name for a boy to document the heritage of the child. However, one group of the Looneys appears to have used the names of generals and high-level political figures as middle names. This group lived in Hawkins County Tennessee during the very late 1700s and through most of the 1800s. Major General Henry Knox (25 Jul 1750 – 25 Oct 1806) fought in the Revolutionary War and was the last Secretary of War under the Articles of Confederation and the first Secretary of War under the Constitution.

Another clue is the oral family history. George Austin William Webb, grandson of James Knox Looney, remembers being told that James' father fought on the side of the Confederacy during the Civil War and died at the Battle of Vicksburg. A search of the list of Confederate dead revealed no Looneys in any of the spelling variants (Luna, Luney,

Lunie, Loonie) at the Battle of Vicksburg. Then a record was found of two Looneys who were traded as Prisoners of War at Vicksburg although they had been captured during an earlier battle at Fort Donelson. Both men served in the 18th Infantry Regiment from Tennessee; a unit raised in Hawkins County.

James K. Looney's race is recorded as black on most of his Census entries but in one of the two entries that were made for him in the 1910 Census, he is recorded as mulatto. Operating on the premise that mulatto meant mixed white and black parentage and the knowledge that James was born during the period of slavery, a search of the 1860 Slave Schedule was conducted looking for a slave holder with the last name Looney who held a woman of childbearing years and a male mulatto child of the right age. This, of course, was based on the assumption that James carried the last name of his slaveholder/father. The part about carrying the name of his father was later proven to be true by the DNA analysis. No matches to these search criteria appeared in Mississippi, however, Tennessee proved to be a different story. There were three matches; a woman named Mary Looney who was promptly eliminated as a possibility for being his father, an 80 year-old man who did not serve in the Civil War named Samuel Looney, and a man named William Carroll Looney who was traded as a prisoner of war at Vicksburg on 23 September 1862. This man had served in the 18th Tennessee Regiment as a Private and been captured at the Fort Donelson near the Tennessee-Kentucky border on 16 Feb 1862. So William Carroll Looney became a candidate of interest.

This William Carroll Looney was born on either 6 or 9 June 1822, (sources differ on this point) Rogersville, Hawkins

County, Tennessee to Absalom David Looney (b. 7 Mar 1790, Rogersville, Hawkins County, Tennessee d. 12 Dec 1862 Hawkins County, Tennessee) and his wife, Sarah Jane "Sallie" Starnes (b. 30 Jan 1799 Craig County, Virginia d. 8 Feb 1874 Hawkins County, Tennessee). William Carroll Looney died of a heart attack on 11 September 1893 in his home near Alpha, a village five miles west of Morristown in Hamblen County, Tennessee.

He was described by a grandchild in this way. *"William Carroll had very dark blue eyes which looked black when he was young because his hair was black. He was not quite six feet tall, and his weight was perhaps 150 to 175; he was never a large man. As I remember his beard was gray, kept trimmed, with his hair reached back from a wide smooth forehead. I was told by my mother he had a cleft chin. He always wore a white shirt and a black bow tie. He rode horseback, even on his rounds over the farm."*

He married Rachel Payne George Johnson (b. 15 Mar 1821 d. of pneumonia; sources are inconsistent on the date with two possibilities 9 Feb 1898 Hawkins County, Tennessee or 18 Jan 1899 Panther Springs, Hamblen County, Tennessee) around 1840. Rachel was a step-daughter of a wealthy gentleman named James Johnson. Upon the occasion of her marriage, Mr. Johnson gifted to Rachel a young female slave named Nancy (b. 1827 Tennessee; both parents born in Tennessee). Nancy lived with the family up until Emancipation and perhaps for some time beyond that. She had 9 mulatto children and was reportedly married to a slave on another farm. William Carroll was once offered $10,000 for Nancy and her children. Rachel refused sell. According to William Carroll Looney family sources, one of Nancy's daughters remained for some time with William's family after

Emancipation. However, she is not recorded as being part of their household in the 1870 Census. She may have married by then and moved on.

Nancy Looney shows up in the 1880 Census still living in District 9 of Hawkins County and she has a daughter (Mary b. circa 1858) and three grandchildren (Fannie b. 1872, Wiley b. 1876, and Meta b. 1878; all born in Hawkins County) living with her. In this Census, she is listed as black and her daughter is listed as mulatto. A boarder named Montgomery Looney (b. circa 1825 Tennessee), listed as black and a farm laborer, is also in the household. It is likely he was also held as a slave by one of the Looney families in the area, but whether there is any blood relation between Nancy and Montgomery is an open question. There are also several other mulatto Looneys living in the same district who are most probably related—perhaps some of her sons. It would be interesting to know if there are any descendants from this line who would be willing to participate in a DNA analysis.

Since William Carroll Looney served during the Civil War, there was a chance he had filed for a pension. A search of the National Archives listed a record for William C. Looney. The record, once received, was a complete surprise. It was a request for anything owed to a William C. Looney who had died on 28 Dec 1862 at Vicksburg. Who was this? The William C. Looney already described obviously did not die at the Battle of Vicksburg and lived for many years following the Civil War. This man was not listed on the casualty list for that battle either. However, it turns out that his death happened prior to the full-scale siege of Vicksburg which may be why he did not appear on that list.

More research revealed that this William C. Looney (not yet sure of the middle name although it may well be Carroll as there are a number of people in this general family line with that name) was born in 1838 in Hawkins County. It looks like he was orphaned at an early age and was living with a relative named Michael Jackson Looney in 1850 although that Census does not list relation to head of household. He had two sisters; one named Mary who filed for any monies due. If he was a nephew to Michael J. Looney, then his ancestral line back to Robert is different than the William Carroll mentioned earlier. More research needs to be done to see if his line can be identified.

In 1860 he lived with John and Elizabeth Miller in District 6, Union County, Tennessee where he helped with the farming. The Raccoon Valley post office served the local area. He travelled back to Hawkins County in order to enlist in Captain Samuel Rhea Gammon's company on 12 September 1862. This William Looney served as a Private in Company B, 60th Tennessee Mounted Infantry, part of Colonel Jonathon Alex Crawford's originally designated 79th Infantry Regiment. He was 6 feet tall with a fair complexion, blue eyes, and dark hair.

In the last month of 1862, Major General Ulysses S. Grant, Commander of the Union Army of Tennessee, ordered Major General William Tecumseh Sherman to capture Vicksburg, Mississippi. Built on high bluffs, Vicksburg controlled traffic on the Mississippi River, a vital artery of communication and supply for whichever side controlled the flow of traffic on the river. What became the Vicksburg Campaign waged over the course of roughly 8 months, and started with an attack from the river to capture the 300-foot bluffs just to the north of town. The defensive positions already developed and manned by Confederate units were reinforced just in the nick of time.

According to a Blue & Gray Magazine article titled "Chickasaw Bayou" by Terrence J. Winschel, Historian, Vicksburg National Military Park, three brigades including the 60th Tennessee Regiment then commanded by Colonel John C. Vaughn, *"pulled into Vicksburg along the tracks of the Southern Railroad during the afternoon and evening of December 27th. They were promptly forwarded to the point of danger and, by daylight of the 28th, were in position along the Walnut Hills."*

The next day Union and Confederate artillery exchanged fire; each pounding the other's positions. By nightfall, William Looney was dead. He died on his first day of action — a raw recruit, most likely killed by shrapnel from an artillery round. He was one of five men of the Regiment killed that day. Fighting raged for the next several days, but in the end the Confederate forces held and Sherman was forced to withdraw.

The Cedar Hill Cemetery in Vicksburg has 5,000 Confederate soldiers interred there who fought during the Vicksburg Campaign and it is most likely William was buried there. Of the 5,000 buried there, 2,400 are unknown. When he was killed, Capt. Gammon certified that William had received no pay except the bounty of $50 and owed the Confederate States $12.25 for clothing.

One might think the second William C. is a sure bet for being the father based on the few clues we have as to who James K. Looney's father was, however, because of the uncertainty that all Looneys who died in the Battle of Vicksburg have been accounted for, more research is needed.

There are now two participants in the Looney DNA Project who show a 71% chance of sharing an ancestor within the last four generations. Researching these lines may help in uncovering collaborating evidence or may lead to yet another possibility. Hopefully over time more information will be revealed and more participants will contribute to the understanding of the Looney bloodlines.

James Knox Looney and Family

James Knox Looney was born in March circa 1853 in Tennessee. The earliest Census entry found so far is that of 1880 when James was boarding with a farmer named Bearl Everett in Township 18, Range 6, Carroll County, Mississippi. This area was served by the post office in Vaiden. Although spelled phonetically in the Census, this name is Burl or Burrell. This becomes of interest shortly. Carroll County turns out to be pivotal in the history of our family. Not only do we find James here, there are other surnames of importance here too: Everett, Kaigler/Kegler, Phillips, and Reed. With regard to the Phillips surname, while Solomon Phillips has not yet been linked to the group of Phillips living right around the Everett and Kaigler/Kegler families located here, it would not be at all surprising to find that his family is one of the neighbors. Family groups tended to intermarry and stay connected across the generations.

James married Nellie Everett on 3 September 1880 in Carroll County, Mississippi. The record of their marriage includes a Marriage Bond. Marriage Bonds were not an uncommon feature of the marriage records during some periods of time and in some counties. Normally a senior male member of the families of both the bride and the groom signed the bond. The purpose of the bond was a guarantee that both parties were eligible for marriage (by age and kinship status (in other words, the applicants were not first cousins or closer) and were not already married to another party). James signed the bond guaranteeing his part of the bargain. His signature indicates he had received some education. Allen Everett made his mark in guarantee for

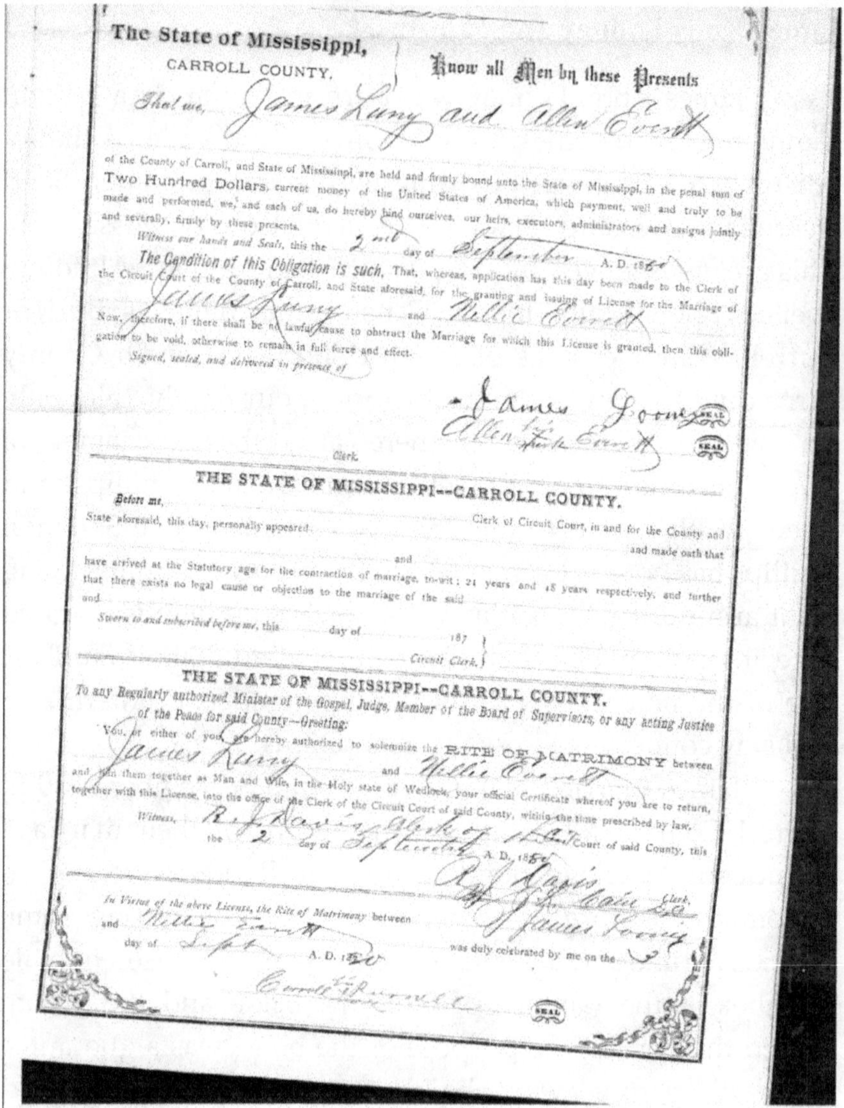

The State of Mississippi,
CARROLL COUNTY.
Know all Men by these Presents
That we, James Luny and Allen Everett
of the County of Carroll, and State of Mississippi, are held and firmly bound unto the State of Mississippi, in the penal sum of Two Hundred Dollars, current money of the United States of America, which payment, well and truly to be made and performed, we, and each of us, do hereby bind ourselves, our heirs, executors, administrators and assigns jointly and severally, firmly by these presents.
Witness our hands and Seals, this the 2nd day of September A. D. 1880
The Condition of this Obligation is such, That, whereas, application has this day been made to the Clerk of the Circuit Court of the County of Carroll, and State aforesaid, for the granting and issuing of License for the Marriage of James Luny and Nellie Everett
Now, therefore, if there shall be no lawful cause to obstruct the Marriage for which this License is granted, then this obligation to be void, otherwise to remain in full force and effect.
Signed, sealed, and delivered in presence of
James Looney (SEAL)
Allen his mark Everett (SEAL)
Clerk.

THE STATE OF MISSISSIPPI--CARROLL COUNTY.
Before me, Clerk of Circuit Court, in and for the County and State aforesaid, this day, personally appeared and and made oath that have arrived at the Statutory age for the contraction of marriage, to-wit: 21 years and 18 years respectively, and further that there exists no legal cause or objection to the marriage of the said and
Sworn to and subscribed before me, this day of 187
Circuit Clerk.

THE STATE OF MISSISSIPPI--CARROLL COUNTY.
To any Regularly authorized Minister of the Gospel, Judge, Member of the Board of Supervisors, or any acting Justice of the Peace for said County--Greeting:
You, or either of you, are hereby authorized to solemnize the RITE OF MATRIMONY between James Luny and Nellie Everett and join them together as Man and Wife, in the Holy state of Wedlock, your official Certificate whereof you are to return, together with this License, into the office of the Clerk of the Circuit Court of said County, within the time prescribed by law.
Witness, R. J. Davis, Clerk of the Circuit Court of said County, this the 2 day of September A. D. 1880
R. J. Davis, Clerk.
In Virtue of the above License, the Rite of Matrimony between James Looney and Nellie Everett was duly celebrated by me on the 3 day of Sept A. D. 1880
Carroll Purnell (SEAL)

Figure 7 *Marriage Certificate for James K. Looney and Nellie Everett.*

Nellie. It is not totally clear what his relationship was to Nellie, but given his age, he is most likely an older cousin or uncle. The marriage was performed by Carroll Purnell who was an African-American farmer in the same area. No religious or judicial title is given on this document or in the Census material. However, it is likely that he was a pastor for a local church.

Let me say before going any further that this family's history is quite complicated and can be confusing. In addition to spelling variants, there are many actual name changes, particularly for the women. There are also entries in official records which are deliberately meant to be unclear and there are entries which conflict with information given at other times. Here is what has been found in the records.

Nellie's last name is recorded as Everett on the marriage record. However, earlier that year, when the 1880 Census was conducted, Nellie was recorded with the last name Parker along with everyone else in her mother's household. She was living with her mother, Charlotte, several siblings, and probably her children, Henry (b. 1877) and Sarena (b. Mar 1880). These children are most likely James's as he living right next door. Additionally, in the 1900 Census, James and Nellie report having been married since 1877. These two children do not show up in the 1900 Census with their parents. It is possible they have married and moved on. It is also possible one or both of them did not live long, particularly Henry since there is another child called Henry born later.

James was not living in Carroll County in 1870. There are no Looneys at all in this county that year which is pretty amazing as they tend to be pretty thick on the ground throughout the South.

Nellie was living in Carroll County in 1870, in fact, it is highly likely that she was born there. In the 1870 Census, she and the rest of her household are listed with the last name Kaigler. This may well be her true maiden name. Living next door is the same Burrell Everett that James is found with in 1880. Burrell is a farm laborer and has his wife and mother, Evaline, living with him. Although the 1870 Census does not list family relationship in the household and no Census records relationships between households, looking at family groups entered in both the 1880 and 1870 Census' for this area, it is very probable that Burrell is Charlotte's brother and Evaline is her mother. Both Burrell and Charlotte were born in Georgia. Evaline Everett was born in Virginia circa 1810. It is probable that Everett is Charlotte's maiden name which she reverts back to later in life. More about Nellie's family line will be explored a bit later in this document.

Both James and Nellie are recorded in the 1880 Census as mulatto. In the 1900 Census they are both recorded as black. The people who conducted the Census made subjective judgments about race. As the "Jim Crow" era lengthened, the idea of labelling people Black, later as Negro, and then Colored, became more and more aligned with the "one-drop" laws. One-drop of African blood put a person in that category and there was less recognition of the mixed ancestry most African-Americans actually had then and have today.

Based on their children's birth locations, James and Nellie moved to the Memphis area between September of 1880 and August of 1885. There is a James Looney listed in the Memphis City Directory in both 1886 and 1887 who is very probably the James Looney we are interested in. He is listed as colored, a laborer, residing at the right rear of 108 4th Street north side of Chelsea. Directory listings of the time often gave descriptive annotations for addresses rather than just a number and street name. Now a man supporting a young family, he would have followed the work. Although James was primarily a farmer, farming can be a fickle, unpredictable occupation and many farmers end up doing additional work to support their families. Memphis was booming and cotton prices dropped quite a bit in the 1880's making it difficult for farmers to support their families.

James and Nellie had 9 children; 7 of whom were living as of 1900. At that time he was living in Enumeration District 49, the west part of Civil District 13, Shelby County, Tennessee with his wife, Nellie, and 6 of his children:

>1. Katherine Looney (b. 18 Aug 1885 TN or MS (sources are inconsistent) m. 15 Feb 1900 to Joe F. Works (b. 1882, TN) d. 13 Aug 1949 Memphis, TN buried White Chapel, Fields Road, Memphis, TN)
>
>2. Henry Looney (b. Aug 1886 TN)
>
>3. Burrell Looney (Note: family members who knew him pronounce the name as it was spelled in the Census entries for Nellie's brother and uncle) (b. 26 Dec 1889 TN m. possibly twice, first to Annie Mae Shavers around 1912 then to Henrietta Beatty, d. 2 Mar 1963 Memphis, TN buried Memphis National Cemetery, Memphis, TN);

4. Lucy Looney (b. 13 Apr 1892 TN m. twice, first to Solomon Phillips around 1913, then to Willie Webb around 1923, d. 2 Nov 1950 Cleveland, OH, buried in Sunflower County, Mississippi);

5. James Looney (b. 22 Mar 1894 TN m. married twice: Eliza (b. 1906 MS) around 1920; later Annie Belle McKinney d. May 1964 Michigan);

6. Martin Looney (b. 23 Jun 1895 Memphis, TN m. Hattie Williams (b. 1900, MS) on 1 Mar 1914, Leflore County, Mississippi, d. 20 Apr 1957 Memphis, TN, buried in Sunflower County, Mississippi).

Also in the household were a son-in-law (Joe F. Works), and his mother-in-law, Charlotte Everett (b. Jan 1830 Georgia, widowed, listed as having had 6 children, 4 of whom were alive in 1900, parents both born in North Carolina according to this entry. This information is not consistent with earlier entries.). So far, there is no further information on the one other child of Nellie and James that is indicated on the Census under the question asking how many children the mother had birthed.

In this Census, James parents' birthplaces are listed as Tennessee for his father and North Carolina for his mother. His parents' birthplaces are quite inconsistent on the Census forms. His mother's birthplace is listed as Georgia, North Carolina, Mississippi, and Virginia in various entries. His father's entries include: Georgia, Kentucky, Mississippi, Tennessee, Virginia, and the Irish Free State.

In 1900, James was renting a farm and farming it with the help of Henry, Burrell, Katherine, and Joe Works.

Something happened in 1902 or 1903, perhaps Nellie died. Tennessee did not start keeping death records statewide until 1908. Memphis starting keeping records in 1848, however, a search of the Memphis database did not reveal Nellie.

The family was still living on the farm just south of Memphis at this time. In the margin of the first 1910 Census in which James appears, is written "west side of Horn Lake Road". This road leads from Memphis into Mississippi. The area was predominately settled by African-American farmers and it is the district in Tennessee which elected the only two African-American Senators to the U.S. Congress from Tennessee—Harold Ford, Sr. and his son, Harold Ford, Jr. The Ford family has a history in this area reaching back into the 1860's.

On 26 December 1903 James applied for a marriage license with "Mrs." Tomanna Mack. However, the marriage did not get completed. This could be for a number of different reasons. There may have been a ceremony but the paperwork never got returned to the county. Perhaps Nellie was still alive and there had been no divorce. Or perhaps Tomanna was still married to the man she wed on 5 November 1899 - William S. Webb. Tomanna's daughter, Lee Ann, is recorded as William's daughter although she was born circa January 1887 and may actually have been fathered by someone else. She becomes important a bit later in the narrative. The surname Mack is actually Tomanna's maiden name,

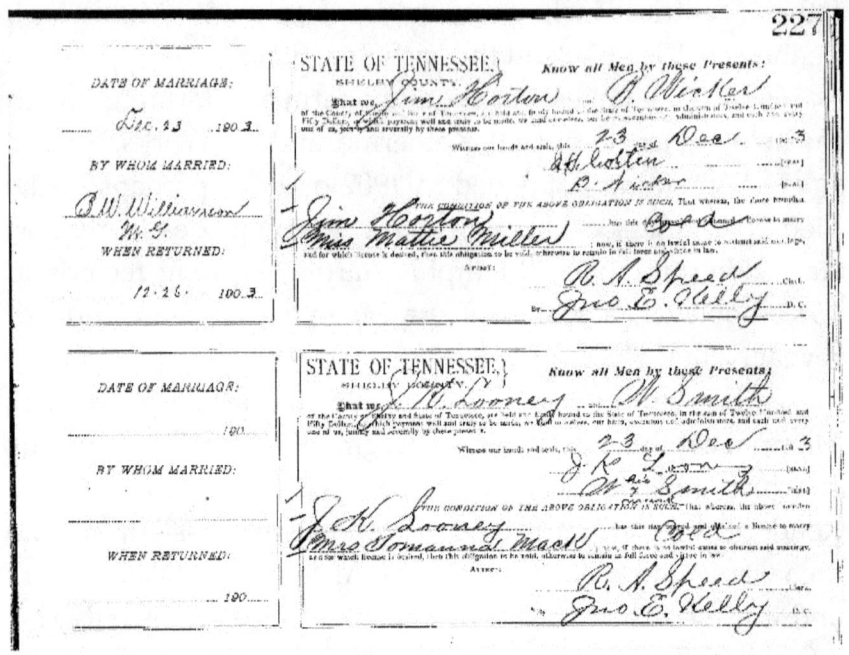

Figure 8 James K. Looney's application for marriage to Tomanna Mack in 1903. The application preceeding his shows how the record would appear once a marriage had been completed.

notwithstanding the "Mrs." title listed on the marriage application.

James and Tomanna lived together as man and wife despite not having a legally valid marriage in Tennessee. Tennessee has never recognized common–law marriages. Later James and Tomanna moved to Mississippi. Mississippi did recognize common-law marriages from the mid-1850's until 5 April 1956, so by that measure James and Tomanna may have had a legally recognized marriage when he died in 1936. It actually was not uncommon for marital documentation to be out of order during this time period. Many people married, left their spouses when it suited them and, without obtaining a divorce, married again when they found someone new. Tracking situations like this was much more difficult then than it is today.

By 1910, James, Tomanna, James, Jr., Lucy, and Martin were living with Tomanna's mother Delia (Hart) Keglar (b. about 1852, Tennessee) in Memphis. This name is spelled in various ways including Kegglor, Kegland, Kaigler, and Kegler. Delia Keglar was a laundress working for a private family. She is listed in the Memphis City Directory as far back as 1897 and, at that time, living in the area of the intersection of Kansas and Kerr Avenue.

Family sources provided the name of Tom Annor for Tomanna. She is not listed that way in any record found thus far. It may have been too unusual for enumerators to spell or she didn't use it regularly. Instead she is listed as Tomanna, Annie Taylor, Anna T., Tom Anna, T. Ana (single letter "n"), and Tomie. To distinguish her from her daughter who was also commonly called Annie, I will use Tomanna. For her daughter, I will use Lee Ann. Only once is Tomanna listed as having an occupation; in the 1910 Census enumerated on 15 and 16 April, she was working as a farm laborer. By the 18th of April that year, the family has moved in with her mother and Tomanna is never listed with an occupation again although family sources say she ran a personal care product company like Madame C. J. Walker's.

James moved from the farm into Memphis to be a timber man. The timber industry in Memphis was booming at the time. In 1912, Tennessee lumber men put in a 60-hour workweek at fourteen cents an hour. There were 32 hardwood mills in Memphis in 1910. James and Burrell were both working in lumber mills. This is also the likely way that Lucy met her first husband, Solomon Phillips, as he was also working in a mill. For a short time, Lucy and Solomon, lived with James just after their marriage in 1913/4.

In 1914 Solomon is listed as boarding with James Looney at the same address that had been given in previous directories for Delia Keglar, although she is no longer listed there.

In 1918, when Solomon registered for the World War I Draft, he was working for the Dixon and Shannon Lumber Company and in the 1920 Census he is working as an "edgerman" in a mill. An edgerman earned much more money than a laborer in a mill. Want ads for workers at the time advertised edgerman positions paying $2 an hour.

Based on the reported birthplace of his son, Cecil, James moved his family to Beat 4 in Leflore County, Mississippi around 1915. His son, James, Jr. moved there too and on 5 June 1917 he registered for the World War I Draft. James, Jr. was living in Itta Bena, Mississippi and working as a farm laborer for W. F. Roberts. Martin Looney stayed in Memphis working as a "wood chopper" until sometime after 1917, but by 1920 he was boarding with his father. When James, Sr. moved to Leflore County, he returned to share cropping.

The domestic arrangements by this time were a bit complicated. James is living with Tomanna as man and wife, however, her daughter, Lee Ann "Annie", is living with them and having children fathered by James. This situation appears to have existed from at least 1910 when their daughter, Eleanor, was born. James fathered at least 7 children with Lee Ann. They include:

    1. Elma (b. 1910 Shelby, Tennessee) (This is the name that appears on the 1920 Census, family

sources know of a daughter named Eleanor. No record of a child named Eleanor has emerged. Instead there is this child and then there is a child named Elnora born in 1929 who shows up in the household of Willie and Lucy Webb on the Mississippi Educable Children listing for 1935. There is no indication in that record of who Elnora's parents are. Family sources believe the youngest of James and Lee Ann's children was Christopher who was born in 1927. A descendant of Eleanor's could help clarify this situation.)

    2. Andrew (b. Tennessee)

    3. Cecil T. (b. 1915 Mississippi)

    4. Robert Emmett (b. 20 Jun 1920 Leflore, Mississippi m. Pearlie Gilbert (b. 23 Jan 1925 Leflore, Mississippi to Fred Gilbert (b. 7 Sep 1894 Morgan County, Georgia d. Jun 1969 Greenwood, Leflore County, Mississippi) and Lillie Bell Booker (b. 8 Apr 1905 Mississippi d. 18 Nov 1982 Bessemer, Jefferson, Alabama) d. 9 Jan 1995 Detroit, Michigan) 28 Oct 1950 Leflore County, Mississippi; had 10 children d. 1 Jan 1967 Detroit, Michigan)

    5. Asa V. (b. 11 Jun 1922 Leflore, Mississippi d. 23 Jul 1989 Detroit, Michigan)

    6. Willie Bell (b. 12 Sep 1924 near Itta Bena, Leflore, Mississippi m. two times first Perry Moore 1942 had 2 children (Ora Jean Moore and Perry Moore, Jr. both deceased); second William B. Flournoy 1953 had 4 children; Willie Bell taught at Poro Beauty College, Detroit and later founded and operated for nearly 30 years her own nationally accredited school of cosmetology and later a beauty salon; she also served

as the local precinct delegate for three terms, as chairperson of a local election board and an appointee of the Detroit City Clerk in the Election Ambassadors Program d. 30 Apr 2004 Detroit, Michigan)

7. Christopher C. H. (b. 2 Feb 1927 (although listed as 2 Feb on his Funeral Program and on his original application for Social Security, in the Social Security Death Index his birth is listed as 20 Feb; probably that is a typographical error) Sunflower, Mississippi m. Corena (spelled this way in Social Security records) or Corinne (spelled this way in Christopher's Funeral Program) (b. 23 Dec 1922 d. 19 Mar 2004 Detroit, Michigan) she had been married previously and had two sons — Samuel "Sammie" Pulliam and Eugen {sic} Pulliam); Christopher worked in the paint shop of an automobile manufacturer d. 1 May 1970 Detroit, Michigan).

James may have had more children. Although 16 children are accounted for here, some family members report there was a total of 22. Additionally, there is a family oral history stating James also fathered children by one of Nellie's sisters. There are four grandchildren listed on the 1880 Census as living in the household of Charlotte Everett who are most probably Rebecca's offspring. This is the Census where everybody in her household is listed with the last name Parker, although they may have used Everett, Kaigler, Looney or even something else in later records. These grandchildren of Charlotte's are:

    1. James H. Parker (b. 1871 Mississippi)
    2. Robert Parker (b. 1873 Mississippi this child is

listed as Black where the other children are listed as Mulatto which may indicate a different father)
3. Cansey Parker (granddaughter b. 1875 Mississippi)
4. Jeremiah J. Parker (b. Sept 1879 Mississippi)

DNA testing of the descendants of these children is probably the only way to know if these children were fathered by James K. Looney. More information on this point may develop over time.

In the 1920 Census, Lee Ann and "Elma" are both listed as daughters of James and are listed with his last name which is spelled "Luny." Lee Ann's marital status is listed as single.

In 1930, Lee Ann and her children are listed with the last name Webb and her marital status is listed as widowed. She is listed as stepdaughter to James. James is sharecropping cotton and the family has moved to Sunflower County.

In the 1940 Census, after James died, Lee Ann "Annie" was listed as the head of the household and she and her children are listed with the last name Looney and Lee Ann's mother is listed as Annie Taylor. The family has moved back across the county line to Leflore County. Lee Ann is listed as a Farmer and her children who are living with her with the exception of Christopher who was 13 at the time, are listed as farm laborers. In reality, Christopher was probably helping with the farm as well. Enumerators were required to list occupations for people age 14 and older. On farms children started to help with farm tasks early in life.

Between 1924 and 1927, James moved his family over the county line into Sunflower County, Mississippi. They lived in the vicinity of Moorhead, not far from Willie and

Lucy (Looney) Webb. Both households would have been quite full. The sharecroppers' shacks were small. During this time, it is not uncommon to see children living with relatives. It was a way of evening out the workload and the number of people within a household. In fact, a child named Elnora (b. 1929) lived with Willie and Lucy for a time in the mid-1930's. It is not clear whose child she was. She is recorded as part of their household in the 1935 survey of Educable Children. Mississippi conducted these surveys aperiodically throughout the period 1850-1894 and then again from 1906-1965. Sunflower County records exist for the years: 1850, 1927, 1931, 1933, and 1935. Leflore County records exist for the years: 1892, 1943, 1945, 1947, 1949, 1951, 1953, 1955, and 1957. These records have not been digitized which makes them time-consuming to search since you must browse the images and there are hundreds of pages in each report.

James worked the fields until one week before he died of lobar pneumonia on 9 May 1936. His death occurred prior to the advent of antibiotics which might have helped him. Penicillin did not become available to the general public until after World War II. Lobar pneumonia is a common complication of the flu or a cold, particularly in the elderly.

His age is recorded as 79 but he may have been as old as 83 given the Census entries. Birth dates for people born prior to official record keeping are more of an estimate than a firm fact. His widow reports his birthplace as Memphis. He obviously lived around Memphis for a long time. Whether or not he was born there requires more investigation. Given the DNA and family stories about who his father was, he may have been born elsewhere and moved to the Memphis area after Emancipation.

He was living at the Milton Barnett Plantation at the time of his death. Farms in the South were most often called plantations. Many of these farms during the early part of the 1900s still had the structures built during the time of slavery. The main house and barns would normally be grouped together. A group of shacks for household and main compound slaves would usually be fairly close to the main compound. Depending on the size of the plantation there might be additional slave quarters located in "camps" throughout the property with convenient access to the fields. Remember these would have been built during a time when your feet and possibly a mule-drawn wagon would have been the only forms of transportation. In fact, living family members remember this still being the case during their early years. It was after World War II that tractors and cars started to penetrate the South. When the Civil War ended slavery, farmers hired workers under the sharecropping system and the former slave quarters became the sharecropper's homes. Now many of these structures have been torn down as farmers use tractors and combines to farm their land. However, there are some shacks still in existence with people living in them in Webb, Mississippi as an example.

Social Security was enacted on 14 August 1935 and taxes to support the program started being collected in January 1937. The first benefits were paid in January 1940. The Federal Insurance Contribution Act authorized the collection of taxes to support this program. The first Social Security number was issued in November of 1936 and so far over 453.7 million numbers have been issued. The first three numbers indicated the geographic area where the number was issued with the remaining numbers being random. Since

2011, the Social Security Administration has revised this approach and now all the numbers are random. There was a push to register people which over the years has resulted in people being registered shortly after birth. But in the early years, it took a little while to get everyone registered.

Although James Looney died before registration started and Lee Ann appears to never have registered, some of their children did. Applicants filled out a form which included the name of the father and maiden name of the mother. Willie Bell applied on 12 March 1946 listing James K. Looney as father and Annie Ford as mother. A short 6 days later, both Asa and Christopher Looney applied on 18 March 1946 listing James Looney as father and Annie Reed as mother. Robert Emmett Looney applied on 17 January 1955. A complete copy of this record is still in the process of being released.

Years later when Willie Belle passed away, her Funeral Program lists her mother as Lee Ann Maggie Elizabeth Ford. There is some thought that there is a connection to the Fords previously mentioned who lived in the same district of Tennessee as James did for many years. While the connection to the Fords is not delineated in any early documentation, it is possible Lee Ann was the illegitimate offspring of a Ford even though Lee Ann is clearly identified as the daughter of William S. Webb in the 1900 Census. Preliminary research into the Ford family has not yet revealed a connection, but much more needs to be done on that line of investigation.

The Slave Holders of the Everett Line

In the first half of the 1800's cotton profits caused plantation owners to migrate westward to the rich dark soils of the "black belt" of Alabama, Mississippi, and as far away as the river valleys of Texas. Government land policy encouraged the settlement and development of these lands through programs granting veterans land patents, cheap sale of public lands, and the Indian removal acts which resettled Indians west of the Mississippi. White settlers brought their slaves with them. It is estimated that 800,000 slaves were moved between 1800 and 1860 from the Atlantic coastal region to work the new farmland. Several lines of our family participated in this movement including the Everett and Kaigler lines. Examining the Census for white families living in the Vaiden area who might possibly have been slave holders led to three families all of whom had inherited from the same man from Georgia.

Tracing these three slave holding families of Turner C. Everett, George C. Everett, and Henry Kaigler led to the discovery of who held Nellie's line of family in slavery and revealed where the family had been located during the early to mid-1800's.

The James Abbington Everett Line

Most researchers cite James Abbington Everett (b. 1 May 1788 Bertie County North Carolina d. 23 Jun 1848 Houston County Georgia) as the son of Henry Everett (b. 1760) and Elizabeth Abbington (b. 1765). However, documentation for this time period is scant and there are a number of Henry Everett's or Averett's living in North

Carolina and Georgia. Additionally, most sources currently list Elizabeth as dying prior to the date of birth for any of the children she is purported to have had, so clearly there is some discrepancy there and more research on this point is needed. His siblings and some of their offspring are listed in his will and included:

1. Charles Everett (b. abt 1780 m. Catherine "Caty" Rents 23 Aug 1810 Amite, MS had 6 children d. abt 1830 Amite, MS)
2. Turner C. Everett (b. circa 1781 d. between 1830 and 1840 Dooly, GA (although not listed in the will specifically, James names Turner C. (b. 1821), George C. Everett, James M. Everett, and Charles H. Everett as nephews, and these four men may be descendants of Turner C. Everett. They would have to have been sired by a male Everett and they were not the sons of James' brother Charles. According to the 1830 Census, Turner may have had as many as 5 sons, although how many of them reached adulthood is an open question.)
3. Nancy Everett (m. Furlow (her husband may have been Robert Furlow (b.1765 NC d. 1845 MS) who is closely associated with Charles Everett. They moved at the same times to the same locations; Robert was the guarantor on Charles' Marriage Bond; one source lists Robert as a first cousin to Charles.) d. before 1848)
4. Patsy Everett (m. Sugars Bynum; had 4 children d. before 1848)

Turner and James both moved into the area of Houston/Pulaski/Dooly counties in Georgia. James had served as a soldier in the War of 1812. He is listed on the Muster Roll of a detachment of Georgia cavalry mounted riflemen under the command of Lt. Col. Allen Tooke which was stationed at Fort Mitchell Hartford and on an "Indian Scout" from the 9th November to the 22d of November 1814 and on a certification of the receipt of "full pay" for his service. A note in this record states the men were probably from Pulaski County. Land grants in Georgia were awarded to veterans of the war and it is likely that James was a recipient. This may also be Turner's situation, although this possibility still requires verification.

There have been numerous boundary changes with these counties and it is possible that even though Turner is listed in Census entries in Dooly and Pulaski counties during the early 1800's, he never actually moved. Turner shows up in the Pulaski County Capt Richard Davies District Tax Digest for 1818. Turner was selected to serve as a commissioner at the founding of the Houston County to superintend the election of five Justices of the Inferior Court. Turner C. Everett is the likely father for Turner C. Everett (b. 1821) who becomes of real interest shortly. Also Dr. George C. Everett lived close to Turner C. Everett near Vaiden in Carroll County, Mississippi. He showed up in Mississippi around the same time as Turner, was also from Georgia, and he named a son Turner. George is also named in the James A. Everett's will as a nephew and may well be Turner's brother, and if not, certainly a cousin.

On 7 August 1820 there is a James Everett living in Pulaski County who may well be the one we are interested in because next door is Peter Greene with whom he is clearly associated with later in life. The household contains: Free White Persons - Males - Under 10: 1, Free White Persons - Males - 10 thru 15: 1, Free White Persons - Males - 26 thru 44: 1, Free White Persons - Males - 45 and over: 3, Free White Persons - Females - Under 10: 3, Free White Persons - Females - 16 thru 25: 1, Free White Persons - Females - 26 thru 44: 1, Slaves - Males - 14 thru 25: 1, Number of Persons - Engaged in Agriculture: 2, for a total of Free White Persons of 11 and 1 total slaves. In the Pulaski Co, GA Minute Book A on page 69, James A. Everett is named as co-signor of a bond in the amount of $8,000 when Peter Greene is given guardianship "to the person and property of Robert M. Ingram".

James A. Everett helped found Fort Valley in Houston County, Georgia. Houston County was established in 1821 from the Creek Cession of 1821. It is named after John Houstoun (b. 1744 d. 1796) who was a member of the Continental Congress and became Governor of Georgia in 1778. John Houstoun pronounced his name "House-ton" and this is the way the county name is pronounced today although the "u" in the last syllable was dropped from the spelling. The very next year, in 1822, it was divided and part of the county became Crawford County named after William Harris Crawford (b. 1772 d. 1834), a U.S. Senator, an ambassador to France, and the Secretary of the Treasury. The Fort Valley area is now part of Peach County, Georgia, formed in 1924 from parts of Houston and Macon Counties, so named for the peach orchards which predominate there. James was a veteran of the War of 1812 and an Indian trader. According to local history books, he arrived in the area of Fort Valley in the early 1820's and started serving as the postmaster as early as 7 December 1825 when Fort Valley was part of Crawford County. Later official documents show he again served as the Postmaster for Fort Valley from 11 January 1834 until Peter B. Greene (who would have been his father-in-law if he had lived long enough) took over 16 May 1836, James took it on again on 15 September 1836 when Peter died, and then Charles H. Everett (he is one of James' nephews) took it over in July 1842. Charles H. Everett is recorded next to James in the 1840 Census.

When the first session of the Superior Court was organized 7 May 1822, the Honorable Thomas W. Harris presiding, the Court was held in the blacksmith shop on the premises of James A. Everett.

He had a large plantation of 12,000 acres according to one history written about the Houston County. The Property Tax Records of 1849 of his estate show a slightly different story. That record shows a total of 16,623 acres owned in Georgia in several different counties including Houston, Crawford, Macon, Dooly, Coweta, Sumpter {sic – should be Sumter}, and Stuart {sic – should be Stewart]. He also owned four lots in the town of Fort Valley which were advertised for sale in the Macon Telegraph on Tuesday, 6 November 1849 on page 4. The probate of his will revealed he owned 600 acres in Alabama and 5,000 acres in Mississippi, both properties being primarily woodland. At least some of his land came to him through the Georgia Cherokee Land Lottery held in 1832.

The 1830 Census records James living in what was then Crawford County and owning 26 slaves – 8 males between the ages of 10 thru 23, 4 males between the ages of 24 to 35, 2 females under the age of 10, and 12 females between the ages of 10 to 23.

In 1830 James served as an Administer of the Estate of Nathan Tanton as noted in the Macon Weekly Telegraph (Macon, GA) on Saturday, February 20, 1830; Volume: 4 Issue: 8 Page: 29 in a notice that in 4 months application would be made to the Ordinary Court of Crawford County to sell estate for the benefit of Nathan Tanton's heirs and creditors. Later that same year, James was called in to appraise a horse belonging to John H. Powell of Captain Alsey Marshall's District. The animal was "tolled" before Peter B. Greene, Esq. who is the father of James's wife Mary Beaufort Greene. The bay mare with her right eye out, a white spot in her forehead, about 5 years old, 5 feet 3 inches high was appraised by James A. Everett and Sampson English to $50 on the 11th of June 1830. The Macon Weekly Telegraph reported the story on 19 June 1830.

He helped found two schools in the area. In 1836 both he and Henry Kaigler, whom you will meet shortly, were trustees of the Fort Valley Academy. And in 1837, he donated $25,000 (equivalent to $609,756.10 in 2014 dollars) to found the Wesley Manual Labor School. The interest alone to be used to fund the salaries of the school officers.

James A. Everett married rather late in life to 15-year-old Mary Beaufort Greene (b. 21 Mar 1823) on 10 December 1838. The couple had 6 children; one of whom was born just before his father's death. Their children include:

1. Sarah Eliza Everett (b. 18 Sep 1838 Fort Valley, Houston, Georgia m. James Persons Flewellen 24 Oct 1854 d. 22 Feb 1881 Independence, Washington, Texas buried Prairie Lea Cemetery section 3, range 1, Brenham, Washington, Texas)

2. James Abbington Everett (b. 25 Aug 1840 Fort Valley, Houston, Georgia d. 18 May 1908 His place of death and burial is in question as there are two entries; one for Marshallville, Macon, Georgia buried Marshallville City Cemetery Marshallville, Macon, Georgia and the other for Oaklawn Cemetery, Fort Valley, Peach, Georgia.)
3. Ann Elizabeth Everett (b. 20 Nov 1842 m. Benjamin Warren Sanford 1861 d. 17 Apr 1917)
4. Theodocia H. Everett (b. 1844 m. Rev. Robert Afton Holland 23 Mar 1864 d. 21 Dec 1893 St. Louis, Missouri)
5. Henry Peter Everett (b. 4 Jun 1846 m. Julia Felder 1870 d. 10 Nov 1914 Houston, Georgia buried Oaklawn Cemetery, Fort Valley, Houston now Peach County, Georgia)
6. John Fletcher Everett (b. 14 Jun 1848 d. 9 Apr 1908 Houston, Georgia buried Oaklawn Cemetery, Fort Valley, Houston now Peach County, Georgia).

Mary Beaufort Greene was the child of James' longtime friend, Peter Buford Greene (b. Jun 1795 Hancock County, Georgia m. Sarah W. Ingram 12 Jan 1819 Pulaski County, Georgia d. 20 Jan 1836 Houston County, Georgia). Peter and his wife Sarah had 6 children who lived to adulthood. They also had at least 4 children who died in infancy.

1. Mary Beaufort Greene (b. 20 Mar 1823 d. 6 Feb 1852; more detail in this section)
2. John Greene (d. 1848)

3. Elizabeth F. Greene (b. 16 Nov 1827 m. Turner C. Everett 18 Sep 1849 Houston County, GA; had 5 children d. 18 May 1878 Carroll County, MS, buried Everett Cemetery, Carroll County, MS)
4. Miles LaFayette Greene (b. 1826 Georgia d. 8 Dec 1865 Houston County, Georgia, buried Oaklawn Cemetery, Fort Valley, Houston now Peach County, GA)
5. William Ingram Greene (b. 1829 d. 1897)
6. Peter Buford Greene (b. 1836)

According to the book titled *First Hundred and Ten Years of Houston County, Georgia (1822-1932)*, in 1840 James A. Everett paid $100 to have a missionary preach to his "colored" people. Reverend James Dunwoody preached at two plantations owned by Brother Everett, one above Fort Valley, the other near Hog Crawl Creek. Such was Rev. Dunwoody's success that he received into the church a large majority of the people to whom he preached; so that at Brother Everett's request, he continued the mission five years in succession.

In the 1840 Census, James's household in Houston County includes: Free White Persons - Males - 20 thru 29: 1 Free White Persons - Females - Under 5: 1 Free White Persons - Females - 5 thru 9: 1 Free White Persons - Females - 20 thru 29: 1 Slaves - Males - Under 10: 2 Slaves - Females - Under 10: 1 Slaves - Females - 24 thru 35: 1 No. White Persons over 20 Who Cannot Read and Write: 2 Free White Persons - Under 20: 2 Free White Persons - 20 thru 49: 2 Total Free White Persons: 4 Total Slaves: 4 Total All Persons - Free White, Free Colored, Slaves: 8. The number of slaves is much lower than one might expect, however, it may be that only those slaves actually housed with the family are recorded and the slaves who are living in closer proximity to the fields are either listed in some other way or not listed at all. Perhaps more research will reveal what accounts for this apparent disparity.

The Alexandria Gazette in Alexandria, Virginia included the following news item on page 2 of its Wednesday, August 6, 1845 issue –

"James A. Everett, Esq. of Houston County, Georgia, has made a donation of $8000 to the Georgia Female College at Macon. The institution has, by the liberality of Mr. Everett, has been entirely relieved from debt. We take pleasure in recording the gifts of wealth to learning."

According to the Property Tax Records of Houston County in 1848, James' estate owned 242 slaves, then in 1849 a total of 263. The Tax Record for 1848 was completed after his death, so it is his estate that was assessed a tax based on this number.

Toward the end, James became ill and he wrote a will in May of 1848. The will is included in the Appendix C in its entirety, but there is one paragraph which is of great interest to our family. James left his mother-in-law two thousand dollars, his gold spectacles, and the use for life of five "negroes" which he named. These are the only slaves identified by name in his will. The names include Early, Caroline, Burrell, Tatnall (this name might be Tarnall), and Jerry. Burrell is of particular interest to our family and will be discussed a little later.

James also specifies his executors which include his brother-in-law, Myles L. Green, his nephew, Turner C. Everett, and a friend, Adolphus D. Kendrick. (As a quick aside, Adolphus also served as a Postmaster in Houston County in the town of Marshallsville.) Turner C. Everett is charged with purchasing more "negroes" as specified in the will to the tune of $32,000 ($969,696.97 in 2014 dollars). James does an interesting thing with relation to these investments – he specifies that these "negroes" cannot be sold or be used to satisfy a debt contract. While he may have specified these measures to ensure the investment did not get squandered, it has the effect of keeping any family groups together. He further specifies *"And in dividing my estate according to this mode prescribed in this item of my will the negroes shall be set off in families and not otherwise unless absolutely necessary."* He clearly intended for family groups to be kept together, instead of selling people off individually.

In addition to providing for his family, James made a number of bequests to support his religious friends and community. He gave money to fund international and domestic missionary work and specified funds for use by two Bishops in their work with the Creek Nation. He also provided money to purchase a "negro man or boy" for two Reverends who were friends of his.

During his lifetime, James was a strong advocate for building a rail line to Fort Valley. After his death, his estate subscribed to 200 shares for the building of The Southwestern Rail Line which was by far the largest investment in the venture. The rail line was built and for many years carried the agricultural products of cotton and peaches to bigger markets.

James died on 23 June 1848 in Houston County, Georgia. His obituary in the Macon Weekly Telegraph (Macon, GA) on Tuesday, July 4, 1848 on page 3 said:

"At Fort Valley, Houston county[sic], on the 23^d ult. of a long and painful sickness, which baffled the kind attentions of numerous friends, and the united efforts of several skillful Physicians, Mr. James A. Everett, in the 61st year of his age.

In the death of Mr. Everett his family and relations have lost a most kind and provident husband, father and friend – his slaves a humane master – and the community at large a generous benefactor.

To a mind naturally keen and discriminating, he added an energy and decision of action, that made him eminently successful – having by his own exertions, accumulated a princely fortune; he has within the last ten years of his life, let thousands and tens of thousands of it go, both as private and public donations."

The 1850 Slave Schedule lists a total of 170 slaves held by James' Estate and his widow, Mary. Mary has 28 slaves listed under her own name, while 142 are listed under Joseph E. Davis, Agent for the estate of J.A. Everett. The slaves range from a 7-month-old girl to a 70-year-old female.

Mary married a second time on 15 January 1851 to Dr. William A. Mathews. It was to be short-lived. Mary Beaufort Greene Everett Mathews died on 6 February 1852; she would have been 29-years-old had she reached her birthday in March. She was buried in Oaklawn Cemetery, Fort Valley, then Houston now Peach County, Georgia. Upon her death, her children were split between Myles and Turner. The girls stayed with Myles. James, Henry, and John were sent to live with Turner C. Everett in Carroll County, Mississippi after their mother's death.

In 1854 the 1,500 acres the estate owned in Crawford County Georgia were valued at $7,500 in the county's Property Tax Digest.

In the January 1855 Term of Houston Ordinary Court, Myles L. Green petitioned the Court to designate appraisers to value and divide the estate as Sarah had married James P. Flewellan (spelled with an "a" instead of an "e" in the probate record). In April of the same year, Myles again petitioned the Court for permission to sell properties not adjoining the main plantation in order to give Sarah her portion.

In the June 1857 Term, David N. Austin petitioned the Court to order a title for land which he had purchased from James A. Everett for $204.33 plus interest which he had paid now in full.

During the June 1859 Term, Myles petitioned the Court for additional compensation because *"during the year 1858 he was at great trouble & lost a great deal of time from his own business in attending & Superintending the plantations belonging to his said Testators Estate and also in attending to the Negroes in their sickness and looking after their safety and comfort."* He was granted $600.

A total of 343 slaves are recorded in the 1860 Slave Schedule for James Abbington Everett's estate. They ranged from a one-month-old boy to an 80-year-old female. Most were in the prime working years of 14 to 40.

In the December 1860 Term, Myles again petitioned for the appointment of appraisers to make a division of the estate due to Ann's marriage to Benjamin W. Sandford.

James and Henry both moved back to Houston County by 25 November 1861 when they joined Company E in the 57th Georgia Infantry Regiment of the Confederate States Army. Henry Peter Everett was just 14 years old when he enlisted to fight. This company was later redesignated Company K. James received a Cross of Honor bestowed on Civil War veterans for his service in this unit.

James also funded the equipping of the Everett Guards which was named in his honor. A. H. Long was made Captain of the unit and Mr. Everett, 1st Lieutenant. This company was in service for 6 months in the Savannah area.

On the 21st of November 1863 the process of dividing the estate was repeated for the oldest son, James Abbington Everett.

After the War, James A. Everett (b. 1840), applied on 30 August 1865 and then received on the 28th of September 1865, a Presidential Pardon for his "taking part in the rebellion against the Government of the United States". His application notes that *"he was not yet twenty-one when the war ended, he was conscripted in the Confederate Army until the close of the war. He returned to being a private citizen – a planter by vocation and has had very little to do with public affairs. His slaves are free. He has accepts the new order of things and will faithfully abide by it."* On the bottom of his application is a note "Worth over $20,000."

Also in 1865 the U.S. collected taxes to defray the cost of the Civil War and James Abbington Everett (b. 1840) was assessed a total of $7 for 2 gold watches and a piano. In 1866 both an income tax and a luxury goods tax were collected. This time James Abbington Everett paid $1 for a gold watch and $52.57 on his income of $1051.50 (a rate of 5%). In July of that same year, he also got to pay $5 for his piano valued at $50. His father's estate paid $86.25 on an income of $1725.

Shortly after the Emancipation (18 December 1865), Myles again petitioned the Court with these words:

"in consequence of the emancipation of the Negro slaves formerly belonging to said estate it is impracticable to keep up & carry on the farms belonging to said estate under this change &

supervision of Overseers as heretofore done – that the freedmen on said farms account be controlled or induced to work faithfully or continually & it will be difficult with their labor to harvest the crops made this year Besides the estate is losing from the deportations of the Negroes on the stock.".

Myles was given leave to sell the estate's personal property as a result. Not long after that, Myles was back in court to request the division of the estate for Theodocia upon her marriage to Robert A. Holland.

Myles died on 8 December 1865. He had spent 17 years administering the estate on James A. Everett, largely on his own as Turner C. Everett had fulfilled his purchasing duties and then moved to Mississippi and Adolphus D. Kendrick had moved to another county in Georgia. Myles not only managed the day-to-day operations and legal necessities, he brought Ann and Theodocia (and probably Sarah before her marriage although no record has been found to definitely state this) into his home after their mother died in 1852.

Then in the February 1866 Term, Adolphus D. Kendrick on behalf of himself and Turner C. Everett petitioned to be released from their duties as Administrators of the Estate and suggested James Abbington Everett, the oldest son, and William I. Green (another of Mary's brothers) be appointed. The petition was granted.

James and William petitioned the Court in the August 1866 Term for permission to sell land in Pulaski County and in and around the towns of Hartford and Hawkinsville. Permission was granted in the October session.

Back in court in January 1867, James and William requested they be allowed to sell 600 acres in Alabama and

5,000 acres in Mississippi. Permission was granted but in the end they did not get an offer they considered fair so they parceled out the land itself to heirs. James's son Henry Peter came of age in June of 1867 and there was another division of the estate.

In July of 1868 as a result of petition to the Court on the behalf of John F. Everett, youngest son of James, an order was given to build

"a good suitable dwelling house & necessary convenient outhouses kitchens negro houses Cribbs Smokehouses Gin house & __ & to purchase for & supply him the said John D. Everett with the necessary stock of horses & mules cattle & hogs corn & meat & necessary supplies & suitable farming utensils & implements to enable him to work & carry on a farm".

John received 3,000 acres and some $5,000 dollars as his settlement. When he came of age the next year, James and William requested a dismissory note as the last will and testament of James Abbington Everett had finally be discharged in full. The note was granted.

In 1870 the oldest son James lived in Houston County with his wife and 3 children, his younger brother John, and John W. Hollinshead (b. 1847 Macon, Georgia to James T. and Nancy J. Hollenshead{sic} d. 17 Sep 1887 Fort Valley, Houston, Georgia; buried Oaklawn Cemetery, Fort Valley, Houston now Peach, Georgia).

On 8 July 1924, the area where James had lived was reorganized into Peach County with Fort Valley as its county seat.

The Turner C. Everett Line

Turner C. Everett was born on 17 December 1821 in Georgia. He was probably the child of Turner C. Everett (b. circa 1781 died between 1830 and 1840), one of the sons of Henry Everett (b. 1760) and Elizabeth Abbington (b. 1765). Turner (b. 1821) fought in the Mexican American War of 1846 to 1848. In 1848 he inherited $5,000 dollars total from his very wealthy uncle, James Abbington Everett. He was also made an executor of the estate and specifically charged with purchasing and managing the "negroes" as directed by the will. Most of the legatees named in the will received an amount of money designated to be invested in "negroes". The total amount to be used in this way was equivalent to close to one million dollars in 2014 dollars.

On 18 September 1849 he married Elizabeth F. Greene. Elizabeth was the daughter of Peter Buford Greene and Sarah W. Ingram who married on 12 June 1819 in Pulaski County, Georgia.

Turner's uncle, James Abbington Everett, married Elizabeth's older sister Mary on 10 December 1838. So Turner was a nephew and would have been a brother-in-law to James Abbington Everett had James lived longer.

In 1850 Turner and Elizabeth lived in District 9, Houston County, Georgia. He owned 14 slaves at that time. By 1860 Turner C. Everett had moved to Police District 5, Carroll County, Mississippi and owned 38 slaves. Turner's brother George C. Everett moved there as well. He was a doctor. George also held small numbers of slaves. George had a large family of eight children including a child named Eveline. This is of interest because it is a relatively unusual name in this geographic area and it is also the name of the oldest known person in the Everett line of our family. When looking at family groups including extended family members, it is common to come across the same names and it was also not unusual to find slaves bearing names which occurred in the family to whom they were enslaved. Again, not proof, just suggestive of a possible relationship.

After Emancipation, Turner C. Everett remained in Carroll County and nearby are the Everett and Kaigler families we are interested in. Although this is indirect evidence of a connection, it was a common pattern for newly freed people to remain in place for the first few years as they had no money to move, no transport other than their feet, and no other way to make a living than continuing to work for the families they had worked for prior to Emancipation.

Other indirect evidence which connects Turner C. Everett to our families of interest are the years and locations of births of various members of both the slave holding and the enslaved families. When these show a similar pattern, one can speculate that the families were moving in conjunction with one another. In this case we can place Turner in Georgia as late as 1851 and in Carroll County Mississippi as early as 1856. Nellie's family follows a similar pattern showing the earliest Mississippi births as occurring in 1854.

Another factor which is also consistent with Turner Everett, George C. Everett, and Henry Kaigler being the slave holders for our families of interest is the Slave Schedule of 1860. Here we look for an alignment of ages and genders (no names were listed on Slave Schedules unless the person was 100 or more years of age). The reason we look at the holdings of these three men is because we know their households inherited from James Abbington Everett. Even during slavery, people often actually did have last names. Some were surnames of previous slave holders.

Based on James A. Everett's will, Sarah (Ingram Greene) Kaigler was granted the use for her lifetime of five named slaves including one named Burrell. After her first husband died, Sarah remarried, this time to a man named Henry Kaigler. Since Turner moved to Mississippi in the early 1850's, it is likely that he brought with him the five people gifted to Sarah.

During the Civil War, Turner enlisted as a Private in Company B, 3rd (Owen's) Regiment Mississippi Infantry Minute Men, Company B (Carroll County Defenders). This Company was raised in 1862 with a 6 month enlistment. There is not much recorded about this unit and it likely functioned as a home defense unit rather than an active operating unit deployed throughout the theater of engagement.

In his request for a Presidential Pardon for his support of the Confederate cause on 22 August 1865, Turner placed the value of his slaves at $20,000. His request was granted on 8 September 1865 when he was pardoned under an Amnesty Proclamation.

Before the Civil War, the Federal government was funded by tariffs charged on goods being brought into the country. Tariffs provided the largest portion of the federal budget, sometimes as much as 95%, until the income tax was permanently established by the 16th Amendment to the Constitution in 1913. To defray the expenses of the Civil War, both an income tax and a luxury goods tax were assessed. The income tax met with stiff headwinds and was declared unconstitutional within a couple of years of its enactment.

The Bureau of Internal Revenue was established in 1862 to collect these taxes to support the operation of the Federal government. The tax on luxury goods lasted a while longer. In 1866 the Bureau of Internal Revenue made a collection of these taxes. Some of these records survive. Turner paid a total of $9.55 for his 2 carriages, 2 watches, and silver plate valued at $575. The Bureau was reorganized and renamed effective 9 July 1953 to the Internal Revenue Service.

Turner C. Everett died on 26 August 1885 and is buried in the Everett Cemetery, Vaiden, Carroll County, Mississippi.

The Henry Kaigler/Kegler Line

Henry Kaigler was born 5 June 1804 in South Carolina. His direct male line is descended from his grandfather Andrew Kaigler who was born in Germany around 1730, emigrated to America in about 1750 or so, and married Katherine Coppelpower. Andrew and Katherine's family included Michael Kaigler who was Henry's father. The family were planters in Sandy Run, South Carolina.

In 1835 Henry is listed as one of the larger slave holders in the Tax Digest for Houston County, Georgia having a total of 21. In 1836 both James A. Everett and Henry Kaigler were listed as trustees for the Fort Valley Academy in Georgia.

Henry married Sarah after the death of her first husband in 1836. Thus he became James A. Everett and Turner C. Everett's step father-in-law. Henry and Sarah moved to Carroll County from Houston County, Georgia before Turner Everett. They arrived sometime before the birth of their eldest son Cowles (pronounced Coals) Mead Kaigler who was born 8 July 1841. In total, Henry and Sarah had 4 children.

1. Cowles Mead Kaigler (b. 8 July 1841 Mississippi)
2. Augustus Kaigler (b. 1844 Mississippi)
3. Artimissa Kaigler (b. 1847 Mississippi)
4. Winfield Kaigler (b. 1851 Mississippi)

There is a record of his purchase of an additional 41.69 acres in Carroll County on 15 April 1853.

In 1860 Henry is listed in the Slave Schedule as holding 42 people (he had 37 in 1850). The increase of five coincides with Sarah's receipt of the five people gifted to her by James A. Everett.

After the Civil War, Henry applied for and received a Presidential Pardon for supporting the Confederacy on 20 October 1865. The policy of the United States government immediately following the Civil War was to allow people to keep their property minus their slaves if they swore an oath of allegiance to the United States. Naturally, most people who had supported the secessionists, changed their allegiance and did so.

In the 1866 Tax Assessments, Henry was assessed for 2 carriages, 2 gold watches, and a pianoforte for a Total Assessed Value of $600, resulting in a Total Tax of $8.00.

Peter Greene, Sarah's son from her first marriage, took in the elderly couple and when the 1880 Census was conducted, they were living with him and his family in Montgomery County, Mississippi.

Henry died on 26 November 1884 and is buried in the Vaiden Cemetery in Carroll County with his wife who died in 1889. Since Sarah died after Emancipation, the five people gifted to her from James A. Everett and their natural increase never did return to the estate of James A. Everett back in Georgia. Instead, they were freed in Mississippi in 1865.

Another factor which supports Henry Kaigler as one of our family's slaveholders is the movement and burial of Allen Everett – the bond guarantor for Nellie upon her marriage. Allen and his family also moved to Montgomery County around the same time as Henry and when Allen died he was buried in the Kaigler Family Cemetery in Carroll County.

Charlotte Everett

In 1870 Charlotte Kaigler is listed as a 30 year-old black woman head of household doing farm labor. Although the surname in this Census is Kaigler, this is Charlotte Everett. There are no marriage records for people who were held in slavery as marriage between or to a slave was not legal. So while she is using the Kaigler last name, there is no documentary evidence to show why. It's not clear if she formed a relationship with one of the Kaigler slaves or used the name as a surname because the Kaiglers were the last family for whom she worked. Later she uses the surname Parker and there is no marriage record in Carroll County to explain this name change either.

According to the 1870 Census she was born circa 1840. Interestingly, Charlotte's birthdate shifts to earlier dates with each of the following Census's. In 1880 her calculated birthdate would be 1835 and in 1900 her birth date is listed as January 1830. Given the birthdates of her likely brother, Burrell, mother, Evaline, and the first child clearly linked to her, Rebecca, the 1840 date is more likely than the 1830 date.

She had a total of 8 children over the years. Her children are listed as mulatto in the 1880 Census, but black in the 1870 Census. DNA results indicate that both James and Nellie were probably of mixed race.
1. Rebecca Kaigler (b. 1854 Mississippi)
2. Susan Kaigler (b. 1856 Mississippi)
3. Walton (or possibly Walter) Kaigler (b.1858 Mississippi)
4. Nellie Kaigler (b. 1864 Mississippi)
5. Lucy Kaigler (b. 1866 Mississippi)
6. Stephen Kaigler (b. 1867 Mississippi)
7. Bearl (Burrell) Parker (b. 1873 Mississippi)
8. Caroline Parker (b. 1879 Mississippi)

Interestingly in James A. Everett's will, a slave named Caroline is gifted to Sarah Kaigler. While Charlotte's child is clearly not the person who was gifted in 1848, she may have been named after the person who was gifted. And given that Burrell was another of the persons gifted and Charlotte lived next to and named one of her children after him, the Caroline mentioned in the will of 1848 may also have been a relation of Charlotte's, possibly a sister. The listing of Georgia as the birthplace for Charlotte and Burrell is another indicator that they, at the very least, were slaves owned by the Everett family and, combined with these other factors, possibly were sister and brother.

Charlotte died sometime between 1900 and 1910. No death record has been located and is quite likely none exists as the state of Tennessee did not start requiring official records of deaths until 1908.

Delia Hart

Let us take the time to follow Delia's history as she is the most distant maternal ancestor in the Tomanna Mack line. The first record of Delia is from the 1870 Census when she is recorded as living with her brother, his family, and her own daughter, Marianne. In this Census, her surname is Hart. At this time, Delia Hart lived in Civil District 13 of Shelby County Tennessee. Civil District 13 falls to the immediate south of Memphis and goes to the border with Mississippi. She was born in Tennessee and it may well be that she was born in Shelby County. She and her 2-year-old daughter Marianne (listed as Maria) lived with Delia's brother, Thomas, his wife, Chena, and their 4-year-old son, Peter. Thomas worked as a laborer, his wife kept house, and Delia worked as a field hand. Right next door is a 48-year-old white farmer named James F. Mack who was born in Tennessee. James is recorded quite distinctly in the 1860 Census and the Tennessee Compiled Census as having the middle initial "T". It is the same man, but it is not clear which initial is correct at this point. By the way, there is another James Mack living in Shelby County during this time period who is a different person altogether, and it is easy to mix these two people up. The one who is **not** connected to our family lived in Memphis and over the years went from a hustler (street vendor) to owning a grocery store.

Ten years later, Delia is again listed as living in Civil District 13. In the 1880 Census, Delia was listed as single and her last name was given as Mack. She had three daughters at that time including Marianne Sellers (b. 1867 TN), Tomanna Mack (b. 1870 TN), and Susan Mack (b. 1871 TN). Delia is not listed in any marriage records for Shelby County for any of her name changes. This time her occupation is listed as Farming. Asked where her parents were born, she cited Tennessee for both of them. Marianne, listed this time as "Mariah Sellars", at age 13 was working on the farm. Tomanna Mack makes her first appearance on a Census having been born in 1870 after the Census was taken. She had attended school within the previous year. Susan Mack, her sister, was 9 years old and also had attended school in the previous year. The whole family is listed as mulatto. It seems probable that James F. Mack fathered Tomanna and Susan, however, there were no birth certificates issued during this time period in this area to confirm this hypothesis. Nevertheless, we may one day learn whether the surname Mack is indeed part of the bloodline, if there are members of the Mack bloodline who participate in DNA testing and a match emerges.

The Census of 1890 burned in a tremendous fire and the records were destroyed so we do not get any insight into Delia's situation then. However, we pick up her trail again in 1895 when she purchased some property and then in 1897 she shows up in the Memphis City Directory. Her surname is now given as Kaigler or various variant spellings. Again no documentation could be found to give a reason for the change and there is no record showing her living with a man named Kaigler.

In the 1900 Census, she was living on Kansas Ave with her daughter, listed as Anna, her son-in-law, William S. Webb, and granddaughter, listed as Annie. Delia is listed as the mother of 6 children with 2 still living as of 1900 (in 1910 she is listed as the mother of 7 with 2 living).

In the 1910 Census, Delia is recorded as owning a house with a mortgage located on 'Elect Ave 1 south of Beatrice Ave' also described as 'Elect southeast corner of Beatrice Ave' according to the Memphis City Directory during the various years she lived there. A search for Elect Ave on Google maps did not reveal its location. It has probably been renamed. Beatrice Ave, however, is still on the map. A property record search for Delia does not show any sign that she actually owned this property. However, it did reveal that she purchased 6 lots from E.E. Meacham in the Arcadian Hills subdivision south of Fort Pickering for $140 on 18 October 1895 which was paid in full on 8 April 1901. She sold these lots to Bessie Baruchman on 28 March 1907 for $425. In 2014 dollars that would be $10,625. She is listed in the Memphis City Directory until 1913.

Before we leave the Looney line, there are four lines of James Knox Looney's children which have been researched in more depth. Lucy Looney's line is included in the section of Willie Coleman/Webb and Lucy Looney. Here the lines of Katherine, Burrell, and Robert Emmett Looney are detailed.

Katherine Looney

Katherine Looney was born on 8 August of 1885 in Tennessee or Mississippi (sources are inconsistent on this point). According to the Shelby County Marriage Records Book U page 149, on 15 February 1900 she married Joe F. Works who was born in 1882 in rural Shelby County, Tennessee. Henry Kaigler, Minister of God, performed the ceremony. This is not the Henry Kaigler who married Sarah Ingram. More research needs to be done on this point.

At first Joe and Katherine lived with James and Nellie working on the farm. The couple had a child named William Henry Works born in 1914 in Tennessee. William Henry had at least two significant relationships. On 7 July 1931 he, with his father as guarantor, applied for a marriage license to Lucinda Norman (the daughter of Rich Norman and his wife Lucinda (Silas) Norman). Although the marriage license in not completed, the couple does appear to have "held out" as married. Lucinda, however, died soon after. She passed away on 30 July 1932 in Memphis, Tennessee and was buried in Chuck Cemetery on 9 August 1932. William Henry married again in 1935 to Ruby Warren. They had at least 3 children and an infant who died at birth on 21 April 1950.

Joe F. Works appears to have married again on 13 April 1919 to Bertha Canada with James H. Pugh M.G. performing the ceremony and acting as guarantor. James H. Pugh was a full-time minister in a Baptist church. He lived at 170 Madder Avenue in Memphis with his wife and 10 children and owned his home.

Katherine died on 13 August 1949 at her home at 3052 Andy Road, in rural Shelby County, Tennessee of a cerebral hemorrhage and paralysis due to high blood pressure. Her home was just south of Memphis' rail yard. According to her Death Certificate, she had lived there 49 years which must be where she and Joe lived once they set up their own establishment. Funeral arrangements were handled by Southern Funeral Home, 440 Vance Ave., Memphis, Tennessee. She was buried in White's Chapel Cemetery located at White's Chapel AME Church on Fields Road,

Boxtown, Tennessee. This is located just south of Memphis and is not far off Horn Lake Road where she had lived with her family in 1900.

Burrell Looney

Burrell Looney was born on 26 December 1889 in Shelby County, Tennessee. His mother had both a brother and an uncle with this name. He lived with his father, mother, and siblings in 1900 as noted in the section on his father. In 1910 he was still with his father and working in the lumber mills of Memphis.

It appears highly likely that Burrell had four children with a woman named Annie Mae Shaner or Shavers. One of these children died at an early age and "Burl Looney" is listed as the father. There are no other Burl or Burrell Looney's listed in the Census in Tennessee at this same time other than the one in our family. It is not clear whether he married her or not – no marriage documentation was found in Shelby County, but perhaps they married in another county. The children included:
1. J. Walter Looney (b. 1913 d. 17 Mar 1936 of pneumonia brought on by influenza, Memphis General Hospital Memphis, TN, 24 Mar 1936 buried in Boxtown, TN)
2. Robert Looney (b. 1914 Memphis, TN)
3. Eddie Looney (b. 1915 Memphis, TN)
4. Burrell Looney (b. 1916 Memphis, TN)

These boys were raised by their maternal grandparents, Edward "Ed" and Florence Shaner or Shavers (the surname is recorded in different ways in the Census material). However, in the 1930 Memphis City Directory Edward Shavers is listed as a laborer living at 890 Lane Ave and there is a woman named Mary Shavers living at that address as well. No relationship is noted in the Directory and the entries are separate. Normally husbands and wives are in a single entry with an annotation denoting the wife. It could be that Mary is another relative of Edward, perhaps a mother or sister. It is not clear what happened to Annie.

On 5 June 1917, Burrell registered for the World War I Draft in Precinct 3 of Shelby County, Tennessee. He was "working for the public" and employed by Charles Ked in Savage, Mississippi which is 51 miles south of Memphis in Tate County, Mississippi. A likely explanation of this is a public works contract for road building or maintenance that had been let out to the said Charles Ked. He lists marital status as married and his nearest relative as "Wife" but gives no name for her. He is described as of medium height and build, with black eyes and hair. He made his mark to affirm his answers.

Burrell was called up and did serve in the U.S. Army. His official military records were destroyed in a catastrophic fire that started on 12 July 1973 at the National Personnel Records Center in St. Louis. It was not until 16 July that the fire department declared the blaze officially out. Approximately 16 to 18 million records were lost in this single event. As a result, when one requests a file for a person whose records were affected by this fire, the file provided is usually a final pay voucher. Such was the case for Burrell. It does give us some information though. He was a Private. He was "outprocessed" or demobilized from 13th Company, 4th Battalion, 159th Depot Brigade at Camp Zachary Taylor,

Kentucky on 9 January 1919. This training camp was opened in 1917 near Louisville and closed three years later. It was built in 90 days on 2,730 acres for a total cost of $7.2 million. The camp contained some 1,700 buildings and housed over 40,000 troops.

He had transferred there two days prior from Camp Grant, Illinois which was located in the southern outskirts of Rockford, Illinois. This camp covered over 18,000 acres and was in operation from 1917 to the late 1940's. The 86th Infantry Division (Black Hawk Division) was formed there. This unit pulled its men from Chicago and other parts of northern Illinois. It was primarily a training camp for infantry soldiers. While the division did not see combat in World War I, some elements did get deployed. In the fall of 1918 the camp was hit by the Spanish Influenza Pandemic which sickened over 4,000 soldiers at the camp. Between the 23rd of September and the 1st of October 1918 over 1,000 of these soldiers died. October 1918 was devastating — more than 195,000 Americans died of the flu in that month alone. A letter written by a doctor on 29 September 1918 stationed at Camp Devens, Massachusetts described the disease progression and its impact this way:

"This epidemic started about four weeks ago, and has developed so rapidly that the camp is demoralized and all ordinary work is held up till it has passed. All assemblages of soldiers taboo. These men start with what appears to be an attack of la grippe or influenza, and when brought to the hospital they very rapidly develop the most viscous type of pneumonia that has ever been seen. Two hours after admission they have the mahogany spots over the cheek bones, and a few hours later you can begin to see the cyanosis extending from their ears and spreading all over the face, until it is

hard to distinguish the coloured men from the white. It is only a matter of a few hours then until death comes, and it is simply a struggle for air until they suffocate. It is horrible. One can stand it to see one, two or twenty men die, but to see these poor devils dropping like flies sort of gets on your nerves. We have been averaging about 100 deaths per day, and still keeping it up. ... It takes special trains to carry away the dead. For several days there were no coffins and the bodies piled up something fierce, we used to go down to the morgue (which is just back of my ward) and look at the boys laid out in long rows. It beats any sight they ever had in France after a battle. An extra long barracks has been vacated for the use of the morgue, and it would make any man sit up and take notice to walk down the long lines of dead soldiers all dressed up and laid out in double rows."

By the time the Pandemic ended more than 600,000 U.S. citizens had died. Experts estimate the world-wide death toll between 21.5 to 30 million people. The U. S. death toll was higher than military casualties for all wars fought in the 20th century. All in all the U.S. military suffered 116,516 deaths in World War 1.

Army units were segregated during this period. Nearly 400,000 African-Americans served in the Army and while some were in the two black combat divisions, most served in labor battalions. These noncombatant soldiers were responsible for tasks like road building, constructing ammunition dumps, cooking, building warehouses, loading the hulls of cargo ships with supplies bound for France, and salvaging materials from the theater of war. It was not until 26 July 1948 that President Truman issued Executive Order No. 9981 which desegregated the military.

African-American soldiers stationed at Camp Grant were prohibited from patronizing many white establishments in nearby Rockford, and so sought relaxation and fun away from the base and formed the Booker Washington Association which was a predecessor to the Booker Washington Community Center. In 1946 Camp Grant was permanently closed. Today much of the land that formed the camp is occupied by the Chicago Rockford International Airport.

Burrell's last pay prior to discharge had been received on 30 September 1918 and processed by Captain M.S. Crosby, Quartermaster Corps, Moline, Illinois. Burrell was entitled to travel pay to Binghampton (also spelled Binghamton), Tennessee which is a neighborhood in Memphis just east of the Memphis Zoo. He had served one enlistment period. His Army Serial Number was 2436655. He had two allotments being taken from his pay — one for "Class A Comp." for $49.50 and a second for "Insurance Premiums C. and D." for $20.70. He did not owe the military any fees. He received $41.25 in cash. He signed his name to acknowledge receipt.

In 1929 he was listed in the Memphis City Directory as living at West Junction with his wife Henrietta and he was working as a laborer at the International Sugar Feed company.

In 1930 he had moved his family to Beat 2 in Sunflower, Mississippi and was sharecropping cotton. He was right next to his sister Lucy and his brother Martin and their families and just down the road from his father and his family. In his household, in addition to three of his children (Lucille, Orlanders (son), and Nellie Grace (recorded here as Grey)), is Lucinda Norman who was listed as a niece. Lucinda does have a relationship with his nephew William Henry Works but she does not appear to be related by blood perhaps more of a niece-in-law. (See the section on Katherine Looney above more detail on Lucinda.)

In 1940 he and his family still lived in Sunflower County, Mississippi and the family has grown to include Martin, Burrell, Dorothy, Roseanna, Myria, and granddaughter, Mary.

Burrell applied for a marriage license on 13 July 1955 (Book O03 page 365). On 14 July 1955, Burrell at age 66 married Henrietta Beatty then age 50 in Memphis, Tennessee. The ceremony was performed by H. M. Roberts, Minister of God. Burrell and Henrietta's children include:

1. Lucille "Dear" Looney (b. abt 1918)
2. Orlanders Looney (b. 20 Nov 1927 Tennessee m. Romiestein Herron (b. 24 Jan 1934, Shelby County, Tennessee d. 25 Nov 2014 Detroit, Wayne, Michigan buried 6 Dec 2014, Woodlawn Cemetery, Detroit, Wayne, Michigan) on 19 Jun 1951 Shelby County, Tennessee; had 3 children d. 12 Aug 1972 Detroit, Wayne, Michigan)
3. Nellie Grace Looney (b. 15 Jul 1929 Mississippi m. Louis Jeffries, Jr. 4 children d. 25 Sep 2011 Tacoma, Washington buried Memphis, Shelby, Tennessee)
4. Martin Looney (b. 1931 d. around 1941/2 in a swimming accident, Mississippi)
5. Burrell Looney, Jr. (b. 14 Mar 1933 Sunflower, Mississippi m. at least three times all in Shelby County, Tennessee first Margaret Delores McGill 8 Sep 1954; second Mary Louise Cooper 22 Jul 1974; third Emma H. Lehman 5 Sep 1992;

served 3 enlistments in the U.S. Army 19 Sep 1952-16 Sep 1955, 21 Nov 1955 to 20 Nov 1958, and 27 Jan 1959 to 24 Feb 1964 d. 15 Jan 1996 Detroit, Wayne, Michigan)
6. Dorothy Looney (b. abt 1935)
7. Roseanna "Rosie" Looney (Living)
8. Elmyria L. Looney (b. 13 Jul 1938 Sunflower, Mississippi m. Solomon Macon Hayes (1922 – 26 Dec 2013); had one child; worked as a hairdresser d. 2 Apr 1994 Memphis, Shelby, Tennessee buried in Section X Grave 14140 West Tennessee State Veterans Cemetery, Memphis, Shelby, Tennessee with her husband)
9. Freddie Lee Looney (b. 20 May 1942 Sunflower County, Mississippi m. at least twice 2 children; served in U.S. Army during Vietnam rose to the rank of Specialist 5 d. 18 Apr 1998 Memphis, Shelby Tennessee buried in Section J Site 5055 of West Tennessee State Veterans Cemetery, 4000 Forest Hill-Irene Rd. Memphis, Shelby, Tennessee)

Burrell died at the Veteran Affairs Hospital in Memphis, Tennessee on 2 March 1963 of bronchopneumonia complicated by diabetes mellitus. His residence was at 400 West Peebles Road, Memphis which is close to where his sister Katherine had lived during her lifetime. His birthplace is recorded as Ensley which turns out to be a street just to the west of the Horn Lake Cutoff leading to Horn Lake Creek. It was noted in the section on his father James that the family had been recorded in this general area. His occupation was listed as retired laborer. He was buried on 11 March 1963 in

Section E Site 91 at the National Cemetery at 3568 Townes Avenue in Memphis. Funeral Arrangements were handled by N. J. Ford Funeral Home, Memphis, Tennessee.

Robert Emmett Looney

Robert Emmett Looney was born on 20 June 1920 in Leflore County, Mississippi. Although one would expect that he registered for the World War II Draft as his brothers Cecil and Asa certainly did, extensive searches did not provide his registration. It is probably there, but has some unexpected factor which makes it difficult to find.

When he was 30 years old, he married Pearlie (Gilbert) Coleman on 28 Oct 1950 in Leflore County before F. H. Smith, Justice of the Peace. They were both living along Route 1 in Itta Bena, Mississippi at the time. The name Itta Bena is derived from a Choctaw phrase "ita bina" meaning 'forest camp'.

Later they moved about 12 miles east to Greenwood, Leflore County, Mississippi. Greenwood is the "cotton capital of the world" and the county seat of Leflore. They had 10 children. They moved to Detroit, Michigan in 1965. Mary Eliza "Mickey" (Webb) Blackmon (one of Lucy (Looney) Webb's children), and therefore half-niece to Robert, helped the family settle into their new home. He died on 1 January 1967 in Detroit.

The Gilbert Line

David Gilbert

David Gilbert was born in 1870 most probably after the Census was taken that year on 1 June. The first Census entry for him is in 1880 Census in the Enumeration District 084, District 285, Morgan County, Georgia at which time he is living with his paternal aunt Fannie (Gilbert) Perryman and her husband, Peter.

Morgan County, named after the Revolutionary War General Daniel Morgan, was established on 10 December 1807. Madison was designated the county seat in 1808. Madison was spared destruction during General Sherman's march to Atlanta because it was the birthplace of pro-Union Senator Joshua Hill who also happened to be a friend of Sherman's brother at West Point. As a result, this area had operating plantations after the Civil War when so much of Georgia had been devastated. This may be a reason for the Gilbert family moving into this area where they might get work as they do not appear to have lived here in 1870.

Peter Perryman (b. circa 1852) and Fannie Gilbert (b. 11 Nov 1852, Georgia—d. 11 Nov 1915, Fort White, Columbia County, Florida) married in Morgan County, Georgia on the 27th of January 1876. Based on the 1880 Census, Fannie was about 21 and Peter about 24 when they married but other entries in different Census takings and other official records make those ages estimates at best. By 1880 they had two children of their own, Joseph, age 3 and Etta, age 1. In addition to raising David Gilbert, who must have been a child of a brother of Fannie, there was another one year-old child named James Parks identified as an adopted son.

Peter Perryman worked for a man named Reuben Miller for at least 12 years, probably longer. Peter is recorded in the Tax Digests of Morgan County as paying one poll tax in the years 1878, 1883, and 1890. In 1890, he paid a total of $1.12 in tax based on one poll tax, $5 worth of livestock and $10 worth of household goods. The equivalent in 2014 dollars would be $29.48. A poll tax was a tax levied on an adult without regard to income and was used, particularly in the Southern States, as a way of controlling the voting population, weeding out poor people who couldn't afford to pay.

David married Ollie Jackson (b. 1872, Georgia d. between 1930 and 1940, Leflore County, Mississippi) on the 27th of December 1888 in Morgan County. The Reverend Randall Coss officiated. Their marriage was recorded in the Morgan County, Georgia Marriage Book 2 (1879-1890) on page 456 on 12 March 1889 by the Ordinary (equivalent to a modern County Clerk) T. B. Baldwin. Sometimes marriage records include more information about the individuals who are getting married but, in this case, the only information is the names, marriage date, and officiating official.

David and Ollie had four children:
1. William Gilbert (b. 1891, Morgan County, Georgia)
2. Maud Gilbert (b. 1892, Morgan County, Georgia)
3. Fred Gilbert (b. 7 Sep 1894, Morgan County, Georgia (see section on Fred for more detail) d. Jun 1969, Greenwood, Leflore County, Mississippi)
4. John Gilbert (b. 1908, Florida).

By 1910, David, and Ollie have moved to Fort White, Columbia County, Florida with their four children and are living next to Fannie and Peter Perryman. Fannie and Peter had moved by 1900 to Suwanee County, Florida and then moved again to Fort White. It isn't clear where David and Ollie were in 1900. Searches of the records were unsuccessful thus far. It is possible there is a spelling error in the original record or its transcription that makes it difficult to search for them. It wouldn't be surprising to eventually locate them either in Morgan County or near Fannie in Florida. David seems to have been close to her while she lived.

Fannie died on 11 November 1915 and is buried in the Heavenly Rest Cemetery, Fort White, Florida. Florida started to issue Death Certificates around this time but no Death Certificate was issued for Fannie. That might have named her parents who would have been David's grandparents and thus furthered our understanding of the family line. One other possibly important clue from the 1910 Census is that David's birthplace is listed as South Carolina. This is not consistent with entries in other Census findings which cite Georgia as his birthplace.

There is an African-American family in South Carolina with the surname Gilbert with a daughter named Fannie of the right age to be the Fannie noted here. However, nothing found so far definitely links these two entries as being the same person.

Alternatively, there is a family listed in the 1870 Census in Houston County, Georgia with a daughter named Fannie who might be the one we are interested in. The family consisted of mother, Susan (b. 1825 Georgia), Fannie, and a brother named Caleb (b. 1854 Georgia). Neither Susan nor

Caleb appear in the 1880 Census which may mean they had died. This would fit what we know of Fannie and David. Once again there is no definite link as yet between the Fannie in this family and the Fannie who is undoubtedly linked to David.

Most likely, this Gilbert family had been slaves of Julius Caesar Gilbert (b. 4 Jan 1821 d. 17 Mar 1895), who had 30 slaves listed in the 1860 Slave Schedule including slaves who are the right genders and ages to fit this family. Julius married Maria Louise West (b. 19 Jan 1835 d. 12 Mar 1910) on 8 December 1853 in Houston County, Georgia. Julius Gilbert was a successful physician and farmer who was commissioned as a Second Lieutennant in Company C, Georgia 1st Infantry Regiment on 18 March 1861. He was promoted to Full Surgeon and mustered out on 15 March 1862. He volunteered again and was promoted to Full 1st Lieutenant on 07 July 1863. He mustered out on 15 February 1864. He joined for a third term on 15 June 1864 and mustered out on 15 May 1865.

After Fannie died, David, Ollie, Fred, and John moved away. In the 1930 Census, David and Ollie are living with their youngest son John and his wife, Annie in District 4, Beat 2, Leflore County, Mississippi. David is listed as 60 years old and he is listed as not working in the Occupation column. It is possible that he was ill or injured and not able to work. John is listed as the head of household and renting the farm. John's wife and mother are listed as working as farm laborers. This is consistent with the way sharecroppers are recorded. David could not read or write but John, his wife, Annie, and Ollie could all read and write.

Fred Gilbert

Fred Gilbert was born on 7 September 1894 in Morgan County, Georgia. According to his Social Security application, he did not have a middle name. He lived and worked at farming with his family first in Morgan County and then Fort White, Columbia, Florida until he moved to Camilla, Mitchell County, Georgia sometime after 1910 and before 1917.

Meanwhile a storm was brewing in Europe which would reshape the lives of millions of people world-wide. The triggering event was the assassination on 28 June 1914 of Archduke Ferdinand, heir to the Austro-Hungarian throne, and his wife, Sophie, by a Serbian. One month later on the 28th of July Austria-Hungary declared war on Serbia and World War I began. It was the start of a string of dominoes. Country after country began declaring war and within months Europe, Australia, New Zealand, and most of Asia were at war. Africa was also impacted as European colonies there participated as well.

World events then became a factor in Fred's life. After the sinking of the Lusitania signaling the use of unrestricted submarine warfare against non-combatants and the Zimmerman telegram from the German Foreign Secretary to Mexico proposing a military alliance with Mexico in order to defeat the United States, the United States declared war on Germany on 6 April 1917. Events moved quickly as the U.S. geared up to fight. A call for volunteers netted only 76,000 men; not nearly enough for the kind of fighting to come, so a draft system was speedily put in place. Three draft registrations were held. The first was on 5 June 1917 for men between the ages of 21-31. The second was held 5 June 1918 for men who had turned 21 since the first registration. The third occurred on 12 Sep 1918 for men between the ages of 18 and 45.

According to Ancestry.com, "In 1917 and 1918, approximately 24 million men living in the United States completed a World War I draft registration card. That accounts for approximately 98 percent of men in the U.S. born between 1872 and 1900. The total U.S. population in 1917-1918 was about 100 million individuals, so close to 25 percent of the total population is represented in these records." From the 24 million who registered, just under 3 million were actually drafted. In all 367,710 black Americans were drafted (13.0% of the total), compared to 2,442,586 white (86.9%).

On 5 June 1917 Fred registered for the World War I Draft. At the time he was 23 years old and described as Negro, tall with a slender build, brown eyes and black hair with all his limbs, hands, feet, and eyes and was not otherwise disabled. He reported he was a natural born citizen born in Morgan County, Georgia. He was working for Camilla's Public Works Department in Mitchell County, Georgia. His supervisor was Capt. C. S. Watts. He was single and had not been in the military before. He had no one depending on him as the sole means of their support and claimed no exemptions from military service.

Over a year later on the 26th of September 1918, Fred was called up for service and reported to Camp Wheeler for training. Camp Wheeler was established 18 July 1917 near Macon, Georgia as a mobilization center for the U.S. Army. It was one of sixteen camps set up for the purpose of training Army National Guard forces to serve with U.S. Army Divisions. It housed up to 43,000 officers and enlisted men in tents and a few temporary wooden shelters. The camp occupied 21,480 acres and cost $3,900,000 to clear and build. It was used to train the 31st Infantry Division. The 31st Infantry Division deployed to Europe in October 1918 but its troops were used as replacements for units already deployed along the front. It did not see action as a unit. The Armistice was declared on 11 November 1918 and the remnants of the 31st Infantry returned to Camp Wheeler in December of 1918 to be demobilized.

Fred was called up in anticipation of the need of replacements and the need to build large training camps for training those recruits. However, his training would not have been completed by the time the main contingent deployed. As a result, he did not serve overseas and was honorably discharged on 1 February 1919. The Camp was decommissioned on 10 April 1919 only to be re-opened in 1940 for World War II. During World War II, wooden barracks buildings were built to house troops.

After release from the military, Fred returned to Camille and, shortly thereafter, on 6 September 1919, he married Viola Bowman. This marriage does not appear to have lasted very long. The couple does not appear in the 1920 Census. And then on 17 December 1923, Fred Gilbert and Lillie Bell Booker applied for a marriage license in Leflore County, Mississippi. Fred and Lillie married on Valentine's Day, 14 February 1924.

Fred and Lillie had two girls:
1. Pearlie (or Pearl Lee as her name appears on some records) Gilbert (b. 23 Jan 1925 Leflore, Mississippi; more on Pearlie in a later section; d. 9 Jan 1995, Detroit, Michigan)

2. Ollie Mae Gilbert (b. 9 Sep 1927 Leflore, Mississippi d. 6 Nov 2012 Brighton, Jefferson, Alabama).

Then in November 1929, things changed dramatically. On 13 November 1929 a capias (warrant for the arrest of) was issued for Fred. He was arrested on the 14th and arraigned on the charge of murder on the 18th. He pleaded not guilty. On the same day subpoenas were issued to four witnesses for the prosecution. Those witnesses included Minnie Booker, his mother-in-law, Will Simmons, Augusta Simmons, and Elbert Lewis. They were called to appear before the court on the 25th of November. William Hemingway Montjoy (b. 5 Dec 1906 d. Oct 1976) who was a young lawyer in private practice at the time defended Fred.

On the 27th of January 1930, Fred was found guilty as charged. On the 7th of February he was sentenced to life in prison. On the 9th of February he was processed into Parchman Farms State Penitentiary in Sunflower County, Mississippi. Despite several hours of searching the courthouse records in Leflore County, the trial transcript could not be located. The record storeroom is in complete disarray. The record probably is there and, perhaps at some point, will be unearthed. The local paper did not print anything about this case which most likely means the victim was also African-American. Other stories in the paper cover the white community, African-Americans are mentioned tangentially as a "Negro" with no name or other personally identifying information.

Parchman is the oldest prison and the only maximum security prison in Mississippi. In 1900 the Mississippi State Legislature allocated $80,000 to buy Parchman Plantation, a

3,789 acre estate for the purpose of setting up a prison. Over subsequent years, a total of 28 square miles of delta land was purchased. The land was covered with undergrowth and woods, but underneath was rich alluvial soil—prime growing land. The prison started operation in 1901 and was largely built by the prisoners. Very quickly, the prison became a money maker for the State.

By the time Fred entered its gates, the inmates of Parchman had cleared the trees and were raising cotton and other crops. Convicts worked 10 hours a day, six days a week. They slept in long, single-story buildings called "cages". The prison was so large and remote, fences and walls were considered unnecessary. On the two Census's which cover this period of Fred's life, he is listed as a laborer on the farm. The farm raised crops including cotton and wheat and livestock including over 500 dairy cows and calves and pigs for butchering. Mules pulled the farm equipment. There were some other modes of employment for prisoners as opposed to farm labor including bricklaying, prison hospital staff, and operating the cotton gin or the sawmill. Additionally some prisoners called "trusty guards" or "trusty shooters" were designated to the help police the prisoners. These prisoners were housed separately from the at-large population.

When Fred was processed at reception on 9 February 1930, basic information was recorded in the Mississippi Convict Register, Volume M, Entry 390. His immediate family of wife, Lillie Bell Gilbert residing in Greenwood, Mississippi, and parents, David and Ollie Gilbert residing in Shell Mound, Mississippi, were listed. Fred is described as 36 years old, weight 166 pounds, height 5 feet 10½ inches, of a medium build with a large mouth, good teeth, and large nose. No comment was recorded in the Health or Disease sections. He had a number of years of education which is very difficult to read but might be 11 or 12 and could read and write. He had a number of scars including a scar on his right wrist, a large blue scar on his left arm, a pit scar below his right eye, a scar below his left eye and scars on both knee caps.

His birthplace is noted as Georgia. His faith is listed as Baptist. His occupation is Farm Laborer. The last column of the Register lists a prisoner's final disposition. In Fred's case, it is unusual. He had been sentenced to Life in Prison on a Capital charge, however, his sentence was suspended on 4 January 1944. Suspension means the fulfillment of a sentence is delayed by order of a judge. Normally a suspension is given before someone is incarcerated, however, in this case it was given after a period of 13 years but prior to the fulfillment of life. There are no explanatory notes about why this action was taken at this time but in 1944 the country was at war and man power had been diverted to the Armed Services. It is possible that farmers and other employers with a need for labor approached the State government to allow for the release of prisoners to serve as workers.

Whatever the back story to his release, Fred was working within the month for a man named H. W. Crowley in Jackson, Mississippi. He was living at 147 W. Davis, Jackson, MS. This location now has a parking lot and is across the street from a commercial property which consists of several large warehouse buildings. It is just to the east of one of the main rail lines in Jackson.

He did not stay there too long. By 1950 he was back in Leflore County living in Itta Bena. His daughters Pearlie and

Ollie were still living there. His parents had most probably died before his release, but as of 1940 his youngest brother, John, and his family still lived there. Fred died in Greenwood, Mississippi in June 1969.

The Lillie Bell Booker Line

Alford and Lillie Gordon

So far very little is known of Alford Gordon and his wife, Lillie. Their names are recorded on Minnie Gordon's Social Security application. She did not remember her mother's maiden name. On various Census entries for Minnie, the birthplaces of her parents are both recorded as Mississippi. Minnie reports being born in Carrollton, Carroll County Mississippi on 14 June 1876 so we can infer that the couple lived there then, however, thus far no Census entries in either 1880 or 1870 have been found which seem to be a record of this family. According to U.S. Census data, the 1860 Carroll County population included 8,214 whites, 13 "free colored" and 13,808 slaves. There was a total of 963 slave holders in the county in 1860; 75 of whom held more than 40 slaves. By the 1870 census, the white population had increased about 15% to 9,497, while the "colored" population had dropped about 16% to 11,550. That drop indicates the number of "colored" people moving into the county was lower than the number moving out. Carroll County was founded in 1833 and named after Charles Carroll, the last surviving signatory of the Declaration of Independence. Although it is part of the Mississippi Delta region, much of the county is hill country.

Minnie Gordon

According to Minnie's Social Security application she was born on 14 June 1876 to Alford and Lillie Gordon in Carrollton, Carroll County, Mississippi. She lived a long and event-filled life. She married John Booker circa 1896 in Tallahatchie County, Mississippi. The marriage record no longer survives at the County Courthouse, so no further information is available about their marriage.

In total, Minnie had ten children as reported in an article written about her. To date, eight children have been found in the records. She and John had two infants who died before 1900. That may account for all ten children, although sometimes people reported, later in life, only the children who survived infancy. It is possible there are two children, not recorded here, that made it to adulthood. Their other children included:

1. Cilla Booker (b. 1899 Mississippi d. probably before 1910)
2. Gilbert Booker (b. 1903 Mississippi d. before Oct 1982)
3. Lillie Bell Booker (recorded as Lydia in the 1910 Census b. 8 Apr 1905 Mississippi (See section about her for more details) d. 18 Nov 1982 Bessemer, Jefferson, Alabama)
4. John Booker (b. 1907 Mississippi d. before Oct 1982)
5. Tom Booker (b. 1909 Mississippi d. before Oct 1982)
6. Handy Booker (b. 1910 Mississippi d. before Oct 1982)
7. Daniel Booker (b. 1912 Mississippi d. before Oct

1982)

8. Egusta Mae "Gussie" Booker (b. 1913 Mississippi m. a man with the surname "Bob" d. 7 October 1969 Long Beach, Los Angeles, California).

In 1900, she and John were living in Beat 1, Tallahatchie County, Mississippi. John was sharecropping and both he and Minnie labored on the farm. By 1910 they had moved to Beat 4 in Tallahatchie County and Cilla does not appear in this Census and may have either died or was living with other family members.

Minnie and John continued to sharecrop. As of 2014 there are still Bookers living in Tallahatchie County who are probably cousins to descendants of John Booker.

Sometime between 1913 and 1920, John died. It may be possible to find his Death Certificate as Mississippi ordered the issuance of Death Certificates starting in 1912. However, compliance was spotty in the early years and it is possible one was not issued. In 1920 Minnie has moved with some of her children to Leflore County and was living with a cousin named Will Stevens. She worked on his farm. Her marital status is listed as widow.

Her daughter Lillie Bell married Fred Gilbert on 14 February 1924 and two grandchildren were born before the next turn in her life. On 18 November 1929, Minnie was subpoenaed to appear as a witness for the prosecution against her son-in-law, Fred Gilbert. Fred was found guilty and sentenced to life in prison. He was sent to prison on the 9th of February 1930. On the 28th of April 1930, Minnie was the head of household, renting a farm and farming cotton. Living with her are her son, Handy, and daughter, Lillie and her two children, and a granddaughter listed as Martha Gilbert who is actually Gussie's child, Martha Lee Smith. Both Ollie and Martha are listed with very specific age information which is rather unusual and was puzzling as their last names were the same. According to the 1930 Census, Ollie was 2 years 10 months and Martha was 2 years 11 months. Discovering that Martha was Gussie's child explained the situation.

Minnie married a second time during the 1930s to a Caldwell, most probably his first name was Tom. The 1940 Census shows Tom Caldwell, wife, and a 12-year-old granddaughter named Martha Lee Smith living right next door to Lillie Bell, Pearlie, and Ollie. Although his wife's name is recorded as Annie, it seems highly likely that the wife is actually Minnie. Mr. Caldwell was a caretaker on a "white folks' plantation". After her husband died in 1960, Minnie moved to California to live with her daughter, Gussie at 905 E. 17th Street, Long Beach, Los Angeles County, California.

On 14 June 1976, a big birthday party was held. She was living with her granddaughter, Martha Harris (née Smith), at 2240 Myrtle Avenue in Long Beach at the time. According to Zillow.com, this Craftsman-style bungalow was built in 1928 and is a multiple family home containing 5 bedrooms and 3 bathrooms. Myrtle Avenue was closed between Hill and 23rd Streets and decorated for the occasion. Jim Ellison and the Soul-Intruders, a soul-rock band played as family, friends, neighbors and local dignitaries celebrated. Her daughter, Lillie Bell Griffin, attended. In 1976, Minnie had 32 grandchildren and 58 great-great-grandchildren. President and First Lady Gerald Ford sent a letter of "Hearty Congratulations". The Third and Sixth District Council Members Renee Simon and James Wilson congratulated her and she received a U.S. flag which had flown over the Capital and a $300 money tree. She reported having been sickly until the age of 12, but not needing to see a doctor again until she reached 100. She liked to sew and piece together quilts.

Minnie died on 9 October 1982 and is buried in Section 5-1, Lot 044, Grave 5S, Woodlawn Memorial Park, Compton, Los Angeles County, California. Her daughter, Gussie Bob, who died 7 October 1969, is also buried there. Established in 1871 as Compton Rural Cemetery, Woodlawn is one of the oldest cemeteries in Los Angeles County.

John Booker

John Booker is a fairly common name. Piecing together information gleaned from the 1900, 1910, and 1920 Census entries, Lillie Bell's marriage certificate, and the article written about Minnie (Gordon) Caldwell, the John Booker we are interested in was born around 1875 in Mississippi and died between 1913 and 1920. Since he was sharecropping in 1900 and 1910, it is probable that his father also sharecropped. There was not much change in the employment opportunities until after World War II, so men usually continued in whatever employment their fathers did.

In reviewing the 1880 Census, there are 5 John Bookers born in Mississippi in the preceding decade. There is also a J. F. Booker, a John Bucker, and a Jack Booker (Jack being a common nickname for John). Several of these candidates appear in the 1920 or later Census and can be taken off the list of consideration. Of these eight candidates, the one who seems a good possibility is a John Booker living in Leflore County, Mississippi with his parents, George A. and Angeline Booker. Due to the missing 1890 Census, there is no intermediate data between 1880 and 1900. Leflore County is bordered by Tallahatchie, Carroll, and Sunflower Counties, all of which show up in various parts of the family history.

To reach a higher level of certainty about this part of the lineage two possible avenues of investigation exist:

1. interviews with a wider number of family members may be helpful and
2. hiring a researcher to determine John Booker's exact date of death so a Death Certificate can be ordered. Based on the enactment of and compliance with a law passed requiring the issuance of a Death Certificate starting in 1912 in the state of Mississippi, there may be one for John.

If this is, in fact, the correct family, then the information on George A. Booker and the Gadens that follows shows the line back to roughly 1791 in Georgia.

Information on what is known about the John Booker who married Minnie Gordon is covered in the section on Minnie.

George A. Booker and Angeline Gaden

Angeline Gaden was born around 1837 in Mississippi. In the 1870 Census she is listed as a 33 year-old farm laborer living in Township 17, Carroll County, Mississippi. She is living with 21-year-old Bubin (sic—this name is probably Rubin) Gaden and 3-year-old Francis Gaden. The 1870 Census does not record the relationships between people living in the same household. Later information shows that Francis is her daughter. Rubin (or Bubin as the name has been transcribed) is most likely a younger brother and not a son. Angeline had another child in 1872 named Robert Porter and then she married George A. Booker circa 1873. George A. Booker was born circa 1835 in Georgia. In the 1880 Census, the family includes Angeline's two children, Frances and Robert Porter, two sets of twins, Jane and Joseph born 1874, and John and Mary born 1877, and Angeline's mother, Charity. It is probable that at least one of the sets of children recorded with the same birth year was not twins. Later records on John indicate a birth year around 1875. By this time the family is living in Leflore County.

Charity Gaden

The Gaden name appears with numerous spelling alternatives including Garden, Gayden, and Gaiden. In the 1870 Census there is a large group of Gadens who are probably all related in Township 17, Carroll County, Mississippi. Charity Gaden is recorded as the mother of George A. Booker in the 1880 Census, however, she is actually his mother-in-law. Her daughter Angeline married George A. Booker. Charity was born in Georgia circa 1816 and both of her parents are recorded as having been born in Georgia. Using the standard generation estimate of 25 years, this would mean this line of the family has been in the United States since at least 1791.

As an added point of interest, the Reed family that connects to the larger family through Lucy Looney's children, Harry and Thelma, also first appears in the records in Carroll County in 1870 as does Lucy Looney's maternal line.

Lillie Bell Booker

Lillie Bell Booker was born on 8 April 1905 in Mississippi (probably Tallahatchie County) to John Booker and Minnie (Gordon) Booker. Her parents farmed cotton. It was a hard life of backbreaking work. A typical sharecropping arrangement was the owner of the land provided the land, a mule team, starter seed, and a dwelling for the sharecroppers. In return, the sharecropper plowed, planted, raised, and harvested the crop. At the end of harvest season once the crop had been sold, the owner would split the profit with the sharecropper. While some split the profits evenly, often the sharecropper was given less than half of the profit being told that *"Negroes only need $500 to live on."* —a comment made after a particularly productive harvest to Willie Webb. The money would have to last until the next harvest.

Lillie Bell would have helped in the fields from an early age. Even very young children helped tend the crop by picking insects off during the growing season. When harvest time came, every family member helped pick the cotton.

She also would have helped her mother with the cooking, laundry, canning, and the kitchen garden which would have been close to the house. Most sharecroppers also had at least a few chickens, perhaps a milk cow, and a hog or two being raised for butchering in the fall. The farm would also have had at least one, but more probably two mules, for pulling the farm equipment.

Lillie Bell married Fred Gilbert on Valentine's Day 1924. See the section on Fred for more detail on the children and this period of their life together in the 1920's.

By the time the enumerator for the 1930 Census visited her mother's house where she was living in April, she is recorded as divorced. No record of this divorce exists in the Leflore Courthouse, but because Fred was then domiciled in

Sunflower County, the record may be there. It is also possible a legally documented divorce was not actually accomplished until after Fred was released from prison in January 1944, because shortly after his release, she married Samuel Griffin of Route 1, Itta Bena, Mississippi on 25 March 1944. She and Samuel are listed four years earlier in the Census of 1940 as married and living in the same household. They were farming in Leflore County.

At some point, Lillie moved to Alabama. She made the trip out to California for the grand celebration of her mother's birthday. She died shortly after her mother, on 18 November 1982 in Bessemer, Jefferson County, Alabama.

She lived at 100 Dolomite Avenue which was in an area called Roosevelt City. Roosevelt City was incorporated in 1967 and was a satellite suburb of Birmingham, Alabama that was traditionally largely populated by African-Americans. It appears to have been absorbed by nearby Bessemer.

She was a member of the local First Baptist Church. According to her obituary, she is buried in George Washington Carver Memorial Gardens, 1020 Minor Parkway, Birmingham, Alabama. Her funeral arrangements were handled by Chambers Funeral Home, Inc. She was 77 years old.

Pearlie Gilbert

Pearlie Gilbert was born on 23 January 1925 (according to her Social Security Death Index and Michigan Death Index entries) in Leflore County to Fred Gilbert and Lillie Bell Booker. She was joined by her sister Ollie Mae on 7 September 1927. When her father was sent to prison, the family moved in with Minnie (Gordon) Booker also living in Leflore.

By 1940, she was living with her mother and Samuel Griffin, her mother's second husband (although their marriage was not official until 1944). She is listed as an unpaid family worker assisting with the farming. She had completed a 7th grade education at this point.

On 15 Feb 1941, Pearlie married Elbert Coleman (b. 21 Mar 1919 in Sunflower County, Mississippi d. 20 Mar 1970 Itta Bena, Leflore County, Mississippi). He was the son of Henry Coleman (b. circa 1883 Mississippi) and was working with his father farming in rural Leflore County in 1940. He had a 5th grade education. Pearlie and Elbert had 6 children according to an entry on PeopleSearch.com from Carl Looney.

On 28 October 1950, Pearlie married Robert Emmett Looney (b. 20 Jun 1920 Leflore County, Mississippi d. 1 Jan 1967 Detroit, Wayne County, Michigan). They were married by F.H. Smith, Justice of the Peace.

The couple had ten children. They left Mississippi and moved to Detroit, Michigan. Pearlie passed away on 9 January 1995 in Detroit.

Willie Coleman/Webb and Lucy Looney

Willie Coleman/Webb

Willie Coleman was born on 5 August 1881 in Pike County, Alabama to Frank C. Coleman and Flora Sanders. The couple wed shortly thereafter in Quitman County Georgia on 18 September 1881. Willie moved with his parents to Sunflower County Mississippi between March 1885 and January 1886.

In 1900 Willie lived and worked on his father's plantation (as most farms in the South were called). He married Ida Jackson on 28 December 1912 and had at least 3 children with her. Their children include:
1. Pernella Coleman (b. 4 Jun 1913 Mississippi m. Reverend Benjamin Mitchell abt 1929 Mississippi; 8 children d. Jun 1983 in Kansas City, Wyandotte County, Kansas buried Mount Hope Cemetery, Kansas City, Wyandotte County, Kansas)
2. Sarah Coleman/Webb (b. 6 Dec 1915, Sunflower, Mississippi m. two times first Payton L. Riley 8 Dec 1933; at least 3 children second unknown first name surname Price; again at least 3 children d. 5 Apr 1997 Monterey, California buried 11 Apr 1997 Mission Memorial Park, 1915 Ord Grove Ave, Seaside, California)
3. Savanna "Dora" Coleman (b. Dec 1919 or Jan 1920)

Ida had another child, Jesse James Burks, who was considered a brother by the entire group of children connected to Willie Webb and Lucy Looney. More on him in the section about the children.

Willie should be registered for the Draft for World War I, however, there were other Willie and William Colemans living in the area and it is not clear which Draft Card might be his. To add more to the puzzle, there is another Willie Coleman living in Sunflower County who married an Ida. This Ida was Ida King and they wed in 1914.

Sometime shortly before the 1920 Census life changed dramatically and Willie changed his surname to Webb. Based on the birth date of youngest daughter by Ida, the incident probably occurred in 1919 or the first few months of 1920. There are at least two versions of what happened. Both will be given here and perhaps more will emerge to show more clearly what happened.

The first version comes from Willie's sons Mack Henry Webb, Sr. and George Austin William "Bill" Webb. In this version, Willie was chased by a group of white men. He was shot. One bullet lodged in his head and he carried it for the rest of his life. During the scuffle, he managed to wound at least one man who later became a Sheriff's Deputy and limped for the rest of his life. He managed to escape by hiding in a body of water and using a reed to breathe. The men who had chased him poured a flammable liquid onto the water and lit it. Willie had some burns as a result. Afterward, he escaped to the small town of Webb, Mississippi where he was helped by the Funderburk family. He went into hiding and changed his name to Webb. When he recovered enough to travel, he moved to Memphis where he played guitar in a nightclub and met Lucy (Looney) Phillips there as she was waitressing at the time. Lucy's first husband, Solomon, was out of the picture and Lucy was a young mother struggling to raise two children on her own. Willie and Lucy married and after a time moved back to Mississippi. When his father Frank Coleman died, Lucy and Bill attended the funeral because Willie thought the FBI might be there to see if he would show. Bill says there were a couple of white men dressed in the way "G" men dressed at the time at the funeral and his mother pointed them out to him.

The second version was written by Samuel Webb, Sr. in his **Family Publication #1**. Samuel is one of Joseph Webb's sons and most probably heard this version from him. Samuel records Willie Coleman's birth year as 1891 however this could easily have been a typographical error. Records show he was born in 1881. Samuel describes him as extremely handsome. Apparently Willie usually had the attention of the women. At one particular gathering, he was having a good time and dancing with a number of women. Some of the men there got jealous. Five of the jealous men slipped away from the gathering and waited for Willie along the route home. They ambushed him, *"...knocking him to the ground, he was stomped in a fierce manner, and beat over the head with thick tree branches that had been obtained from the woods. Believing that he was finally unconscious, together the attackers drug Willie face down to the muddy swamp waters to suffocate. Satisfied with their handiwork, the would-be assassins departed. After their prolonged departure, Willie drug himself from the muddy waters and went into hiding. Within a one week time period he emerged from hiding several times. Each time he emerged, he retaliated against the men that had attempted to bring his life to an end. Within a one week time period, the fate that had been intended for Willie had been reversed towards his attackers. Although deaths of African-Americans of that time meant very little to white authorities, Willie Coleman decided that it would be best to leave the state of*

Mississippi altogether. He changed his last name from Coleman to Webb and put great distance between himself and the state of Mississippi."

Whatever the truth of the matter, Willie lived the rest of his life as Willie Webb. Following this incident, Willie fled to Memphis, Tennessee where he lived for about 6 years. While there, he worked in the evenings at a juke joint or club playing guitar. It was at work that he met Lucy (Looney) Phillips who was waitressing. It is not certain what happened to Solomon Phillips; the section about him has what is known.

Willie and Lucy teamed up, and after a couple more years in Memphis, moved to the eastern part of Sunflower County near Moorhead, Mississippi just over the county boundary from her father and brothers. Willie returned to sharecropping. The family lived on Section 16 Plantation for a number of years. In the later part of 1935, they moved back up to Memphis for a short while. Given Lucy's history of miscarriages, this move may have been prompted by needing medical care during the pregnancy of their last child. By 1940 the family was back in Sunflower County. The couple had 6 children who survived to adulthood. As mentioned Lucy also had a number of miscarriages and there are two children who died in infancy. The first child listed here appears to have been their child based on the child's Death Certificate, although no family source remembered mention of him. The second child which died in infancy has the opposite situation – many family members have heard of the child and no Death Certificate has been located as yet, although there is still hope one might be found. The challenge with finding it at the moment is the way Death Certificates can be searched in Mississippi. A fair amount of information, including a narrow window of when the death may have occurred, is required before one can locate it. The children of Willie and Lucy include:

1. Willie Webb (b. 27 Sep 1923 Arkansas d. 7 Jan 1924 Memphis, Shelby County, Tennessee buried Shelby County, Tennessee buried 8 Jan 1924 Union-Forever Cemetery, Shelby County, Tennessee)
2. Joseph Garlin Webb (b. 23 Apr 1925 Memphis, Shelby, Tennessee m. Louise Wilson 25 May 1944 Sunflower County, Mississippi 9 children; 2 additional relationships resulting in 2 children d. 1997 Cleveland, Cuyahoga County, Ohio buried 30 Jun 1997 Cleveland, Cuyahoga, Ohio)
3. Flora Webb (b. 1927 Sunflower County, Mississippi m. 3 times first Alex Randle 23 Nov 1942 Sunflower County, Mississippi 1 child; second C. M. Funderburk 1 child; third Willie Lee Perry, Sr. 28 Mar 1946 Greenville, Mississippi 6 children d. 2001 Detroit, Wayne County, Michigan)
4. Bernice Webb (b. est Jan 1930 Sunflower County, Mississippi m. Isaac Briggs 5 Sep 1948 Sunflower County, Mississippi 8 children d. 23 Apr 1991 Indianola, Sunflower County, Mississippi buried 1 May 1991, Moorhead, Mississippi)
5. Mack Henry Webb (b. 1 Apr 1931 Sunflower County, Mississippi m. two times; first Ruth Mae Barnes 24 Jan 1951 Cleveland, Cuyahoga, Ohio 7 children; second Sandra Ossman 30 Jul 1998 Columbus, Franklin, Ohio no children d. 8 Feb 2008 Columbus, Franklin County, Ohio buried 14 Feb 2011 Section 36 site number 874 Dayton National

Cemetery, Dayton, Ohio)
6. Mary Eliza "Mickey" Webb (b. 2 Aug 1934 Sunflower County, Mississippi; unions with first Willis Norman Taylor 2 children; second Samuel Pulliam 1 child; m. Clarence Blackmon 1955 Detroit, Wayne, Michigan 5 children d. 31 Oct 2014 Detroit, Wayne County, Michigan buried 8 Nov 2014 Detroit Memorial Park West, Detroit, Wayne, Michigan)
7. George Austin William "Bill" Webb (living)
8. Raymond Webb (birth and death dates unknown)

Willie died on 6 April 1968 in Indianola, Sunflower County, Mississippi at his home on 309 Mill Street, Indianola, Mississippi. He was living with his third wife, Lula Mitchell, at the time at the time of his death. According to his Death Certificate he was 86 years old. He was buried on 14 April 1968 at Old St. Rest Cemetery which about 3 miles north of Indianola according to his Death Certificate. Internet directions from Indianola are: take Hwy 82E, 7 miles east from Leland to Delta Western, turn north at intersection past railroad, take first right onto Fairview Road, 4 miles north, cemetery on right. Funeral arrangements were made by Hull Funeral Home, Indianola, MS which is now Byas Funeral Home.

The Ida Jackson Line

Edmund Jackson

Ida's father was Edmund Jackson (b. 1866 Mississippi). According to the 1900 Census, both of his parents were born in Alabama, however in the 1910 Census his parents are listed as having been born in Mississippi. He was a sharecropper. On a transcribed listing of marriages, Edmund is listed twice. It turns out that one listing is for his marriage and in the second listing, he is actually a witness.

On 4 Aug 1887 he and a man named Simon Fleminster posted a marriage bond of $100 for the impending marriage between Edmund and Lena Giggle (this is the way the surname was spelled on the bond although this name also appears as Gigger or Geiger in other documents related to this family). He married Adlena "Lena" Gigger on 5 August 1887 in Sunflower County, Mississippi. The ceremony was officiated by Minister William Stephens. William Stephens was another member of the African-American community established just to the east of Shaw, Mississippi. He owned his farm as did Frank C. Coleman and Major G. Gigger, a relative on Ida's mother's side. Most pastors supported their families through work other than the church.

Although indexed as a marriage record for Edmund Jackson, he was actually the witness on the Marriage Affidavit for an application for marriage between Silas Jackson and Tish Giggle on 24 March 1893. For some reason no license was issued and the marriage did not happen. Silas Jackson (b. 1874 Mississippi) was the son of Abram Jackson (b. 1855 Virginia) and his wife, Norah (b. 1855 Alabama). He had at least a brother, Moses (b. 1872 Mississippi) and a sister, Perla (b. 1878 Mississippi).

There is perhaps some discrepancy about Lena's date of birth which is recorded as 1876 in one of the Census entries. That would have made her 11 years old at the time of their marriage. On the 1910 Census, she is recorded as the mother of 12 children, 9 then living. In the 1920 Census, more

children appear. The listing below is a combination of all Census data. Their children include:
1. Anthony Jackson (b. 1889 Mississippi)
2. Almus Jackson (son) (b. 1891 Mississippi)
3. Chalmus Jackson (daughter) (b. 1891 Mississippi)
4. Ida Jackson (b. 1896 Mississippi d. around 1927)
5. Thomas "Tommy" Jackson (b. 1898 Mississippi)
6. Isaola Jackson (b. 1901 Sunflower, Mississippi)
7. Allen Jackson (b. 1903 Sunflower, Mississippi)
8. Joy Jackson (b. 1904 Mississippi)
9. Tololo Jackson (at least that's what the name looks like on the Census) (b. 1905 Mississippi)
10. Lavel Jackson (b. 1913 Sunflower, Mississippi)

Henry Gigger

Henry Gigger was born in 1835 in South Carolina. Around 1860 or so probably while in Alabama, he married a woman named Charlotte also from South Carolina. They had nine children.
1. Alonzo Gigger (b. 1862 Preston, Sumter, Alabama)
2. Mary Gigger (b. 1865 Preston, Sumter, Alabama)
3. Henry Gigger (b. 1868 Preston, Sumter, Alabama)
4. Mary Gigger (same name as #2 – perhaps the first Mary died) (b. 1871 Preston, Sumter, Alabama)
5. Nicholas Gigger (b. 1872 Preston, Sumter, Alabama)

6. Major G. Gigger (b. 1873 Preston, Sumter, Alabama m. at least twice first Florida Thompson 22 Mar 1896 {note: he signed the Marriage Affadavit on 22 Mar; the date for the Rites of Marriage is overwritten and might be 28 as opposed to 22}, Sunflower County, Mississippi second Delia Meyer (b. 1885 Mississippi) 28 Feb 1903, Bolivar County, Mississippi; marriage performed by Reverend S. G. Gigger)
7. Adlena "Lena" Gigger (b. 1876 Preston, Sumter, Alabama m. Edmund Jackson 5 Aug 1887 Sunflower County, Mississippi)
8. Charlotte Gigger (b. 1877 Preston, Sumter, Alabama m. John Williams 23 Jan 1898 Sunflower, Mississippi)
9. Bessie Gigger (b. 1880 Preston, Sumter, Alabama)

Charlotte died before 1900 as Henry is then a widower farming in Beat 4 of Sunflower County which is the same area the Frank Coleman and young Willie Coleman yet to be Webb are living. On 22 January 1901, Henry applied for a marriage license and on 27 January 1901 Henry married Mollie Grammar. M. L. Peacock swore there was no legal cause to obstruct the marriage. The marriage was officiated by Reverend M. J. Jackson.

Here there is another piece of confusion. There is a marriage record for a Henry Gigger to Mary Hare on 13 February 1893. Perhaps she had died before 1900 when Henry was listed as widowed. Or perhaps the Henry Gigger who married Mary Hare was the son listed above.

Unfortunately, nothing leaps out in a records search, so this will take more effort to resolve.

In 1910, Henry and his family lived next door to Frank C. Coleman; by 1930, his son Major Gigger with his wife Delia are the ones living one farm over from Frank Coleman.

Ida Jackson, granddaughter of Henry Gigger, was Willie Coleman's first wife before he changed his name. As noted above, Ida was born around 1896 in Mississippi, probably in Sunflower County. Her family lived near the Coleman family slightly east of Shaw, Mississippi. Shaw is on the border of Bolivar and Sunflower Counties.

According to her youngest child, Reverend Jesse James Burks (b. 9 Feb 1923 Sunflower, Mississippi d. 26 Dec 2013 Chicago, Cook County, Illinois), she became ill and arranged for her children to be cared for by relatives before she died in 1927. No Death Certificate was found in the Mississippi Department of Archives and it is possible she left the state to seek medical care elsewhere. Jesse and his sister, Dora, initially lived with Ida's great-uncle Major G. Gigger and his wife. The Giggers were quite strict and while in their teens both Jesse and Dora moved on to other relatives. Sarah ended up with her father and Lucy while she was in her teens once they had moved back to Sunflower County. Pernella Coleman married Benjamin Mitchell about the time of her mother's death.

Lucy Looney

Lucy's early life was discussed in the section on her father James Knox Looney. We'll pick up her story when she married her first husband, Solomon (in the records he sometimes appears as "Sol" and in the family he is referred to as "Saul") Phillips. Lucy and Solomon married around 1913 although there is no record of this marriage in Shelby County, Tennessee where they were living at the time. It may be that they married in Mississippi or possibly they went across the Mississippi River to Arkansas where there was no waiting period. Following their marriage, they lived for a year or two with Lucy's father. Solomon is listed as a boarding with James Looney at the "Elect south east corner of Beatrice Ave" address.

Lucy and Solomon had two children.
1. Harry Gordon Phillips (b. 21 Jul 1914, Memphis, Shelby County, Tennessee m. Inell Reed 10 Dec 1932 Indianola, Sunflower, Mississippi d. 23 Mar 2001 Cleveland, Cuyahoga County, Ohio, buried 28 Mar 2001 Cleveland, Ohio)
2. Virda Thelma Phillips (b. 1916, Memphis, Shelby County, Tennessee m. Sebren Reed 1933 Sunflower, Mississippi d. 1960 or 1962 Detroit, Michigan)

Something happened to Solomon in late 1922 or early 1923 which will be discussed in more detail in his section. The result was that Lucy was on her own with two young children by 1923. She worked as a waitress at a juke joint and that is where she met Willie Webb who was playing guitar at the same place. Although no marriage record has yet been found, they joined forces and started their family. Lucy had eight children who lived to adulthood. She also had a number of miscarriages and babies who died in early childhood. One of these may well have been an infant who was born on 27 September 1923 and died of ileocolitis on 7 January 1924.

Ileocolitis affects the small intestine, known as the ileum, and the colon. It is characterized by considerable weight loss, diarrhea, and cramping or pain in the middle or lower right part of the abdomen. It causes malabsorption of nutrients and there are frequently ulcers along the bowel wall. Willie Webb, Jr. was born in Luxora, Mississippi County, Arkansas. The town is and was largely inhabited by African-Americans. It is across the river from Shelby County, Tennessee. The father of the child is listed as Will Webb born in Alabama and the mother is listed as Lucy Webb born in Tennessee which is consistent with our Willie and Lucy Webb. Willie Webb, Jr. died in the hospital in Memphis, Tennessee. The child was buried in Union-Forever Cemetery which was located on Horn Lake Road south of the Illinois Central Railroad yards. It was a cemetery serving the African-American community operated until the 1970's when it was closed and later bulldozed over by the city. Horn Lake Road was where Lucy had lived with her family in the late 1800's and early 1900's.

If this child was indeed one of Lucy's children, it is possible that this may have been the start of her interest in helping women deliver healthy babies.

In the 1940 Census, Lucy is listed as having a 5th grade education. According to various family sources, she was well respected for being a learned person. In fact, she became a midwife and delivered hundreds of babies in Sunflower County, Mississippi. The Sunflower County Health Department had a certification program for midwives. African-American women were trained by the hospital staff in child delivery practices. They received annual training. They wore a uniform, a pin for their lapel, a black leather bag loaded with the necessary equipment, and reference books on childbirth and pregnancy. When Lucy first started delivering babies the fee was $10, but that increased over the years and later she was paid $25 per birth. It was an important source of income for the family. She did not work in the fields with the rest of the family. She did the housework and was on call for deliveries at any time of the day. Her son, Bill, remembers knocks on the door in the middle of the night with the request that "Miss Lucy" come to the bedside of a woman in labor. She was also frequently called in by the doctors for difficult births like when the baby presented in the breech position. She was a tiny woman with small hands who could more easily do the repositioning necessary to safely deliver such a baby. Bill describes her as "not more than 90 pounds soaking wet". She had long, straight hair and her skin tone was quite light.

Lucy died on 2 November 1950 at the Cleveland Clinic in Cleveland, Ohio where she had traveled to receive medical care. She suffered from Type II diabetes, but her death came from meningitis. She was taken back home to Mississippi for burial.

Solomon "Sol" or "Saul" Phillips

Solomon Phillips is what is known in genealogy as a "brickwall" meaning a researcher finds a little bit but struggles to break the "wall" down to find anything further. Identifying his parents and siblings is difficult. Finding out what happened to him in the end is also being problematic. The period of time covered by the records found thus far only covers 1914 to 1922. Nevertheless, some things from this time are quite clear.

Solomon was born in Mississippi on 17 August 1880. This was after the 1880 Census was conducted so he does not appear in that Census. The next Census was lost in a fire, so we are not able to pick up his trail then.

The oldest record for him thus far is the listing in the 1914 Memphis City Directory where he is boarding with James Looney at the same address that James lived at in 1910 with his mother-in-law, Delia Kegler. We know he and Lucy started their family in 1914 with the birth of Harry.

He may have known James and Lucy's brother, Burrell, through his work at a sawmill.

In 1916 and 1917, Solomon is listed as living at 4 and 6 Kansas Street respectively, south of Fields in Memphis. Then in 1918 he moved the family to Silverage Avenue one house east of Castex. On 12 September 1918 he registered for the World War I Draft. At the time he was a laborer working for the Dixon and Shannon Lumber Company on South Ragan at the corner of 8 Parkway in East Memphis. His next of kin was Lucy. He is described as a Negro of medium height, slender build with black eyes and hair and missing part of the middle finger of his right hand.

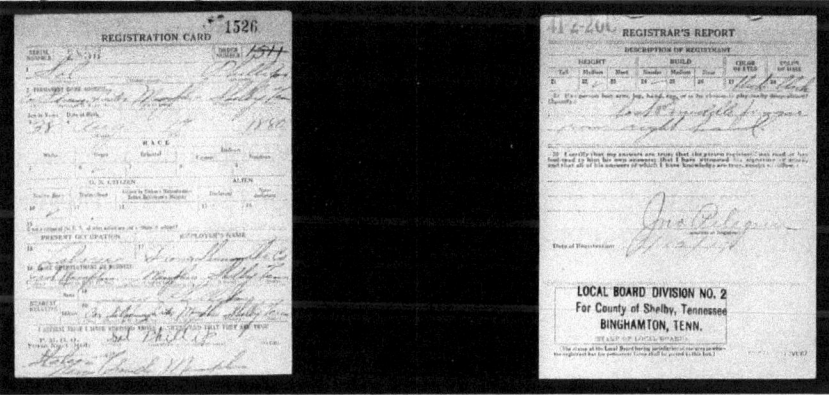

Figure 9 *World War I Draft Registration for Solomon Phillips.*

Solomon and Lucy stayed at the house on Silverage through at least 1921 and might also have been there in 1922. In the 1920 Census, Solomon is listed as mulatto. He was able to read and write. He had moved up in the sawmill and was working as an edgerman. An edgerman cuts flitches and cants (rough-cut boards resulting from the first round of cutting of a log) to various widths using a group of shifting circular saws. An edgerman must have excellent lumber grading skills and a good understanding of the relative value of each lumber grade and dimension so he can minimize waste and maximize the value of the finished boards. Edgermen are paid more than laborers because of the difficulty and danger of the job.

In 1922 he changed his occupation and opened a barbershop at 1584 Florida Ave. The location was perfect for a barber. There were businesses all around him including five lumber companies.

After that he no longer appears in the Memphis City Directory. Bill Webb heard that Solomon was chased and fell from a bridge. Harry Phillips, however, does not list his father as deceased on his marriage application in 1932 although it is clear he would have known to do so as his wife, Inell, lists her mother as deceased.

DNA test results for Phillips line have not yet resulted in any near matches except for our Webb line which, of course, we would expect. Perhaps as more people get tested, matches from the Phillips line will emerge.

The Children

Pernella Coleman

Pernella Coleman was born on 4 June 1913 in Mississippi, most probably in Sunflower County, to Willie Coleman and his first wife, Ida (Jackson) Coleman. She married Reverend Benjamin Mitchell (b. 1907 Mississippi d. abt Apr 1971 Kansas City, Wyandotte County, Kansas) about 1929 in Mississippi. The couple had 8 children including Robert Lee Mitchell (b. 25 Jan 1934 Sunflower, Mississippi d. 16 Jul 2011 Kansas City, Wyandotte, Kansas buried 23 Jul 2011). Pernella died in June 1983 in Kansas City, Wyandotte County, Kansas. She was buried in Mount Hope Cemetery.

Sarah Coleman

Sarah Coleman was born on 6 December 1915 to Willie and Ida Coleman in Sunflower, Mississippi. After her father disappeared and her mother died, she was raised for a while by relatives of her mother, Ida. When her father moved back to Sunflower County, he and Lucy raised her during her late teens and her surname was changed to Webb. Sarah's name is spelled both Sara and Sarah in the various records related to her. The "Sarah" version is the one used in her obituary, so that's the one used here.

On 8 December 1933 she married Payton L. Riley (b. 26 Mar 1909 Sunflower, Mississippi lived in Memphis, Tennessee for much of his life d. 26 Nov 2004 Byhalia, Marshall, Mississippi a small town about 33 miles south-east of Memphis) of Sunflower City, son of Allen (b. circa 1885 Mississippi) and Tinny or Tennie (b. circa 1878-1880 Mississippi) Riley. Allen and Tennie had at least 4 children:

1. Allen J. Riley (b. 1905 or 1913 (there is a discrepancy in the records) Mississippi)
2. Ethel Riley (b. 1907 Mississippi)
3. Payton L. Riley (b. 1909 d. 2004 (read this section on Sarah for more detail))
4. Bertha T. Riley (b. 1916 Mississippi)

Sarah and Payton stayed in Sunflower at least through 1935, but moved before 1940. Payton's occupation in 1940 was a Mattress Maker for the U.S. Bedding Company working in Memphis, Tennessee. He worked 50 weeks a year and earned $685. He and Sarah and their 4-year-old son rented a place on the rear of Number 14 Florida Street for $7 a month. The Memphis City Directory for 1940 lists their home address as 12 East Bean Alley. East Bean Alley is a short dead-end street off Florida Street. The area has been rebuilt since that time and East Bean Alley now has a small manufacturing building belonging to Applied Industrial Technologies making bearings on the left side of the alley and a parking lot on the right side of the alley. Sarah had a 6th grade education which was not uncommon for the time. Most people in the United States had 6 to 8 years of education. High school educations were much less common at this point in history.

In 1941 they lived at the same address, but Payton's occupation changed to laborer.

Sarah had at least 6 children; 3 with Payton, and from their surnames, 3 by another husband with the surname Price.

By 1960, she had moved to Kansas because that is where she was when she applied for her Social Security Number. It would not be surprising to learn she moved to the Kansas City area to be close to her older sister, Pernella. At some point she reverted to using the surname Webb.

Sarah Webb moved to Seaside, California about 1973 and lived there the rest of her life. Sarah died on 5 April 1997 in Monterey, California at the Beverly Health Care Center. She, like so many of our family, was an avid Bible-reader and devout Christian. Her funeral service was held on Friday, 11 April 1997, and she was buried in Mission Memorial Park after the ceremony held at the Monterey Peninsula Mortuary Chapel at 1915 Ord Grove Avenue, Seaside, California.

Savanna "Dora" Coleman

On the 1920 Census, there is a Savanna Coleman listed as a 4-month-old baby with her mother Ida and sisters. This name was not familiar to the oldest surviving members of the family. They remembered a child of Ida's named Dora. This may be the same person. In fact, Jesse Burks reports that his older sister, Dora, and he were raised by the same family after Ida's death. So far, no other mentions in any records have been located for either Savanna or Dora which can be confirmed to be for this particular person. Hopefully more will emerge as other family members contribute to this history.

Jesse James Burks

Jesse James Burks was born on 9 February 1923 in Sunflower, Mississippi to Ida (Jackson Coleman) Burks and her second husband. When his mother died around 1927, he and Dora were initially taken in by Ida's maternal uncle Major G. Gigger (or Geiger) (b. abt 1873 Preston, Sumner, Alabama m. 28 Feb 1903 Boliver County, Mississippi) and his wife, Delia (b. abt 1885 Mississippi). Major G. Gigger owned his farm with a mortgage at the time but by 1940, he was sharecropping. He probably either lost his farm or had to sell it to settle debts during the Great Depression as so many others did during the same time period.

Jesse, who later became a pastor, used to climb up on the farm wagon and preach to the farm animals.

The couple had no children of their own. They lived close to Frank Coleman (Willie Webb's father) and Jesse remembered visiting the Coleman household on Sundays. The Giggers were a strict Christian couple and both Dora and Jesse left in their early teens. Jesse joined his father's family which moved to Chicago, Illinois.

On 28 Dec 1945, Jesse enlisted as a Private First Class in the U. S. Army Air Corp (which became the U. S. Air Force in 1947). He was married at the time. He had a grammar school education and was working in the manufacture of electrical machinery and accessories. He served at McChord Field in Washington State.

After his service he returned to Chicago. He died on 26 December 2013. He is buried in Section 6A Site 1546 at Abraham Lincoln National Cemetery in Elwood, Will County, Illinois.

Harry Gordon Phillips, Sr.

Harry Gordon Phillips was born on 21 July 1914 in Memphis, Shelby County, Tennessee to Solomon (most often called "Saul" or "Sol") and Lucy (Looney) Phillips. The family was boarding with Lucy's father, James Knox Looney that year. Sometime between 1922 and 1925, Solomon disappeared from the picture and Lucy married Willie Webb.

The Webbs moved to Sunflower County, Mississippi between 23 April 1925 and 25 September 1927.

Harry married Inell Reed on 10 December 1932 in Sunflower County, Mississippi. The Reed line is explained in some detail in a section devoted to the Reeds. The couple had 14 children and raised a grandchild as their own. Several of their children have passed away including Willie B. (Phillips) Smith, Nettie B. (Phillips) Jones, Eugene Phillips (who died as a toddler while the family was still in Mississippi), Virda Thelma (Phillips) Ashley, and Inell (Phillips) Mahone.

In the early years of their marriage, Harry and Inell lived with his mother and her household. Harry and Inell are listed with the Webb household in both the 1933 and 1935 Educable Children (Mississippi) survey of Sunflower County, Indianola, Township 19, Range 4.

After the end of World War II, Harry started using a tractor rather than driving a team of mules to cultivate the cotton fields and take the men of the plantation to town on Saturday nights. Town meant the small rail stop of Sunflower. To the people living out in the country where there was no electricity and one went to bed with the sun, Sunflower seemed a glamourous place at night with lights twinkling against the inky black sky. Sunflower had two stores, a juke joint, and a cotton gin and warehouse right outside of town. The school served as the church on Sunday and was also located just outside of town. While Inell allowed her oldest daughters to go into town on weekends, the younger children only got to go about once a year.

During the 1940's the family sharecropped and moved to different houses a couple of times. It was a common pattern for sharecroppers to move in December after the harvest was in and the landowner had "settled up". People talked with their neighbors and found out which land owners could be relied on to pay what was owed. In addition to raising the cash crop of cotton, the family also maintained a large garden. They grew green beans, corn, tomatoes, sweet and white potatoes, collard, turnip, and mustard greens, peanuts, and Crowder beans. Inell canned the green beans, tomatoes, corn, and a vegetable soup she made. She also canned peaches and apples in slices. The fruit was purchased from a farmer who made the rounds each year in his truck.

Canning done during this time period was primarily hot water bath canning. This works very well for fruits, jams, jellies, pickled vegetables and high-acid vegetables like tomatoes. Canning is a relatively new technology for preserving foods. People have dried, salted, and fermented foods for thousands of years. Canning came along in the early 1800's. In 1795, Napoleon Bonaparte offered a reward of 12,000 francs to whomever could develop a safe, reliable food preservation method for his constantly traveling and hungry army. Nicholas Appert introduced a method of canning involving heat-processing food and sealing the food in glass jars reinforced with wire which was first proven in tests conducted in 1806. In 1810 he was awarded the prize. By the time the Civil War started glass food preservation jars with metal clamps and replaceable rubber rings had been invented. In 1858, John Mason invented a glass container with a screw-on thread molded into its top and a lid with a rubber seal. William Charles Ball and his brothers got into the food preservation jar business in the late 1800's. Alexander Kerr invented the easy-to-fill wide mouth jars in 1903. Then in 1915, he developed a metal disk with an attached gasket held in place by a threaded metal ring – the modern 2-piece canning lid still in use today.

There have been a number of methods of canning – hot water bath, steam, solar, oven, and pressure. Steam, solar, and oven are not recommended, so the two methods home cooks used regularly are hot water bath and pressure canning. Pressure canning is required for most vegetables, and all meat, dairy, and seafood in order to kill the botulism spores which can survive the hot water bath method. The first pressure canner for home use was the "Thermo-Chief" available in 1896, however at $76.85, it was too expensive for most home cooks. In 1915 National Presto started marketing large-size pressure cookers specifically for use by housewives. By 1917 the USDA had determined that low-acid foods could only safely be processed by pressure canning. By 1941 pressure canning was practiced in many U.S. households that could afford to buy the canners. Production of pressure canners which were made with aluminum came to a halt during World War II. It was after the War that pressure canners became widely available.

The family also grew dry corn which they would pick, shuck, and shell and then take it into town to get milled into corn meal. A treat was to roast sweet potatoes or corn in the husk in the coals of the wood stove.

There was a big barn on one of the places they lived which housed horses, cows, mules, hogs, a milk cow, and chickens. The cow was milked twice a day. The "sweet" milk was the whole milk before the cream and fat had been separated and turned into butter. Buttermilk and corn bread was another family favorite. At this time, the family did have an icebox to store the milk. Inell made biscuits and corn bread, but did not bake yeast breads. It was not until the family moved to Cleveland and was able to shop in grocery stores that "sandwich" bread became part of their diet.

When the sharp chill of frost filled the air, it was time to butcher the hogs. To preserve the meat to last throughout the coming winter, it was either salted, brined, or smoked. Salting and brining are fairly simple. To salt pork, cut the meat in 4- to 6-inch slabs. For every 12 pounds of meat mix together ½ pound pickling salt and ¼ cup brown sugar. Coat all pieces in the salt/sugar mix. Sterilize a 2-gallon crock. Pack the meat tightly in the crock and cover tightly with cheesecloth. Keep the meat at 36 degrees for at least a month then wrap in moisture-proof paper. Brining is similar. Pack the meat slabs in a sterilized crock; cover with a brine of 3 quarts water, 1 pound pickling salt, and ½ cup brown sugar. Weight down the meat so that every little bit is covered. Store for a week at 36 degrees. Remove the meat, stir the brine, and repack the meat each week for 4 weeks. If the brine is thick or stringy, wash each piece of meat, sterilize the crock, and pack in fresh brine. A common breakfast on plantations during both slavery and later during the sharecropping era was salt pork, cornbread, and milk if available.

The children did go to school when it was in session, but school for African-American children in the Deep South at this time was not in session very much. School was only held when the children (and the teacher) were not needed to work in the fields. It was therefore held in a couple of short sessions per year. Cotton harvesting starts in August and continues through December. Planting usually started in mid-March.

The cotton harvest brought every man, woman, and child out to the fields. Young children were given a "croaker" sack which was a small bag, often an old potato sack. Older children had a larger sack and adults had the largest sacks which trailed behind them secured by a single shoulder strap. An average adult picker could harvest 150 to 200 pounds of cotton a day. Exceptional pickers might get around 300 pounds. It was a grueling 12 hours out in the weather from hot sun in the summer to frosty days by the end of the harvest season. Pickers were bent over, trying to avoid pricking one's fingers on the dried cotton burr and the sting from a packsaddle worm. When the sack was full, it was tied off, and weighed. The sacks were transported to town to be ginned and bailed. Workers were paid from $1 to $3 per hundred weight.

Soon after his mother died on 2 November 1950, his brother Joe convinced Harry to move north. In 1951 Harry and Inell loaded up their 1941 Chevy with their worldly possessions and children and drove to Cleveland. The children now attended a full school year. Harry found work at the Distillata Bottling Company and stayed with the company until he retired. He enjoyed baseball, bowling, and fishing.

He died on 23 March 2001. His Funeral Service was held 28 March 2001 with the arrangements entrusted to Watson's Funeral Home, 10913 Superior Avenue, Cleveland, Ohio. Reverend Bertram B. Lewis, Sr. Pastor of Beautiful Savior Church officiated.

Inell devoted her life to raising her children. She enjoyed playing bingo and an occasional trip to the casino. She died on 5 March 2011. Her Funeral Service was held on

12 March 2011 with funeral arrangements handled by Watson's Funeral Home. Dr. C. Jay Matthews, Pastor, officiated. She is buried in Cleveland Memorial Gardens, Highland Hills, Ohio.

As previously mentioned several of Harry and Inell's children are deceased.

Willie B. Phillips was born on 4 September 1933 in Sunflower, Mississippi. In 1949 she met and married Flim Smith, Sr. in Mississippi. The family moved to Toledo, Ohio in 1953. The couple had 8 children. Willie died on 6 July 1988 while at Mercy Hospital in Toledo. Her Funeral Services were held on 12 July 1988 at the Dale Funeral Home Chapel, 572 Nebraska Ave., Toledo, Ohio. Reverend Willie L. Knighten officiated. She was interred in Section 34, Row 16, Grave 1 at Forest Cemetery, 1704 Mulberry, Toledo, Ohio.

Nettie B. Phillips was born on 10 March 1935 in Sunflower, Mississippi. She was baptized at Zion Rock Baptist Church in Sunflower. In 1951 she married W. C. Jones and moved to Cleveland, Ohio. The couple had 9 children. Nettie was employed at the Metropolitan General Hospital. She died on 13 January 1982 following a short illness at St. Vincent Charity Hospital. Her Funeral Service was held on Wednesday, 20 January, 1982 at the House of Wills Funeral Chapel, 14711 Harvard Avenue, Cleveland, Ohio. Reverend Frank Futrell officiated. She was interred in Section 23, Lot Number F, Tier Number 4, Grave 11 at Highland Park Cemetery, 21400 Chagrin Boulevard, Highland Hills, Ohio.

Virda Thelma Phillips was born 13 July 1943 in Sunflower, Mississippi. In 1951 the family moved to Cleveland, Ohio. Virda graduated from Jane Adams High School and attended the Jane Adams Practical Nursing

Program. She did her nursing internship at MetroHealth. Virda passed the State Boards in the top 10% of her class and became a Licensed Practical Nurse in 1964. She married Monroe Ashley, Jr. on 16 July 1965 and had one child. Virda worked in the field of nursing for over thirty years going the extra mile to see that her patients received the absolute best care. She was a devoted fan of sports, music, and old movies. She died on 6 October 2003. Her Funeral Service was held on Saturday, 11 October 2003 at Rogers Funeral Service, 13201 Euclid Avenue, East Cleveland, Ohio. Pastor William Q. Pilkington officiated. She was interred at Cleveland Memorial Gardens.

Inell Phillips was born 14 April 1947 in Sunflower, Mississippi. After the family moved to Cleveland, she attended the Cleveland Public Schools and graduated from John Hay High School. She continued her education at Cuyahoga Community College where she received her Associates Degree in Accounting. She worked for Jones Day Law Firm, Baker Hostetler & Patterson Law Firm, Squires, Sanders and Dempsey Law Firm and Young, Tarolli, Sundheim, and Covell Law Firm. She married Thomas Carver Mahone in 1967 and the couple had 2 children. She loved to read, travel, bowl, and play bingo, casino, and video games. She passed away on 24 July 2013. Her Funeral Service was held on Saturday, 27 July 2013. Arrangements were handled by Rogers Funeral Service, Inc. 13201 Euclid Avenue, East Cleveland, Ohio. Reverend Horace Glover officiated. She was interred at Cleveland Memorial Gardens, 4324 Green Road, Bedford Heights, Ohio.

John "Johnny" Edward Phillips, Sr. was born 2 November 1950 in Sunflower, Mississippi. He graduated in

1969 from East Technical High School in Cleveland with honors in electricity. He worked for a short time with Western Electric Company before he entered the U. S. Army on 5 May 1970. Two years later he married his high school sweetheart Vivian Razor on 26 August 1972 and the couple was blessed with 2 sons. He worked from 1972 to 1975 at The White Motor Company until he was one of the employees affected by a large lay-off. He had a passion for working with his hands and enjoyed carpentry, painting, roofing, and wallpaper hanging until he developed lupus and arthritis. He was known for his kind heart and easygoing attitude. On 29 August 2001 at Louis Stokes Veterans Hospital (Wade Park), Johnny passed away. His Funeral Service was held on Wednesday, 5 September 2001. Arrangements were handled by Pernel Jones & Sons Funeral Home, 7120 Cedar Avenue, Cleveland, Ohio. Reverend Cornelius E. Edwards, Pastor of Dunham Ave. Christian Church, officiated. According the Veterans Affairs records, he was buried at Riverside Cemetery 3607 Pearl Road, Cleveland, Ohio 44109.

Lawrence Allen Phillips was born on 29 July 1952. He attended the Cleveland Public School system and graduated from East Technical High School. He worked for Ford Motor Company and the Water Company. He married Allene Haynesworth in 1975 and the couple had 2 children. He died on 12 March 2008. His Funeral Service was held on Wednesday, 19 March 2008 at Rogers Funeral Service Chapel, 13201 Euclid Avenue, East Cleveland, Ohio. Reverend Dr. Herbert Gater, Jr., Pastor of the Avon Avenue Baptist Church, officiated. Lawrence was buried at Cleveland Memorial Gardens, 4324 S. Green Road, Highland Hills, Ohio.

Alvin "Spanky" Phillips was a grandson of Harry and Inell's who was adopted and raised by them. Alvin was born on 27 March 1954 in Cleveland, Ohio to Laura Phillips and Jack Rouser. Alvin earned his high school diploma through the Cleveland Public School system. He attended Westside Institute of Technology where he received his Certification in Electrical and Building Maintenance. He served in the U. S. Army and after he returned to civilian life, he worked at various jobs, including the U.S. Postal Service. He married Pamela Glenn in 1976 and had 2 children. He was a fun-loving, caring, down-to-earth person who was blessed with the gift of gab. He enjoyed traveling and spending time with his family. He passed away on 9 November 2010. His Funeral Service was held Tuesday, 16 November 2010 at Pernel Jones & Sons Funeral Home, 7120 Cedar Avenue, Cleveland, Ohio. He was interred in Section 11 Plot 2918 at the Ohio Western Reserve Cemetery, 10175 Rawiga Rd, Rittman, OH 44270. Dedicated in 2000, the Ohio Western Reserve National Cemetery was the 119th National Cemetery created and covers 273.1 acres.

Annette Phillips was born 6 October 1960 in Cleveland, Ohio. She attended Cleveland Public Schools and graduated as Salutatorian of her class at East Technical High School. She attended Tuskegee University on a scholarship where she majored in Chemical Engineering. In pursuit of her degree, she worked as a co-op on various projects for the NASA Research Center. While at the university she met her future husband Grant Logan. They married and were blessed with 2 children. She worked for 12 years as a medical transcriptionist for Elyria Medical Hospital. Although she wished to continue working, complications from lupus and arthritis made it difficult. Annette enjoyed reading, listening to music especially gospel, swimming, playing bingo, and spending time with her loved ones. On 13 February 2007 at just 46 years old, Annette passed away. Her Funeral Service was held on Saturday, 17 February 2007 at the Central Bible Baptist Church 2285 Noble Road, Cleveland Heights, Ohio. Pastor Elizabeth Jones of St. Monica United Faith Church officiated. Annette was interred at Cleveland Memorial Gardens 4324 S. Green Road, Highland Hills, Ohio.

Virda Thelma Phillips

Virda Thelma Phillips was born in 1916 in Memphis, Shelby County, Tennessee. At the time the family was living on Kansas Street four houses down from Fields Street. She moved with the rest of the family to Sunflower, Mississippi between 1925 and 1927. She went by the name Thelma.

She married Sebren Reed, Sr. (b. 16 Dec 1912 Mississippi d. 6 Oct 1988 Detroit, Wayne County, Michigan) in Sunflower County on 10 December 1932. The wedding was performed by Reverend Peter Craig. Both Thelma and Sebren list Indianola as their address. Based on interviews with family members and Census data, they were living near one another slightly to the east of Indianola. The servicing post office was probably Indianola. The couple had 3 children.

Thelma and Sebren are listed with the Webb household in both the 1933 and 1935 Educable Children (Mississippi) survey of Sunflower County, Indianola, Township 19, Range 4. It was a very full household. They moved to Detroit, Michigan between 1945 and 1947. So far, no death record has been found, but a family source believes Thelma passed in the early 1960's while in Detroit.

Sebren Reed, Sr. was born on 12 December 1912 in Sunflower, Mississippi to Arthur and Minnie Reed. After moving to Detroit, he worked for Chevrolet Gear & Axle. After Thelma's death, he remarried in 1964 to Ilene Windham. The couple had 3 children. Sebren died on 6 October 1988 in Detroit, Michigan. His Funeral Service was held on Tuesday, 11 October 1988 at Barksdale Northwest Chapel, 7321 Puritan, Detroit, Michigan. Pastor L. A. Puckett officiated. Sebren was buried at Detroit Memorial Park, 13 Mile & Ryan Road, Warren, Michigan.

Two of Thelma and Sebren's children have passed.

Margaret Reed was born on 19 September 1934 in Sunflower, Mississippi. In the 1940 Census, she lived next door to her parents and brother in the household of Minnie Ann Minton (b. between 1873 to 1877 Mississippi). Minnie is identified as Margaret's aunt. More research is required to identify what the exact relationship was. Minnie's age places her in Arthur Reed's generation, but no connection has emerged as yet to Arthur. Interestingly, Minnie and her husband and children lived close to James Knox Looney, James Looney, Jr., and Martin Looney and their respective families in 1930. She would clearly have known the extended family.

Margaret moved to Detroit with her family. Margaret's Funeral Program cites the move north as happening in 1947, however, her brother Sebren's Funeral Program lists the move as occurring in 1945. In 1953 she married Howard Fox. The couple had 5 children. She died suddenly on Monday evening, 20 April 1970 about 8:00 p.m.

Her Funeral Service was held on Saturday, 25 April 1970 at Greater Love Tabernacle Church of God in Christ, 9780 Quincy Street, Detroit, Michigan. Bishop William Rimson officiated. Arrangements were handled by Thompson Funeral Home and she was interred at Detroit Memorial Park.

Sebren Reed, Jr. was born on 26 March 1937 in Sunflower, Mississippi. Sebren earned his G.E.D. from Detroit Public Schools. He owned a gas station, auto collision shop, and a licensed cab service. He earned a certificate in Refrigeration and Cooling from Highland Park Community College and an auto mechanic's license from Cass Technical Evening School. He was employed by Chrysler Corporation for 11 years and ultimately retired from the City of Detroit as a licensed auto mechanic. His personal interests included fishing, gardening, listening to jazz, and cooking.

He married Shirley and had 3 children. He died on 1 June 2014 in Detroit, Wayne County, Michigan. He had been living in Marquette, Michigan. He was buried on 6 June 2014 in Forest Lawn Cemetery, 11851 Van Dyke Street, Detroit. Arrangements for the funeral were handled by Swanson Funeral Home, 806 E. Grand Blvd., Detroit, Michigan.

The Reed Line

Noah Reed

Noah Reed was born around 1848 in Mississippi. Both of his parents had also been born in Mississippi so this family line has been in the United States since at least the 1820's. There is no record of Noah Reed as a free man of color. Free men of color constituted a very small percentage of the African population in America at this time. The most likely scenario is that he was born a slave on a small plantation. Large plantations kept records some of which survive, but most small plantations did not keep many records and those that they did keep were not saved after Emancipation on 18 December 1865, or if the plantation was sold, or after the owner died. It is highly likely the family line was in the U.S. prior to the end of legal importation which was banned effective 1 January 1808.

So far, it has not been possible to firmly identify Noah's slave holder. If he remained in the same area after Emancipation as so many former slaves did due to lack of financial resources to move, it is possible he had been part of a large plantation operation owned by the wealthy R. D. Crowder who lived in the more healthful environment of Yalobusha County on an estate valued at $5,000 with personal property valued at $100,000 (for a total of $3 million in 2014 dollars). The plantation in Police District 1 of Carroll County had 59 slaves housed in 10 shacks. The property would have been run by an overseer.

However, if Noah used the name of his last slave holder as his surname, which historians estimate between 15% to 30% of former slaves did, there are at least two other possible contenders for slave holder. The first is a man named George W. Reed who lived in Tallahatchie County just north of Carroll County. In 1860, George owned 10 slaves including two who would have been the right ages for Noah and his brother, Sebren. George moved his wife Deborah and six children to Mississippi from Roane, Tennessee where he had married Deborah Cobb on 9 April 1816. George was originally from North Carolina where he was born in 1798. Deborah died in 1850 of cholera. In fact, by 1860 George had only one son living with him, George W. Reed, Jr. It is unclear whether he lost more family members to cholera or they married and moved away.

In 1860 George reported two mulatto slaves as fugitives: a man of 35 and a girl of 16. The remainder of his slaves are listed as black and include the two boys previously mentioned. When the Civil War started in 1861, men enlisted in large numbers. There are two George W. Reed's, one G.W. Reed, and a George Reed who enlisted in various Mississippi units. Further research might reveal if any of these were the George W. Reed we are interested in and/or his son. The reason for examining this family in such detail is the family story of Noah's brother, Sebren Reed, having fought and died in the Civil War.

There was no record of an African-American named Sebren Reed on either the Union or the Confederate side. There were 166 black regiments formed on the Union side, designated at first with "Colored" or "African Descent" appended to the regimental title. Later all became "U.S. Colored Troops". On the Confederate side, it was not until the last months of the war when a desperate need for manpower finally made the Confederate Congress officially call on slave owners to make up to a quarter of the slaves in any one state available for military service. In the end only two companies of black soldiers were enrolled, and they had no part in fighting before the Confederates were forced to surrender. Nevertheless, there are several possibilities for the family story. The first is that no record was created due to the mass confusion, particularly later in the war. The second is that Sebren went to war as servant to a white soldier. Historians estimate between 30,000 to 100,000 African-

Americans served the Confederacy in this way. These men cooked, cleaned, carried and cared for gear, and, when necessary, may have fought alongside their white companion. Often, these men would have been childhood playmates as the plantations were widely separated so visits between owners were infrequent and children of both races living on the same plantation played together. Serving the Confederacy in this way was not a matter of choice or statement of support for the ideals for which the war was being fought. The slaves who were brought to the battlefield to serve their master or master's son had no option in the matter. And once on the battlefield, men fight for survival.

No grave has yet been found for Sebren and it is highly likely that there is not a marked grave. A total of 620,000 men died during the conflict; 260,000 Confederates. While the Union soldiers who died were often buried properly and national graveyards were established during the War to meet the need, Confederate soldiers were considered traitors to the Union and, if their bodies were in area controlled by the Union after the battle, as was often the case, they were frequently buried in mass unmarked graves.

Another factor which led to unmarked burials was simply the rate at which manpower was eliminated during this war. Units often did not have good records of who was with them during a particular fight, replacements were often the first to die because of their lack of experience, and nobody knew who they were. Additionally, some of the carnage was unrecognizable due to the injuries sustained. For these reasons, even soldiers who were buried by the Confederates in local graveyards were frequently listed as unknown.

There is an interesting sidelight though brought up by the search for Sebren Reed and that is that there is a line of white Reeds originating out of South Carolina which also named family members with this name. However, the recording of this name in this family is spelled Seaborn or Seabourn which may have started with a child who was literally 'born at sea'. Noah named one of his son's with this name and that person also was recorded in the 1940 Census as Seaborn.

There are two Seaborn Reed's recorded as having fought in the Civil War. Both of these men are white. One served in Company B, 4th Arkansas Cavalry organized in December of 1863 at Little Rock, Arkansas for the Union. He died on 10 January 1864 before the unit engaged with the enemy. It would not be surprising if he died from disease as 2/3's of all casualties during the War succumbed to dysentery, typhoid, malaria, and cholera among other ailments.

The other man was Seaborn H. Reed who served in a unit which was renamed during the conflict and so he is listed in Company L of both the 2nd and 48th Infantry Regiment. He hailed from Oktibbeha County, Mississippi and a search of the slave schedule shows this family did not hold slaves.

There was another fairly large plantation owned by an Ann Reed in the southern part of Carroll County who would be another possibility for a slaveholder of Noah Reed. It may be that more details will emerge as time goes on which will narrow down the field of candidates.

Let's go back to Noah. About 1870, he married Delilah also called Lila. They started their family of 13 children right away with a son named Eckford. Noah was a tenant farmer in Township 21, Range 4 of Carroll County, Mississippi. He

appears to have stayed near Carrollton (which is the northern county seat of this unusual county which has two county seats; the southern one is Vaiden) for at least 30 years. Noah and Delilah had 13 children. They are:
1. Eckford Reed (b. 1870 Carroll County, Mississippi m. 2 times Annie B. circa 1904 (7 children) then Della or Delia between 1920 and 1930 (at least 4 children) d. before 1940 when his wife is listed as a widow in the Census)
2. Walter Reed (b. 1873 Carroll County, Mississippi)
3. William Reed (b. 1874 Carroll County, Mississippi)
4. Caroline Reed (b. 1876 Carroll County, Mississippi)
5. John Reed (b. 1877 Carroll County, Mississippi)
6. Alpia Reed (b. 1879 Carroll County, Mississippi)
7. another William (b. 1882) possibly the first died young
8. Benford Reed (b. 1884 Carroll County, Mississippi m. 2 times Dora circa 1914 (1 child) then Vera circa 1921 (4 children))
9. a child listed as Luthus but the name could be Luthur (b. 1886 notice this is the same year as the next child; either these children were twins or this child was actually born in 1885)
10. Arthur Reed (b. 1886 Carroll County, Mississippi d. possibly before 1940)
11. Belle Reed (b. 1888 Carroll County, Mississippi)
12. Seborne Reed (recorded here as listed in the 1900 Census) (b. 1894 Carroll County,

Mississippi m. Clara circa 1915 (at least 2 children))
13. Noah Reed (b. 25 Feb 1897 Carroll County, Mississippi m. Vera (Benford's wife) sometime between 1930 and 1940 and raised at least 8 children - Benford's children and his own; d. 20 Jan 1984 buried Mount Elam Cemetery, Carroll County, Mississippi).

Tenant farmers led hard scrabble lives. The landowner provided a shelter, often poorly maintained, and normally a wagon and a mule or two. The farmer was responsible for planting and harvesting. The cotton was then taken to town, baled and stored in warehouses next to the rail line. A lone adult male might be rented 40 acres to farm; a larger family group with a number of sons might manage double that.

The tenant shacks were small, wooden buildings. The entire family shared what little room there was. Typically the house had a wall to separate a front room from the kitchen area and one or two bedrooms which would be located to the rear of the house. The shacks were not insulated and you could see through the floor boards to the earth below. People papered the bare wood walls with newspapers to stop the wind whistling through the house. Many had a front porch which was often rotted and leaning dangerously. Outhouses were located out back.

The "kitchen" was typically a stove, perhaps a sink, more often a washbasin, a table and a shelf or several hooks. Most homes also had a large iron pot located outside in the yard which was used to do laundry and large cooking jobs.

Farmers who could afford to kept chickens, a milk cow, and raised a hog or two for butchering in the fall. A kitchen garden of vegetables might be kept close to the house. Mothers preserved food for the winter including canning quantities of green beans, tomatoes, and peaches which were a favorite. In addition to making preserves, wives also made peach wine which was enjoyed as well.

Arthur Reed

Arthur Reed was born around 1886 in Carroll County, Mississippi. He was the 10th child of his parents Noah and Delilah Reed. At age 14 he was already helping to work the farm. In the U.S. at that time it was common for children of 14 to be treated as adults in the sense of being expected to do a full day's labor (perhaps for pay, although in farming families the money often went to the family and not the individual). Most children living on farms worked for their parents. Some did get paid when cotton picking time rolled around and they were paid based on the weight of the cotton they picked.

The Civil War made a huge impact on this country; many of the schools, hospitals, and government buildings and records were destroyed, particularly in the South. It took a long time to rebuild the infrastructure. Immediately following the end of the Civil War, there was an effort to establish schools for African-American children and for about 10 to 15 years, a number of African-American children did go to school. By the time Arthur was born, schooling was hard to come by and many people, both black and white, of this period never learned to read or write. There is some question about whether or not Arthur received any education since the data on the various Census's where he is found are inconsistent.

On 16 February 1908, Arthur married Minnie Lott in Carroll County. His father, Noah Reed, personally appeared before the County Clerk to verify there was no legal cause to obstruct the marriage. Justice of the Peace H. P. Mullen performed the ceremony. As a brief aside, the name Minnie is a common nickname for Mary. There are a number of nicknames for Mary; some of which seem to have nothing whatever to do with the root name. The nicknames for Mary include: Mamie, Mattie, Mimi, Minnie, Mae, May, Molly, and Polly. Arthur and Minnie had 5 children according to Census entries.

1. Catherine (b. circa 1911 Tennessee (that's what is listed on the 1920 Census but this may not be accurate))
2. John "Jake" (b. 24 Jan 1911 Carroll County, Mississippi m. 2 times first Annie Bell Baker circa 1925 second Maggie d. 17 Jun 1984 Indianola, Sunflower, Mississippi buried Riverside Memorial Gardens, Indianola, Sunflower, Mississippi)
3. Sebren (b. 16 Dec 1912 Mississippi m. 2 times Virda Thelma Phillips 1933 Sunflower, Mississippi (3 children) then Ilene Windham (3 children) d. 6 Oct 1988 Detroit, Wayne, Michigan)
4. Inell (listed as Inez) (b. 28 Nov 1916, Carroll County, Mississippi m. Harry Gordon Phillips 10 Dec 1932 Indianola, Sunflower, Mississippi (15 children), d. 5 Mar 2011 Cleveland, Cuyahoga, Ohio)
5. Senior (b. 1921 Mississippi)

On 5 January 1917 at the age of 24 to the best of his knowledge (although if the data reported in the 1900 Census was accurate, he would have been 31), Arthur registered for the draft in Carrollton. At the time he was working as a road hand for Carroll County. He was married and had a number of children although the number is illegible. Based on a combination of the 1920 and 1930 Census, he probably had 3 children at that point. He is described as short and stout in stature with brown eyes and black hair and no missing limbs or digits.

A Noah Reed shows up in the Memphis City Directory of 1918 who may have been Arthur's youngest brother because by 1920 Arthur is living in Memphis with his wife, Minnie, and daughter, Catherine, who was 8 years old at the time. The other children were probably staying with other relatives at the time. It was not uncommon for a member of a family to move to find work and then be joined by other family members. Memphis was a booming town in the early 1920's with lots of jobs for willing workers.

Arthur found work as a laborer at a sawmill. Interestingly, this could be when Arthur and Minnie Reed met Solomon "Sol" and Lucy Phillips. Harry and Thelma Phillips would have to wait to meet their future spouses until both families (Lucy was by then married to Willie Webb) ended up in Sunflower County, Mississippi between late 1925 and 1927.

In 1920, Arthur and Minnie lived on the north side of Silverage 10 west of Kansas. That description puts the house close to the corner of Silverage and Pennsylvania. The housing stock currently in this area dates from 1945 through the early 1960's.

Sol and Lucy lived on the same street on the north east corner with Castex. The houses are both on the north side about a block apart.

In 1921, Arthur and Minnie moved to 938 Emmie Street and Arthur was working as a carpenter. They lived there long enough to be listed in the 1922 Memphis City Directory at the same address and then moved on to Sunflower, Mississippi.

By 1930, Arthur and Minnie were living in Sunflower County, Mississippi with their children Jake, Sebren, Inell (listed as Inez), and Senior.

They had a boarder named Frank Harris, living with them as well. Catherine is not listed in this Census entry. She would have been old enough to have been married. It is also possible she had died. Malaria, typhoid fever, tuberculosis, and influenza were rife in Mississippi during this period.

When Harry Phillips married Inell Reed in Indianola, Sunflower County, Mississippi on the 10th of December 1932, Minnie Reed had already passed. The young couple went to live with Willie and Lucy Webb. It was a full house by 1933 when they were joined by Sebren Reed who married Thelma Phillips, Lucy's daughter by her first husband. Both the 1933 and 1935 Educable Children Records (Mississippi) list the two young couples plus Joseph and Flora Webb as being in the Webb household. The code number 8 in their entries denotes their reason for not attending school in that year was due to marriage.

Although Sebren and Inell (who are covered in early sections) moved North during the Great Migration, Arthur and Minnie's son John (almost exclusively known in the family as Jake) stayed in Mississippi. In 1930 he lived with his parents in Beat 2 of Sunflower County. He was married at least twice. His first wife was Annie Bell Baker whom he married after 1930. In 1935 he lived in Leflore County. In the 1940 Census he was recorded as living with his wife, Annie Bell, one of his children, and his mother-in-law, Phebee {sic} Baker, in Beat 2 of Sunflower County. According to that Census, Jake had a 7th grade education. He was renting a farm which meant he was sharecropping. Sometime after 1940 he married Maggie. He had 3 children all told; his son, Ben D. Reed, predeceased him. Jake was an active member of the Mt. Carmel Church under Reverend Thomas. Mount Carmel was located at 1200 Bates Avenue in Indianola. He served faithfully as secretary and deacon under the leadership of Reverend Cooks and Reverend Shields. At some point he moved into Indianola, the Sunflower County seat, and lived at 506 Cleveland Street. He departed this life after an illness at the South Sunflower County Hospital on 12 June 1984 at 7:00 a.m. His Funeral Service was held on Sunday, 17 June 1984 at the Mount Carmel Missionary Baptist Church, Indianola, Mississippi. Reverend E. Shields officiated. Arrangements were handled by Dillon Funeral Home. He was buried at Riverside Memorial Gardens, Indianola, Sunflower County, Mississippi.

The Lott Line

Rafe Lott

Rafe Lott was born in about 1835 in Mississippi. His first Census entry is in 1870 when he was living in Carroll County, Mississippi. On the same Census sheet is Jacob Lott who was born about 1815 in Tennessee. This African-American farmer has a personal estate of $115. He was married to a woman named Mary (b. 1840 Tennessee). It is possible that Jacob is the father of Rafe or an older brother or cousin. Mary is most likely not his first wife given the large age difference.

Rafe was a farm hand and he may have been able to read and write. The Census enumerator has placed marks to indicate being unable to read or write in the columns for this data for some of the people on this sheet, but not by any of the people in Rafe's household. All of the other occupants in his household are most probably his children. The 1870 Census does not list family relationship to head of household which would make the conclusion more definite. It does not look like his wife was alive by this time. His children include:

1. Louisa Lott (b. 1853 Mississippi)
2. Austin Lott (b. 1854 Mississippi)
3. Cressey Lott (b. 1854 (this is the year listed in the Census which is the same as Austin's; but the actual birth could have been in 1855) Mississippi)
4. Reuben Lott (b. 1856 Mississippi m. Fannie Davis in Carroll County, Mississippi)
5. Dennis Lott (b. 1858 Mississippi)

While Rafe and his oldest three children were recorded as "Farm Hand"; the youngest two were listed as "Farm Laborer".

Reuben Lott

Reuben Lott was born about 1856 in Mississippi to Rafe Lott. No record yet discovered indicates who his mother was.

Reuben Lott lived with Henry Davis and his family including his daughter Fannie (b. 1867 Mississippi) in 1880.

He was working as a farm laborer for Henry. Henry's wife, Maria, at that time is clearly not his first wife as there is a stepdaughter named Becky (b. 1874 Mississippi) living with him. That indicates that Fanny's mother is somebody else. Also of interest on this Census is the next door neighbor – Martha Lott. Martha has eight children living with her. No husband was present and he may have died or left the family. In any case, she may have been the wife of one of Reuben older brother's. Further research may give more insight into Martha.

Reuben Lott married Fannie Davis on 3 March 1881 in Carroll County, Mississippi. The couple had at least the following children.

1. Henry Lott (b. 1883 Carroll County, Mississippi)
2. Johnie {sic} Lott (b. 1885 Carroll County, Mississippi)
3. Maria Lott (b. 1887 Carroll County, Mississippi)
4. Minnie Lott (b. 1892 Carroll County, Mississippi m. Arthur Reed 16 February 1908, Carroll County, Mississippi d. bwt 7 May 1930 and 10 Dec 1932 Mississippi)
5. Thomas Lott (b. 1894 Carroll County, Mississippi)
6. Boyne (recorded as Bong in 1900) Lott (b. 1896 Carroll County, Mississippi)
7. Seargant {sic} (recorded as Nine in 1910) Lott (b. 1898 Carroll County, Mississippi)
8. Magie (spelling as on 1910 Census) Lott (b. 1902 Carroll County, Mississippi)
9. Fannie Lott (b. 1904 Carroll County, Mississippi)

Reuben appears to have lived his life in Carroll County. More research may reveal when he died as it looks likely that he lived past 1912 when Mississippi mandated the creation of death records.

Joseph Garlin "Joe" Webb

Joseph Garlin Webb was born on 23 April 1925 in Memphis, Shelby County, Tennessee. Although his Death Certificate lists Mississippi as his birth place, early Census entries, his application for a Social Security Number, and his brother, Bill, identify Tennessee as his place of birth. In addition to Census entries, the Webb family also shows up in the 1933 and 1935 Educable Children Records (Mississippi) for Sunflower County, Township 19 Range 4. In the 1935 edition, Joe is listed since he was of school age. He was 10 years old and attending school.

He worked on his father's farm when he was young. In the 1940 Census at age 15 he is recorded as having completed the 6th grade. That Census included a section on where entrants had been living in 1935 and the family had been in Memphis, Tennessee for at least part of that year, although clearly the family was in Mississippi when the Educable Children survey was conducted.

On 22 August 1942, Joe applied for a Social Security Number. At the time he was living at 1102 Union Street, Greenville, Mississippi. He was 17 years old and unemployed.

At age 19, he married Louise Wilson, age 17, daughter of Square and Lorena Wilson on 25 May 1944. His mother, Lucy Webb, signed the affidavit as to the age of the marriage applicants. Joe was living in Moorhead and Louise was living in Sunflower, both towns in Sunflower County, Mississippi. The ceremony was officiated by Reverend J. W. White.

Joe and Louise had 3 of their children (these 3 have all subsequently passed away) while still living in Mississippi. The last of the children to be born while in Mississippi was Lorraine "Cute Eyes" Webb who was born on 28 April 1947. The family moved to Cleveland, Ohio before 3 September 1948 when Louise applied for her Social Security Number. At that time the family was living at 2181 E. 38th Street.

He and his brother, Harry Phillips, both worked for Distillata Company located at 1608 East 24th Street, Cleveland, Ohio. Established in 1897, originally the company was City Ice/Distillata. After World War II, the companies split and Distillata concentrated on soda pop and distilled water in glass returnable bottles. In 1965 the company added spring water to their line of products. Then in 2006 they added coffee. Most recently, Distillata has added water filtration to their service offerings. For a short while, their brother Mack Henry Webb, Sr. also worked there. Joe retired after 39 years.

Joe and Louise were married for 31 years before they divorced on 16 January 1976. They had 9 children; some of whom are now deceased.

Joe had at least three other relationships and at least two of these relationships resulted in a child.

Joe died on 24 June 1997 at a long term care facility and was buried on 30 June 1997. His funeral ceremony was held at the United House of Prayer for All People at East 89 Cedar, Cleveland, Ohio.

As previously mentioned several of Joe and Louise's children are deceased. Those who have already passed include Joseph Webb, Jr., Versa Lee Webb, Lorraine (Webb) Smiley, and Emmanuel (Webb) Shabazz.

Joseph Webb, Jr. was born on 26 May 1944 in Greenwood, Leflore County, Mississippi. He attended Cleveland Public School System. He married and had 4 children. He died on Wednesday, 27 January 1982. His funeral was held on 2 February 1982 and conducted by Cummings and Davis Funeral Home, 13201 Euclid Avenue, East Cleveland, Ohio.

Versa Lee Webb died as an infant before the family left Mississippi. The spelling of this name varies quite a bit in the places this child has been mentioned. The spelling used here is just one of the variations.

Lorraine Josephine "Cute eyes" (Webb) Smiley was born 28 April 1947 in Mississippi. She graduated from John Hay High School in Cleveland. She earned as Associates Degree in Business Management at Cuyahoga Community College and was certified as a Computer Specialist through Cambridge College of Ohio. She married Eddie Smiley, Sr. (b. 1 Nov (Veteran Affairs data) or 30 Apr (Social Security Administration data) 1930 (both sets of records use the same Social Security Number; it is unclear which is correct) served in the U.S. Army from 19 Mar 1953 to 14 Jun 1955 d. 22 Feb 1972 Cleveland, Ohio) who preceded her in death. The couple had 5 children. She was a caring person who contributed greatly to the welfare of her community through active involvement. She became a Child Care specialist and volunteered in many of the inner city schools. She also established her own prison ministry. She spent many hours volunteering for such organizations as the Murtis Taylor Human Services Center, Handicap Co-op, Feeding the

Homeless Services, Ohio State Young Scholars Program, 4-H Club, School Community Councils, Meals on Wheels, and Community Action Meetings. Lorraine died on 18 November 1996. Her funeral was held at the United House of Prayer for All People located at 8713 Cedar Avenue. She was buried in Highland Park Cemetery, 21400 Chagrin Blvd., Cleveland, Ohio on Tuesday, 26 November 1996. The Pernel Jones Funeral Home handled the arrangements.

Emmanuel A. "Spider" Webb was born on 17 May 1949 in Cleveland, Ohio. He graduated from East Tech High School in 1967 with a 4.0 grade point average. He joined the Air Force and served a 4-year tour. At some point he changed his surname to Shabazz. He returned to Cleveland and started driving trucks for Laub Bakery. It was through driving his delivery route he met the love of his life, Bessie Fleeton (b. 14 Aug 1944 Letohatchie, Alabama to Ethel Jones and Robert Fleeton, graduated Calhoun High School, moved to Cleveland in 1961, d. 20 May 2011 Cleveland, Ohio buried 26 May 2011 Cleveland Memorial Gardens, arrangements by Pernel Jones & Sons Funeral Home). They married and raised 5 children. In 1978 he moved his family to 93rd on Anderson where he stayed for 30 years. He was President of the Street Club. In addition to his other talents, Emmanuel also enjoyed carpentry. Emmanuel then worked at Ford Motor Company from which he later retired. He died on 9 July 2012 and was buried on 18 July 2012 in the Cleveland Memorial Gardens. Funeral arrangements were handled by Pernel Jones & Sons Funeral Home, 7120 Cedar Avenue, Cleveland, Ohio.

The Wilson Line

James Wilson

James Wilson was born in June of 1870 in Mississippi. He married Liza Howard (b. Apr 1869 Mississippi) around 1888. They had at least 5 children.
1. Liza Ann Wilson (b. circa 1890 Mississippi)
2. James Wilson, Jr. (b. circa 1891 Mississippi)
3. Square Wilson (b. 2 Jun 1894 Sidon, Leflore County, Mississippi)
4. Carry Wilson (b. circa 1897 Mississippi)
5. Ida Wilson (b. circa 1898 Mississippi)

In 1900, James was sharecropping in Leflore County. In addition to their children, Liza's sister, Nettie Howard (b. Jan 1876 Mississippi) was living with them. Nettie is recorded as single and that suggests that Liza's maiden name was Howard as well. Living next door was Zack Wilson (b. Jun 1875 Mississippi m. 1898) and his wife, Artense (b. Dec 1883 Mississippi). Zack may be James' younger brother or a cousin.

Square Wilson

Square Wilson and Lorena King married around 1913. In 1917 he registered for the World War I Draft. According to his draft registration he was married with two children at that time. He was living and working in Itta Bena, Mississippi. He was employed by Wier and Gillen at farming. He is described as short, of medium build, with black eyes and hair. He was able to read and write because he signed his draft card and spelled his name with a double "ll" – Willson.

In the 1930's and 40's, Square was sharecropping with the help of his large family of 12 children. The family remembers 10 children and it is possible some of the children recorded in the Census did not reach adulthood. The birth years are approximate since the Census information varies and the dates you see here are according to the 1920, 1930, and 1940 Census information. Square and Lorena had the following children:

1. Susie B. Wilson (b. circa 1913 Mississippi widowed before 1930)
2. William C. Wilson (b. circa 1914 Mississippi)
3. Isaac Wilson (b. circa 1915 Mississippi)
4. Theaola Wilson (note: this child is transcribed as Thomas in one census, but if you examine the original document, the name is the same as in the other Census entries) (b. circa 1917 Mississippi)
5. Ethel L. (Recorded as "Ethel Mai" in 1920) Wilson (b. circa Jan 1920 Mississippi)
6. Gladys Wilson (b. circa 1924 Mississippi)
7. Mary "May" Wilson (b. circa 1925 Mississippi)
8. Clinton Wilson (b. circa 1926 Mississippi m. circa 1939 to Sarah (b. circa 1925 Humphries, Mississippi))
9. Louise Wilson (b. 25 May 1927 Morgan City, Leflore, Mississippi m. 2 times first Joseph Garlin Webb second Lawrence Gene Grissom d. 30 Dec 2003 buried 6 Jan 2004 Cleveland Memorial Gardens, Cleveland, Ohio)
10. Eugene Wilson (b. circa 1928 Mississippi)

11. Wesley (recorded as N. Z. on 1940 Census) Wilson (son) (b. circa 1930 Mississippi)
12. Square "Frog" Wilson, Jr. (b. circa 1931 Mississippi d. 26 Feb 2009 Cleveland, Cuyahoga, Ohio buried 5 Mar 2009 Cleveland Memorial Gardens, Cleveland, Ohio).

The King Line

Lewis King

Lewis King was born around 1851. In 1900 he and his wife, Anna, lived near Greenwood, Leflore County, Mississippi. He was sharecropping and his wife was helping him farm. In the 1900 Census they are both recorded as black and in the 1910 Census the whole family is recorded as mulatto. Additionally, in the 1910 Census the data regarding the birth location for Lewis and his wife is different than in the 1900 Census. It looks like the enumerator in the 1900 Census just filled out the form with Mississippi as the birth locations for everyone on the sheet. As this is fairly unlikely, the 1910 Census where there are many different locations recorded throughout the Census sheet seems to provide locations which are more likely to be what was reported to the enumerator in each individual case. Lewis is recorded as being born in Alabama as was his father and his mother was born in North Carolina. Anna or Annie was also born in Alabama, her father and mother both in Georgia.

They had married between 1875 and 1878. Anna had given birth to 7 children so far; 5 of whom were living at the time. Their children included:
1. Minnie King (b. 1880 Mississippi)

2. Henry King (b. 1882 Mississippi)
3. Lewis King, Jr. (b. 1882 Mississippi)
4. Oscar King (spelled Oskar in the 1900 Census and Osee in the 1910 Census) (b. 1889 Mississippi)
5. Mary King (b. 1894 Mississippi)
6. Lorena King (recorded as Lou in the 1900 Census and Lou B. in the 1910 Census) (b. 1895 Mississippi).

Louise Wilson

Louise (nicknamed both "Dear" and "Lou") Wilson was born on 25 May 1927 in Morgan City, Leflore County, Mississippi to Square Wilson (b. circa 1896 Mississippi) and Lorena (King) Wilson (b. circa 1898 Mississippi). On her application for a Social Security Number, Louise lists Greenwood, Mississippi as her birthplace. It is the nearest town of any size, Morgan City being little more than a crossroads at the time she was born. Louise's Social Security Death Index entry lists her year of birth as 1926, but all other sources found thus far list 1927. Morgan City is south of Itta Bena on Route 7 by a little less than 10 miles. It is a small town with a current population of 350. Itta Bena is where much of our family hailed from.

After her divorce from Joe, Louise met and married Lawrence Gene Grissom on 26 June 1979 according to Cuyahoga County Marriage Record Certificate Number 32903 in Volume 9883. This date is listed in Louise's Funeral Program as the date Lawrence died so there was clearly a misunderstanding when that was written.

Louise and Lawrence raised his son Martin Grissom, one of 6 children by Lawrence's previous marriage.

She worked at St. Alexis, the Cleveland Clinic, St. Vincent Charity Hospital, Brush High School, and Kaiser Hospital where she retired.

Louise died on 30 December 2003 and her funeral was held on 6 January 2004 at the United House of Prayer for All People, 8713 Cedar Avenue, Cleveland, Ohio. Her Death Certificate lists her mother's maiden name as Cane, however, both Samuel Webb in his "Family Publication #1" and Census data support the surname of King. She is buried at the Cleveland Memorial Gardens, 4324 Green Rd, Cleveland, OH 44121. Cleveland Memorial Gardens was established in 1999 and is 29 acres in size. The city of Cleveland owns and operates the cemetery.

The Grissom Line

Thomas Grissom

Thomas Grissom was born in March 1873 in Pontotoc, Mississippi. Before May of 1887 his family moved to Arkansas. About 1897 he married Callie (b. Apr 1878 Arkansas). In the 1900 Census he was recorded as living in Cherry Valley, Cross County, Arkansas. He reported his father's birth place as South Carolina and his mother's as Virginia. He was farming. He continued to live in this area through at least 1910. He and Callie had at least 4 children.

1. Fred Douglas Grissom (b. 29 Nov 1896 Cherry Hill, Cross County, Arkansas)

2. Osie (this is the spelling in the 1900 Census) Grissom (son b. 1899 Cherry Valley, Cross County, Arkansas)
3. Zelma Grissom (b. 1903 Cherry Valley, Cross County, Arkansas)
4. Verneda Grissom (b. 1908 Cherry Valley, Cross County, Arkansas)

Also living with the family in 1900 was Thomas' younger brother Willie Grissom (b. May 1887 Arkansas).

Cross County was formed on 15 November 1862. It is named for Confederate Colonel David C. Cross who was a political leader in the area. Colonel Cross settled in the area in the 1840 and became a very wealthy man; owning 85,000 acres making him the most extensive landowner in the county. The county seat is located in Wynne. The township of Mitchell includes the small community of Cherry Valley which had 651 people in the 2010 Census.

Fred Douglas Grissom

Fred Douglas Grissom was the son of Thomas and Callie Grissom of Cherry Valley, Cross County, Arkansas.

On 5 June 1918, Fred registered for the World War I Draft. His Draft Registration gives important details about him. On his registration he listed his birth date as 29 November 1896. He was born in Cherry Valley, Arkansas. His father was born in Pontotoc, Mississippi. He was working for himself. He listed his mother as his nearest relative. He is described as tall with black eyes and hair.

Fred and Ophelia Bedford married on 20 October 1920 in Cherry Valley, Cross County, Arkansas. Ophelia died on 1

February 1925 in Franklin Parish, Louisiana. The couple had at least one child.

    1. Lawrence Gene Grissom (b. 24 Dec 1923 Franklin Parish, Louisiana d. 2 Aug 2003 Cleveland Cuyahoga County, Ohio)

The lands of Louisiana were first explored by the Spanish in the late 1700's. In 1803, the United States secured the Louisiana Purchase. On 26 March 1804 it was officially designated the Louisiana Territory. Louisiana entered the Union on 30 April 1812. The administrative units serving sections of the state were named parishes rather than counties. Franklin Parish was created on 1 March 1843. It was named in honor of Benjamin Franklin. Cotton was grown in Franklin Parish near the river systems that flow through it which provide easy transportation to market. In 1859 a rail line was built to the tiny settlement of Delhi which was originally called Deerfield. After the Civil War, cotton production was abandoned and converted to forest growth. In 1868 Richland Parish was formed by combining parts of Franklin, Carroll, Morehouse, and Ouachita Parishes. Delhi was incorporated in 1882 and, according to "Biographical and Historical Memoirs of Louisiana" (Vol. II, Goodspeed Publishing Co., 1892), at that time boasted *"nine general stores, two drug stores, two livery stables, two hotels, one steam-gin, a good public school, and churches of Methodist, Presbyterian and Catholic."*

    Fred married again shortly after Ophelia's death; this time to Manella or Marzella Blair (b. 1900 Louisiana). In 1940, he was still farming. The couple and their children lived along Rodgers Lane in Franklin Parish, Louisiana. Rodgers Lane is a short east-west connecting road between routes 859

and 17. It is south of Delhi, Louisiana by about 8 miles. Their three sons included:
1. J. L. Grissom (b. 1925 Louisiana)
2. Lavern Grissom (b. 1927 Louisiana)
3. Fred Grissom, Jr. (b. 1932 Louisiana)

Also living in their household was Manella's 85-year-old widowed mother, Carnelia Blair (b. 1855 Louisiana).

Lawrence Gene Grissom

Lawrence was born in Franklin Parish, Louisiana on 24 December 1923 to Fred Douglas Grissom and his wife, Ophelia (Bedford) Grissom.

On 30 June 1942 when Lawrence registered for the WWII Draft, he was living on Route 1 in Delhi, Louisiana. He listed his father as his nearest relation. He was working for Mr. Ted O'Neal in Delhi, Richland Parish, Louisiana. Lawrence was described as negro, 5 feet 5 inches tall, weighing 155 pounds, brown eyes, black hair with a dark brown complexion. He had no obvious physical characteristics (meaning scars, birthmarks, or missing appendages).

He died on 2 August 2003 at 6:09 a.m. at the University Hospital, Cleveland, Ohio. He was 79 years old. His mother's maiden name was listed as Bedford on the Death Certificate. He was an Army veteran. He was buried in Riverside Cemetery, Cleveland, Ohio.

Flora Webb

Flora Webb was born on 25 September 1927 in Sunflower, Mississippi. Flora married three times. On 23 November 1942 she married Alex Randle in Sunflower County in a ceremony officiated by the Reverend Isaac C. Randle. Alex was the son of Isaac C. Randle (b. abt 1896 Louisiana m. Marie about 1919) and his wife, Marie (b. abt 1892 Mississippi). Isaac and Marie had at least 4 children.
1. Malisey Randle (b. abt 1920 Mississippi)
2. Elof Randle (b. abt 1923 Mississippi)
3. Alex Randle (b. 23 Jun 1923 Mississippi d. 18 Sep 2008 Benton Harbor, Berrien, Michigan; buried North Shore Cemetery, Hagar Township, Berrien County, Michigan)
4. Louiase Randle (b. abt 1928 Mississippi)

Alex's father and mother were living in the town of Sunflower at the time of their son's marriage. Alex was 19 at the time and living in Clarksdale, Mississippi. Flora was only 15. The couple had one child. The marriage did not last long.

Flora next married C. M. Funderburk. They had a daughter they named Joyce S. Funderburk (b. 13 Mar 1946 Sunflower, Mississippi d. May 2011 Flint, Genesee, Michigan). Very little is known about C. M. Funderburk and this is a family line that requires more information to research further.

Although her Funeral Program lists 28 March 1946 for her next marriage, the Washington County Marriage Register records her marriage on page 116 to Willie Lee Perry on 24 February 1947 in Greenville, Mississippi by Justice of the Peace William McD. Megget (his middle name is probably a surname from his maternal line). Willie's address at the time was 108B Ginn, Greenville. Willie's father, Charlie, was in Sunflower but his mother, Myrtle Lee, was living in Jackson, Mississippi. Flora's surname of Funderburk is spelled Funderbuarke. She signed the application with this spelling. This surname has at least 12 variant spellings with the most frequent variants in the records found thus far being: Funderburk, Funderburke, Funderburg, and Funderberk. The most common one is Funderburk and this is also the way living relatives in this line currently spell this name, so that is the version used here.

Willie Lee had played basketball in the local high school along with Flora's brother Joe. Flora and Willie stayed together the rest of her life. They had 6 children of their own and raised Flora's children by previous marriages and raised an additional child. They bought a home in Detroit in 1955. Flora worked for 43 years at the Central Overall Supply Company. The Central Overall Supply Company supplied and laundered overalls for businesses like car dealers and manufacturers. As an interesting side note, General Manager Ben Harold testified on 31 July 1958 before a Senate committee investigating the infiltration of the mob into the linen and laundry business in Detroit, Michigan. It appears Central Overall Supply Company had lost business to a mob-supported laundering business called Star Coverall Company to the tune of $312,000.

In 1994 tragedy struck when their daughter Charlene (b. 9 Feb 1957, Detroit, Michigan m. Karl Stanley Bivings 18 Oct 1974 d. 4 Dec 1994, Detroit, Michigan buried 10 Dec 1994 Forestlawn Cemetery, Detroit, Michigan) died.

Flora died on 10 August 2001 in a traffic accident. She was buried on 17 August 2001 at Forest Lawn Cemetery, 1185 Van Dyke, Detroit, Michigan.

Some of Flora's children have passed already including Joyce S. (Funderburk Perry) Beavers, Michael Perry and Charlene Bivings.

Joyce S. Funderburk was born on 13 March 1946 (1948 according to her Social Security Death Index Entry) to Flora and C. M. Funderburk in Sunflower County, Mississippi. She was raised by Flora and Willie Perry. She married Herman Lee Beavers (b. 11 Oct 1942 Ohio d. 27 May 1982, Detroit, Wayne County, Michigan). The couple had 2 children. Joyce died on 8 May 2011, Flint, Genesee County, Michigan.

Michael Perry was born 13 January 1950 in Detroit, Michigan to Flora and Willie Perry. He attended the Detroit Public School System. He graduated from Kettering High School. He received a basketball scholarship to attend Selma University. He married on 23 September 1972 and had 2 children. He worked for Chrysler for 35 years and retired in 2005. He died on 16 April 2006. His funeral was held on 21 April 2006 at the New Greater Zion Missionary Baptist Church, 12530 Mack Ave, Detroit. Swanson Funeral Home handled the arrangements. He is interred at Forest Lawn Cemetery, 11851 Van Dyke Street, Detroit, Michigan.

Charlene Perry was born 9 February 1957 in Detroit, Michigan to Flora and Willie Perry. She attended the Detroit Public School System, but later received her GED and earned a Certificate for Nursing Assistant. She married Karl Stanley Bivings on 18 October 1974 and had 3 children. She died on 4 December 1994. Her funeral was held on 10 December 1994 at Swanson Funeral Home which made the final arrangements. She is buried at Forest Lawn Cemetery, 11851 Van Dyke Street, Detroit, Michigan.

The William Lee Perry Line

F. Perry

F. Perry was born in 1847 in North Carolina. He married Mary (b. 1852 Georgia) around 1877. In the 1880 Census, he is listed as mulatto and his occupation is Minister. In the 1910 Census, Mary reports having given birth to 11 children, 4 of whom were alive as of 1910. Unfortunately, the 1890 Census was destroyed in a fire, it might have provided more insight into their children. However, a combination of the 1880 and 1910 Census entries do give some information. He and Mary had at least the following children who lived long enough to be documented:
1. Tilena Perry (b. 1878)
2. S. Nathaniel Perry (b. 1879 Livingston, Madison, Mississippi)
3. Clara Perry (b. 1892 Mississippi)
4. James H. Perry (b. 1894 Mississippi)

S. Nathaniel Perry

S. Nathaniel Perry (b. 1879 Livingston, Madison, Mississippi) married Ida (b. 1888 Mississippi) around 1903 in Mississippi. They had at least the following children:
1. Walter (b. 1902 Mississippi)
2. Charlie (b. 1906 Mississippi).

They had also had a child who died in infancy.

In 1910 S. Nathaniel Perry was living in Beat 1, Hinds, Mississippi with wife, sons, widowed mother Mary (b. 1854

Mississippi; had 11 children, 4 alive as of 1910), his sister Clara (b. 1892 Mississippi), and brother James H. (b. 1894 Mississippi). Nathaniel was sharecropping with the help of his wife, sister, and brother. His mother moved back to Madison County by 1920 where she lived with her son James H. Perry and his wife Elberta I. (b. 1897) and their family. In 1930 she was still with her son James. James and Elberta I. had at least the following children:
1. Mary F. Perry (b. 1918 Mississippi).
2. Thomas J. Perry (b. 1922 Mississippi)
3. Fred Perry (b. 1926 Mississippi)

Willie Lee Perry

Willie Lee "Big Dad" Perry was born on 26 August 1924 to Charlie and Myrtle Lee Perry of Sunflower Mississippi. He was the eldest child of 22 children. Some of his siblings were named in the Census and others were listed in Willie's Funeral Program. This does not account for all 22 children. However, the partial list of the children includes:
1. Willie Lee Perry (b. 26 Aug 1924 d. 9 Nov 2011)
2. Arthur L. Perry (b. 1928 Mississippi)
3. Dorothy Perry (b. 1933 Mississippi)
4. Josy Bee Perry (b. 1935 Mississippi)
5. Inez Perry
6. Jimmie Perry
7. Vergie Perry
8. Bertha Mae Perry
9. Charlie Perry, Jr.
10. David Lee Perry
11. Frank Perry
12. Red Perry

In the 1940 Census, Charlie Perry's wife is listed as Annie Lee Perry. This woman was a different age than what Myrtle would have been based on her entry in the 1930 Census so it looks like Charlie had married again.

Willie enlisted as a Private on 30 March 1943 to serve in the U.S. Army during World War II. He reported to Camp Shelby, Mississippi for initial training. He was single without dependents working as a farm hand and possessed a grammar school level education according to his enlistment record. He worked for over two decades as a construction worker for the City of Detroit. After his retirement, he became a paper carrier for the Detroit News. He had many talents including baking, cooking, fishing, and hunting.

He died on 9 November 2011. His parents and 12 of his siblings predeceased him. He was interred at Forest Lawn Cemetery, Detroit, Michigan. Swanson Funeral Home at 806 E. Grand Blvd., Detroit, Michigan arranged the funeral.

Bernice Webb

Bernice Webb was born in 1930 in Mississippi. At age 18, she married Isaac Briggs on 5 September 1948 in a ceremony officiated by Reverend Isaac C. Randle (Flora's father-in-law at one point). On the marriage application, her parents, Willie and Lucy, are recorded as living in Blaine, Mississippi which is a tiny farming community 11.5 miles north of Moorhead, Mississippi. Isaac Briggs was 24, his father, Tom Briggs, was deceased and his mother Julia Briggs, was living in Sunflower, Mississippi which is a small town which is roughly halfway between Blaine and Moorhead. Children in Blaine and Sunflower attend school in Moorhead which is probably where Bernice and Isaac met. The couple had 7 children.

Bernice died on 23 April 1991 at South Sunflower County Hospital in Indianola, Mississippi at age 61. Her funeral was held on 1 May 1991 at Quon Chapel Moorhead Baptist Church, Moorhead, Mississippi. Her brothers Joseph Webb, Mack Henry Webb, Sr., and Bill Webb were able to attend the funeral. She is buried at Pine Ridge Cemetery in Moorhead.

The Isaac Briggs Line

Isaac Briggs was born circa 1924 in Mississippi to Tom and Julia Briggs. His father had at least 5 children:
1. Lee Briggs (b. 1902 Louisiana)
2. Bettie Briggs (b. 1913 Louisiana)
3. James Briggs (b. 1919 Louisiana)
4. Mary Briggs (b. 1920 Louisiana)
5. Isaac Briggs (b. 1924 Mississippi)

Julia may have been Tom's second wife given the age of the son named Lee and the long break between Lee and Bettie; alternatively, she was very young when she started to have children. The family moved to Mississippi between 1920 and 1924 when Isaac was born. By 1940 Julia was a widow and sharecropping with the help of the children listed here.

There is a listing for an Isaac Briggs who died on 30 January 2003 in Indianola, Sunflower County, Mississippi. This Isaac is probably the Isaac of interest but the date of birth is listed as 24 October 1921 (as opposed to the 1924 referred to in the Census and Marriage Application records). Further investigation is required to ascertain whether this is the correct person.

Mack Henry Webb, Sr.

Mack Henry Webb, Sr. was born on 1 April 1931 in Sunflower, Mississippi to Willie and Lucy Webb. His father sharecropped and his mother was a mid-wife. The farm had a barn with mules, a milk cow, hogs, and chickens. His mother canned fruits and vegetables and made peach wine — a popular drink for the adults. As a young boy Mack tasted this homemade brew from a glass left unattended by an adult family member. It made his throat burn, and racing to a hiding place under the house he cried himself to sleep. Searchers worried he had fallen into the nearby swollen river, but were relieved when toward morning Mack crawled from beneath the house wiping sleep from his eyes.

He attended school in nearby Moorhead, Mississippi and helped out on the farm. He ran track in high school. Shortly after his brother Joe had settled in Cleveland, Mack joined him in about 1949. For a short time, Mack worked at Distillata with his brother Joe. Mack became a member of the United House of Prayer for All People which was to figure strongly throughout his life. While he and another young man were working outside the church, two pretty young girls came flouncing along the sidewalk. Mack singled out Ruth Mae Barnes and thus started a love story of over 45 years.

Mack's mother, Lucy (Looney) Webb, came up to Cleveland to receive medical treatment at the Cleveland Clinic. When she died on 2 November 1950, she was taken back to Mississippi for burial. Mack married Ruth soon after on 24 January 1951 in Cleveland, Ohio. Among other activities, Ruth enjoyed playing sports. She had been on the track team in high school participating in pole vaulting and sprints. She played softball for many years at church socials.

Mack enlisted in the Army almost immediately after getting married as jobs in Cleveland at the time did not offer much. While he attended Basic Training, Ruth stayed in Cleveland in an apartment in a building owned by Joe Webb. By that time Mack's brother, Harry, and his family had also moved to Cleveland and were living in the same building.

Ruth was pregnant with their first child and missing Mack tremendously. Much to Mack's surprise, she showed up at his Basic Training unit at Fort Dix, New Jersey. The sergeant was good enough to give him time off to see his wife, but she had to go back to Cleveland while he finished his training. To fill her lonely hours, Ruth taught herself to "beat the drums". Many a Sunday, she would keep the tempo in the band and her husband would preach from the altar. With seven children of her own in the church sanctuary, she mastered "the look" which could stop a child's foolishness at 50 paces.

Mack's first enlistment lasted two years during which time he served in the Korean War. He left the military and went back to Cleveland only to find employment conditions there much the same. So he decided to re-enlist and this time, he made a career of the military. Serving in the military requires many changes of station and often means separation from family and so it was for Mack and Ruth. In 1953 the family was in Fort Jackson, Columbia, South Carolina, then back to Cleveland for the family, then Fort McPherson, Atlanta Georgia in 1958, onto Fort Monroe, Virginia from about 1960 to 1963, by 1967 another stint at Fort McPherson, then the family went to Cleveland while Mack went to

Vietnam in 1968 followed by a tour in Greece, then back to Fort McPherson in 1970 until June of 1972 when the family moved to Columbus, Ohio for his final stationing as an Army Recruiter. By this time, he had worked his way through the ranks and was a Sergeant First Class. He had worked in artillery, the infantry, as a mess sergeant, and as a General's orderly for two different Generals.

The family lived at several locations in Cleveland during the various times they were there. At one point they lived at 2070 E. 83rd Street; at another point in time they were on East 93rd Street. There were relatives on both sides of the family in Cleveland and many cousins to play with.

Mack kept up his involvement with the House of Prayer and while the family was stationed at Fort Monroe, he served as the Youth Pastor. He is still remembered by church members there. He later gained the title Apostle.

While Mack was in Vietnam, his father passed away. Mack was given compassionate leave and made the trip home to attend the funeral. He arrived in Cleveland and then traveled with his brothers Joe and Bill (who had come in from Detroit), and Joe's son, Emmanuel, to Indianola, Mississippi. While he was in the States, the area where he was stationed in Vietnam had Agent Orange sprayed on the surrounding terrain. He returned to Vietnam after the funeral. His son remembers waving goodbye from a rail stop in Cleveland.

On 19 September 1972 Mack and Ruth bought a house at 3457 Petzinger Road in Columbus for $5,020. On 29 March 1983 they refinanced the house. And then again on 16 April 1987, when it was worth $32,500. The house was sold on 3 July 2001 for $78,000. It was a small house of 884 finished square feet with one bathroom for a family of 9. The house is a split-level with an unfinished basement. Upstairs is a living room, kitchen, dining room, and 2 bedrooms. Mack divided the basement with framing and paneling to create two rooms to be shared by his daughters, a laundry room, and a recreation room. Summers in Ohio are steamy but the house did not have central air conditioning like most houses built at this time. Instead a fan was kept humming in the kitchen and a window air conditioner was installed in the dining room.

It was a busy and happy home; filled with song and laughter. Ruth directed the Webb Singers and rehearsals happened almost daily in the small kitchen. Each child was strictly schooled in their musical part for each song. Solos were distributed throughout the group since the whole family had musical talent.

Christmas was a big celebration in the Webb household with presents piled high around the tree in the living room. Ruth cooked delicious and plentiful meals. Special occasions called for roast beef, ham, and a turkey, a full assortment of sides, and lots of desserts —pies, cakes, cookies, candy, and ice cream were all on offer. In the summer, there was barbequed ribs, fried chicken, mashed potatoes, green beans, corn-on-the-cob, coleslaw, and sweet potato pie; just to name a few. The kitchen was always in action, often late into the night, as Ruth often cooked for the House of Prayer as well.

A few years after his arrival in Columbus, Mack became the pastor of the House of Prayer in Cincinnati. He made the round trip from Columbus to Cincinnati daily for over 20 years. Often Evening Service attendance consisted of him, his son, and a few faithful members. On Saturdays, it was his practice to do the weekly grocery shopping at

Rickenbacker Air Force Base (AFB). Accompanied again by his son, they would go to the barbershop and then fill the car with groceries from the commissary.

The base had started as Lockbourne Army Air Field in 1942 with the mission of training pilots. In 1946, the primary unit at the base was the all-Black 447th Composite Group, also known as the Tuskegee Airmen. In 1947, the 477th Composite Group was inactivated and its personnel and equipment reassigned to the 332nd Fighter Group, one of the first all-Black flying units in the newly created United States Air Force. On 13 January 1948 the base was re-designated Lockbourne Air Force Base. Then on 18 May 1974 the name was changed to Rickenbacker Air Force Base to honor Columbus native Eddie Rickenbacker, the leading American fighter pilot of World War I. The base was part of the Strategic Air Command (SAC) with reconnaissance and refueling wings on station. The base was transferred from the Strategic Air Command to the Air National Guard and re-designated Rickenbacker Air National Guard Base on 1 April 1980.

Mack tried to share his rural roots with his children. Some attempts were more successful than others. One Easter he brought home a couple of fluffy yellow chicks. The family was entranced. About two months later, the chickens made their appearance as the main dish for dinner. No one would touch their meal; they just wept. His little garden plot went over much better. He dug up a small patch of ground and planted tomatoes, greens, and green beans. He also put in a grape vine and a strawberry bed.

Mack also did much to keep the family cars running. Although there was no garage at the house, the driveway was frequently the place of oil changes and other more extensive car repairs. Naturally, these repairs needed to be effected most often when it was raining, snowing, or just down right cold with an icy wind to freeze fingers trying to delicately tweak a spark plug or set a timing chain.

Mack was a patient, compassionate man but even his patience could be tried. You knew he had reached his limit when you heard any phrase containing the word "Chief" as in, "Look, Chief".

In December of 1985 tragedy struck when daughter Yvonne was found collapsed in a coma one morning on the floor of her apartment with her toddler curled up beside her. She passed away soon afterwards. Mack and Ruth adopted her child and raised him.

After he retired from the military, Mack continued to work. He found employment at Len Immke Buick near the Columbus International Airport and then hired onto the support staff of the Columbus Public Schools now renamed to Columbus City Schools.

Then Ruth suffered a heart attack. She died on 2 April 1996 in Columbus, Ohio. She was buried with much sorrow on 6 April 1996 in Evergreen Cemetery located at 1401 Woodland Avenue, Columbus, Franklin County, Ohio.

Mack traveled for a couple of years with the House of Prayer Council; helping the Bishop with his visits to local Houses of Prayer across the country. An important part of the work of the Council is checking the finances of each house and making sure the paperwork is as it should be.

Mack married again on 30 July 1998 to Sandra A. Ossman, the owner of a children's daycare center now called Little Scholar Learning Center on Groves Road. He had a small stroke about 18 months later. Then he developed

Alzheimer's. Mack died on 8 February 2011 in Columbus, Ohio. His Funeral Service was held at the United House of Prayer for all People, 1731 Greenway Avenue in Columbus on Saturday, 12 February 2011. Final arrangements were entrusted to Smoot Funeral Services, 1166 Parsons Ave., Columbus, OH 43206. He was buried with full military honors on Monday, 14 February 2011 in Section 36 site number 874 at the Dayton National Cemetery on 4100 West Third Street in Dayton, Montgomery County, Ohio.

Of Mack and Ruth's 7 children, one passed away at an early age. Yvonne Denise Webb was born on 19 July 1958 at Fort McPherson, Atlanta, Georgia. She attended public schools in Virginia, Georgia, Cleveland, and Columbus, Ohio. She was an active member in the House of Prayer and sang in both the Singers of Faith and the Webb Singers. She had one child. She suffered from lupus. At the age of 27, she died on 28 December 1985 in St. Anthony Hospital, Columbus, Ohio. She had been living at 57 N. 22nd Street at the time. Her Funeral Service was held on Friday, 3 January 1986 at the United House of Prayer for all People, 832 Fairwood Avenue, Columbus, Ohio. Apostle W. C. Cloud officiated. Final arrangements were handled by McNabb Funeral Home. She was buried at Evergreen Cemetery, Columbus, Franklin County, Ohio.

The family also lost another member in grandchild Anita Shepherd. She was born on 19 April 1974 to Hezekiah Hosea and Lucy (Webb) Shepherd in Washington, D. C. She moved to Ohio at a young age and started her education in the Ohio school system. Friends and family nicknamed her "NeNe" and "Ladybug". She later returned to Washington, D. C. where she graduated from Dunbar High School. She attended the Washington School of Cosmetology. She was an active member of the House of Prayer all her life and gifted with a strong alto voice. She and her husband had two children. She died on 26 May 2006 when her heart transplant failed. She was 32 years old. Her Funeral Service was held on Saturday, 3 June 2006 at the United House of Prayer for all People at 1731 Greenway Avenue, Columbus, Ohio. (There are two Houses of Prayer in Columbus — that is why you see two different addresses.) Apostle J. Walker officiated. Final arrangements were handled by J. Martin Smith Mortuary, 1173 East Hudson Street, Columbus, Ohio. She was buried at Glen Rest Memorial Estate, 8029 East Main Street, Reynoldsburg, Franklin County, Ohio.

The Ruth Mae Barnes Lines

The Hunter Line

James "Jimbank" Hunter

James "Jimbank" Hunter was born around 1840 in either Mississippi or South Carolina. Sources cite different information. In 1870 in the area served by the Hazlehurst Post Office of Copiah County, Mississippi Jimbank lived with his wife Millie (b. 1846). Millie is recorded as mulatto; Jimbank is recorded as black. He was working on a farm at the time. The area that became Copiah County was relinquished by the Choctaw Indians in 1819. Copiah is from a Choctaw Indian word meaning "calling panther". The county was organized on 21 January 1823 as Mississippi's 18th county. Hazlehurst is the county seat. The county is south of Jackson, Mississippi. Although initially planters grew cotton here, around 1870 farmers started to produce tomatoes and later cabbages on a commercial scale. In fact, by the 1930s, the town of Crystal Springs had earned the title "Tomato Capital of the World". There is an annual Tomato Festival celebrated on the last Saturday in June.

In 1880 the family was in Halls Hill, Beat 4 of Copiah County and included three children.
1. Candacy Hunter (b. 1875 Mississippi)
2. Millie Hunter (b. 1878 Mississippi)
3. Richard Hunter (b. Jan 1880 Mississippi)

Jimbank was working as a farmer by then; as opposed to a "worker on a farm". Actually this difference in description might not have meant much change. The first description probably means he was paid a wage for his work on the farm. The second probably means he was sharecropping. In both cases he may well have been working the same ground for the same owner and perhaps even the person who had owned him prior to Emancipation. This would not be an unusual situation at all during this period of time.

Halls Hill turns out to be a short lane off Old Port Gibson Road. Halls Hill Church is at the corner of the lane and road. The lane is, even now, a dirt track. The road is a two-laner with asphalt on a good portion of it, but around Halls Hill it is a bit wild looking and the asphalt in that area is old, crumbly, and a reddish looking finish rather than the shiny, dark, charcoal black of a recently maintained road.

There are no Hunters listed as slaveholders in Copiah County in the 1870's but there are several listed in Hinds County which is the county bordering Copiah to the north.

More research may reveal something more about Jimbank and Millie.

Richard Hunter

Richard Hunter was born in January 1880 in Copiah County, Mississippi. He married at least three times. His first wife was Matilda Harper (b. Mar 1888, Mississippi d. probably between 1916 and 1918) whom he married around 1903.

In 1910, Richard Hunter was a sharecropper engaged in general farming. The family was living along Cumberland Road in Beat 5 of Webster County. In addition to their own children, Richard had two nephews living with him, Willie and Wesley Harper. Both his wife and his then 5-year-old son, Sam, are listed as laborers on the farm.

Richard and Matilda had 5 children.
1. Sam Hunter (b. 1905 Mississippi)
2. Ruth Mae Hunter (b. 24 Sep 1907 Webster County, Mississippi m. Nathaniel Barnes 14 Aug 1923, Blaine, Sunflower, Mississippi: had 6 children; more detail in her section d. 17 Apr 1985 Cleveland, Cuyahoga, Ohio)
3. Ruby Hunter (b. 1909 Mississippi)
4. Otis Hunter (b. 15 Jul 1910 Mississippi m. at least 2 times, first to Mary Lee (b. 1888 Mississippi) second to Rosie d. 5 Jun 1995 Ruleville, Sunflower, Mississippi)
5. Sherman Hunter (b. 5 Jun 1912 Mississippi m. at least 1 time Eula Mae (b. 1917 Mississippi) d. 22 Jan 2008 Ruleville, Sunflower, MS)

6. Annie Mae Hunter (b. 1916 Mississippi m. Richard Pruitt).

By the time Richard married Clara Williams on 20 December 1918 the family was living in Beat 4 of Sunflower County, Mississippi. This is the same Beat where we found Frank C. Coleman and Willie Coleman during this same time period. It is possible that the two families would have known of each other at least and possibly even knew each other better through church or school.

Richard had married again by 1930 to his third wife, Sally. By 1940 he was widowed and living with his son Sherman and his family still in Beat 4 of Sunflower County, Mississippi.

The Harper Line

Randall R. "Ran" Harper

Randall R. "Ran" Harper was born about September 1833 in Mississippi. He is first recorded in the 1870 Census in Township 21, Range 11 of Choctaw County, Mississippi. Choctaw County was formed in 1833 from land ceded by the Choctaw Nation. There are two possible derivations of the name. The first is from the Indian word "chahta" which means separation, most likely referring to the separation of the Choctaw tribe from the Chickasaws. The second is that the name comes from the first leader of the tribe, Chief Chocta.

The county was large and covered 1,080 square miles. The original county seat was Greensboro which gained a reputation for duels, hangings, and murders. During the Civil War, Federal troops burned much of the town to the ground. This county was divided later several times to form new counties. In 1871 a large chunk of Choctaw County was taken away and used to create Montgomery County. On 6 August 1874 the northern part of it was used to form Sumner County now known as Webster County. Randall lived in Choctaw during this turbulent period. In fact, the area that he lived in 1870 is part of what becomes Webster County. This area is north of the Black River. Parts of Grenada and Calhoun Counties were also from Choctaw County. The town of Chester was designated as the new county seat. In 1885 the town of Ackerman was built along the Illinois Central Railroad. Two years later it became the second county seat.

Randall was living with his family and farming. He was married to a woman named Darcus (b. 1837 Mississippi). The couple had at least 5 children.
1. Nancy A. Harper (b. 1859 Mississippi)
2. John Harper (b. 1862 Mississippi)
3. Joseph Harper (b. 1866 Mississippi)
4. Caroline Harper (b. 1870 Mississippi)
5. Martha Harper (b. 1873 Mississippi)

In 1880 the family moved to Beat 5 of Clay County, Mississippi. Clay County was named after U. S. Secretary of State, Henry Clay, and created on 12 May 1871. Clay County would have been quite a move to make back then. However, it is located along the same Illinois Central rail line that runs through Choctaw County, so perhaps the family rode the train. The county seat is West Point. Ran listed both of his parents' birthplaces as Georgia. In the next Census he lists his father's birthplace as Alabama. His sons, John and Joseph, were laborers on his farm. He also had a daughter-in-law named Araminta (b. 1862 Mississippi) living with the family. Most probably this is John's wife.

By the time the next Census which has survived was taken in 1900, big changes have occurred. First of all, he had moved his family back to near where we found them in 1870 only now it is called Webster County, Mississippi. He now owned a farm and was working as a blacksmith. He had also married again. He married Henrietta Annamae Washington (b. Feb 1869 Mississippi) on 5 February 1886 in Clay County, Mississippi. The couple had at least 3 children.

1. Matilda Harper (b. Mar 1888 Mississippi see section on Richard Hunter for more detail)
2. Rosa M. Harper (b. Apr 1890 Mississippi)
3. Rena M. Harper (b. Apr 1892 Mississippi)

Since Randall Harper owned the farm in Webster County, there is hope that with a property record search, we will learn more about the location and size of the property he and the family inhabited. More to come on that in future editions of this work.

Ruth Mae Hunter

Ruth Mae Hunter was born on 24 September 1907 to Richard Hunter (see previous section on Richard Hunter) and Matilda Harper (b. Mar 1888, Mississippi d. probably between 1916 and 1918). There is conflicting information on her birth year. The birth year listed here is the one she provided in her application for Social Security. However, the Social Security Death Index lists 1906 and the Ohio Death Index lists 1908. The 1907 date is consistent with her Census entries. Ruth was probably born in Webster County, Mississippi as the family was living there in 1910.

Ruth was known as "Rutha" when she was a toddler and "Ruthie Mae" when she was a young woman. She married Nathaniel "Ned" Barnes on 14 August 1923 in Blaine, Sunflower County. In that record Ned's first name is recorded as "Man". According to the record, the ceremony was officiated by Reverend G. E. Garrett. Unfortunately, a search for this man did not reveal any record that looked likely. The couple had 6 children.

1. L.V. Barnes (b. 24 Dec 1924, Sunflower, Mississippi d. 2 Oct 1982, Cleveland, Cuyahoga, Ohio)
2. Frederick "Jack" Barnes (b. est 1926, Mississippi d. 8 Jan 1974 Cleveland, Cuyahoga, Ohio)
3. Gertha Lee "Beauty" Barnes (b. est 1927 Mississippi d. 16 Dec 1981 Cleveland, Cuyahoga, Ohio)
4. Nathaniel "Nate" Barnes (b. 1930, Mississippi may still be alive and living in Mississippi)
5. Julia Lee "Bae" Barnes (b. est 1932 Mississippi may still be alive living in Cleveland, Cuyahoga, Ohio)
6. Ruth Mae Barnes (b. 7 Jul 1934 Blaine, Sunflower, Mississippi m. Mack H. Webb, Sr. 24 Jan 1951 Cleveland, Cuyahoga, Ohio; for more detail on Ruth see the section on Mack H. Webb, Sr. d. 2 Apr 1996, Columbus, Franklin, Ohio).

By 1930 she and her children L.V., Frederick "Jack", Gertha Lee "Beauty", and Nathaniel "Nate" were living with her brother-in-law, Jesse Barnes and his wife, Lemmie, and their son, J. B., and daughter, L. C.. They were living in Beat 2, Leflore County, Mississippi. Jesse was sharecropping cotton. Cotton was the big crop in the Delta region of Mississippi in the 1910's through the 1950's. Sharecropping was the primary method of raising the crop as it required large amounts of labor. After WWII, tractors and mechanized processing reduced the need for labor and many people who had been sharecropping headed north to factory jobs in the Midwest.

By 1932, Ruth was living with her husband again as they have another daughter Julia Lee "Bae" (b. est 1932 Mississippi may still be alive living in Cleveland, Ohio). They moved back to Blaine in Sunflower County before the birth of their next daughter Ruth Mae (called "Ruthie Mae" as a child).

In 1935 they lived in Leflore County. They moved again to Coahoma County, which is close to Memphis, Tennessee, sometime after 1935. The family was still raising cotton in 1940. Ned, Ruth, and their sons, LV and Fred "Jack", all worked the fields. Coahoma County was established on 9 February 1836. The name comes from a Choctaw word meaning "red panther". The county seat is Clarksdale. There are entries for a Nate Barnes living in Clarksdale in the late 1990's which may have been Ruth's son Nate.

For those of you who are interested in getting a sense of what life was like on a cotton plantation, Clarksdale offers a unique inn. The old Hopson Plantation has been turned into an inn featuring sharecropper shacks as accommodations and the cotton gin and various other outbuildings one would find on a typical plantation. The Shackup Inn does, however, cater to modern expectations and includes lots of features not available to our ancestors including indoor bathrooms, heating and air conditioning, coffee makers, refrigerators, and microwaves. Just imagine the buildings completely stripped and falling apart and you get a more accurate idea of what these shelters had to offer. If you are traveling in this area, Webb, Mississippi has some sharecropper shacks still occupied and much more like what families would have inhabited in the 1930s and 1940s.

By 1950 the family was living in Cleveland, Ohio. Ruth worked as a cook in "eating and drinking places". At some point, Ned left the family and did not return.

In 1972 she lived at 1598 E. 85th St, Cleveland, Ohio 44106. This single family home was built in 1900 and has 1745 square feet of living space with 4 bedrooms, 1 bathroom, and a detached 1-car garage. It was located across the street from John W. Raper Elementary School which was razed to the ground in 2014.

She died on 17 April 1985 at age 77 in East Cleveland, Cuyahoga County, Ohio. Her siblings Annie Mae, Otis, and Sherman were alive at the time of her passing. She was buried on 22 April 1985 in Highland Park Cemetery in Section 30, Lot No. A, Tier No. 24, Grave No. 15. Highland Park Cemetery was established in 1904 and has 160 acres of lawn and trees. It is still active and has over 134,000 graves.

The Barnes Line

Ned Barnes (b. 1877)

Information on the first relative in this line is sparse because only two records have been found thus far that are without doubt about him; a WWI Draft Registration and an entry for the 1920 Census. Nevertheless, these entries do give us some information.

The name "Ned" is a nickname for Nathaniel. Other nicknames for Nathaniel include Nathan, Nate, Tate, and Ed. Although with the limited documentation discovered for Ned there is no way to verify this, it is probable that his given name was Nathaniel and Ned was what he was commonly called.

Ned Barnes was born on 1 September 1877 in Mississippi. Both of his parents were also born in Mississippi. He married Julia (b. abt 1885 Mississippi). Further research is needed to determine whether or not this was his only marriage. It is possible he was married at least twice. Two factors suggest that possibility; one is the lack of a record in 1910 of the family unit, and second is the gaps in birthdates for the children. The gaps in the birthdates may, alternatively, show miscarriages, stillbirths, or losses of infants. He had at least 6 children.

1. Martha Barnes (b. 1902 Mississippi m. 7 Dec 1919 to Walter Hemphill ceremony by Rev. Allen Brock)
2. Matilda Barnes (b. 1904 Mississippi)
3. Jessie Barnes (son b. 1906 Mississippi)
4. Nathaniel "Ned" Barnes (b. 1908 Mississippi m. Ruth Mae Hunter on 24 Aug 1923 Blaine, Sunflower County, Mississippi)
5. Mary Barnes (b. 1913 Mississippi)
6. Lenora Barnes (b. 1920 Mississippi)

On 12 September 1918 at the age of 41, Ned Barnes registered for the draft for World War I. He was farming in Isola, Humphreys County, Mississippi for a white farmer named Will Switzer. Ned is described as being of medium weight and build. His eyes and hair were black.

Humphreys County is the most recent of Mississippi Counties having been formed 28 March 1918, not long before the WWI Draft Registration. The county was formed by assembling parts of several other county: specifically 155 square miles from Washington County; 18 square miles from Sharkey County; 22 square miles from Sunflower County; 143 square miles from Yazoo county; and 74 square miles from Holmes - making Humphreys County a total of 412 square miles. The county was named for former Mississippi Governor Benjamin Grubbs Humphreys who governed from 1865 to 1868. Although most residents at the time of formation were engaged in general farming with cotton being the cash crop, the county now produces more farm-grown catfish than any other county in the United States. It accounts for about 60% of all farmed catfish production with roughly 40,000 acres devoted to catfish ponds.

Isola is a tiny town located at the border of Sunflower and Humphreys Counties. In the year 2000, the town had a population of 768. It is on the banks of Lake Dawson. The name "Isola" came from the word "isolated" since the location at the time the community was founded was remote. Although it is only about 16 miles from Indianola even at the start of the 1900's, this was a sparsely populated area with few roads, no nearby rail line, and no connected waterway system. Travel would have been a hard slog by foot or horseback. A review of maps displaying boundary changes, shows if Ned was living in the same location in 1910 as he was in 1918, he would have been in Washington County.

On 6 May 1920 when the Census was enumerated in his area, Ned was still farming and living in Humphreys County Mississippi with his family.

Nathaniel "Ned" Barnes (b. 1908)

Nathaniel "Ned" Barnes was born in 1908 in Mississippi. He married Ruth Mae Hunter on 14 August 1923. The entry for Ruth Mae Hunter includes all information known about Ned – which is not very much.

Mary Eliza "Mickey" Webb

Mary Eliza Webb was born on 2 August 1934 in Sunflower, Mississippi. She was known as "Mickey". Shortly after her mother died on 2 November 1950, Mickey and her brother Bill moved to Detroit to live with their sisters, Flora and Thelma respectively. Mickey married Clarence Blackmon. She attended three colleges in Detroit: The University of Detroit, Wayne State University, and Marygrove College. She earned her Bachelor of Arts Degree in Fine Arts and Education. She taught elementary school, mostly at Edmonson Elementary School, for over 35 years. She loved to tell jokes and riddles.

Mickey had seven children in total; two of whom died before her.

Leon Webb was born 6 May 1953 to Mickey and Willis Norman Taylor (d. before 1986). He attended Murray Wright High School and Schoolcraft College and was active in the athletic department. Later he was employed by Valeron Corporation, Troy, MI. He died suddenly on 4 March 1986 in Detroit and was interred Woodlawn Cemetery, 19975 Woodward Avenue, opposite the Michigan State Fairgrounds, between 7 Mile Road and 8 Mile Road, in Detroit, Michigan on 10 March 1986.

Danny Earl Taylor was born 12 May 1954 also to Mickey and Willis Norman Taylor. He was educated in the Detroit Public School System and graduated from Murray Wright High School. He first worked for the Admiral Chrome Company, Detroit from 1971-1979 as shipping and receiving supervisor. Later he was employed by Velron Corporation in Troy, Michigan as dip room operator, operating robotic equipment. After the corporation closed, he opened his own restaurant "Mr. Delicious". He attended Leviticus Missionary Baptist Church. He never married.

Danny died on 20 January 2007. He was buried on 27 January 2007 at Lincoln Memorial Park, 21661 E. 14 Mile Road, Clinton Twp., Michigan 48035.

Mary Eliza passed away on 31 October 2014 and was interred at Detroit Memorial Park West, 25200 Plymouth Road, Redford, Michigan 48239.

George Austin William "Bill" Webb

George Austin William Webb is known as "Bill". As of this writing, he is still alive and sharp as a tack. He has helped tremendously in the research for this family history, sharing his memories and contributing to the DNA picture. His ability to recall names, dates, and locations has been invaluable in locating records.

Bill had three children one of whom has passed away.

Darrell Thomas was born on 24 February 1956 in Detroit, Michigan. Darrell had 10 children by 10 different mothers. Hopefully mention of this helps those children or their descendants when they start researching their family history. Surname changes between generations particularly on the male lines can be quite a research challenge. People often know who their father and grandfather are, but the names of ancesters further back in their lines are unknown. Hopefully, this mention will provide the needed link. Darrell died on 21 March 2015. His funeral service was held at Mt. Zion Baptist Church, 3600 Van Dyke, Detroit, MI 48214.

Appendix A — Meaning and Origin of Surnames in this Family

Barnes — Three possible origins. First, a Middle and Old English origin of a topographical or occupational name for someone who lived or worked at a barn. Second, an Anglo-Saxon and Old Norse origin meaning the son or servant of someone in the upper classes. Third, an Irish origin meaning the descendant of Bearan, a byname meaning "spear".

Briggs — This is a variant of the more common name Bridges. Two possible origins. First, from the early medieval English topographical surname for someone who lived near a bridge, or from a metonymic occupational name for a bridge keeper. Building and maintaining bridges was one of the three main feudal obligations in the Middle Ages, the others being the bearing of arms when required and the maintenance of fortifications. Second, a locational name from the Flemish city of Bruges, meaning "bridges", which had important trading links with England in the Middle Ages.

Burks — Two possible origins both being locational. First, from the French 'de Burgo' or 'de Burgh', signifying "of the borough". Second, from the Middle English 'burk', meaning 'fort'.

Coleman — Three possible origins. First, an old Irish and English origin derived from a compound of Gaelic elements meaning "white dove". Second, an Anglo-Saxon origin for an occupational name for a burner of charcoal or gatherer of coal. Third, an English personal name used to describe someone of dark complexion.

Everett—It has its sources in both the Old English pre-7th century personal name 'Eoforheard' and the Germanic personal name 'Eberhard', both composed of the elements 'eber', translating as 'wild boar' and 'hard' meaning brave or strong. Spelling variants include Averett and Avery.

Flournoy—From the French; it is probably a topographic name for someone who lived in a place where flowers grew. This name is associated with Huguenots who settled in Virginia.

Ford—This is an Old English name and one of the earliest topographical names referring to a person who lived by a shallow place along a river where one could cross.

Funderburk—Americanized spelling of the German "von der Burg" meaning 'from the castle'; it is an occupational or topographic name for someone who lived and worked at a castle. Also spelled Funderburg.

Hunter—From the Old English pre-7th Century word "hunta", from "huntian", meaning to hunt, with the suffix "-er", meaning one who does or works with. The term was used not only of hunters on horseback of game such as stags and wild boars, a pursuit in Middle Ages restricted to the ranks of the nobility, but also as a nickname for both bird catchers and poachers.

Kaigler/Kegler/Keglar—From German; nickname for an enthusiastic skittles player; from the Middle High German word "kegel" for 'skittle ', or 'pin'.

Jackson—It is a patronymic formed from the personal names Jaques or John, both originating from the ancient Hebrew "Yochanan", meaning "Jehovah has favoured me (with a son)". The name as a personal name was first introduced by returning Crusaders from the Holy Land in the 12th century.

Variant spellings include Jackson, Jacson, Jagson, and Jaxon.

Knox — Of Scottish or English origins. In all cases it is either a topographical name for someone who lived on a hilltop, derived from the pre-7th century Old English word "cnocc" or the similar Gaelic "cnoc", both meaning a round-topped hill, or it may be locational from one of the various places called "Knock" found in both Scotland and Northern England.

Llewellyn — This is an ancient surname of Old English and Welsh pre-7th century origins. It derives from the Celtic elements "llyw" meaning "leader" and "eilun", meaning "the likeness to". There are researchers who claim that the first element does not mean leader but lion, however as the lion is also regarded as the king of the beasts, it results in a similar meaning.

Looney — An Anglicized version of the Gaelic "luan" meaning warrior. It was a personal name meaning hound and as such was a nickname for a fast runner.

Perry — Two possible origins. The first is residential for someone who lived by a pear orchard, or more probably one who owned such a place. The name derives from the Old English pre-7th century word "pirige", meaning pear-tree. The second possible origin is Welsh and a patronymic form of the medieval given name "Herry". This is a form of Henry, and when fused with the Welsh patronymic prefix of "ap" produces "Ap Herry" leading to the pronunciation "Perry".

Phillips — Of early medieval English origin, this is one of the many surnames generated by the male given name Philip, which came from the Greek "Philippos", a compound of "philein" meaning to love, and "hippos" meaning horse; hence, "lover of horses". Philip of Macedon, father of Alexander the Great, was a famous bearer of the name, and its popularity throughout Greece and Asia Minor and subsequently in Western Europe, was largely due to him. The name was given to five Kings of France. It entered England via France in the 12th Century. John Phillips, who embarked from London in the ship "Merchant's Hope", bound for Virginia in July 1635, was one of the earliest recorded namebearers to settle in America.

Randle — At least two possible origins. First, from the Middle English given name "Randel", a diminutive of the personal name "Rande", to which was added the Norman French diminutive suffix "-el"; meaning little, to give Little Rand or more likely son of Rande. Rande meaning shield, was a first element in many pre-7th century Anglo-Saxon and Germanic compound personal names, such as the popular Randolph. Second, a form of the Old English personal names Randwulf or Randulf, themselves from the Norse-Viking name "Rondulfr", and derived from the elements meaning shield and wolf.

Reed — At least three possible origins. First, an Old English nickname for a person with red hair or a ruddy complexion. Second, an Old English topographical name for someone who lived in a clearing in woodland. Third, an Old English locational name from any of various places called Read or Reed.

Sanders/Saunders — At least three potential origins. First, a derivative of the Greek personal name Alexander, meaning "the defender", and which was first recorded in 2000 BC. It was introduced into Britain by "Crusaders" and other pilgrims, from the Holy Land, in the 12th century AD. Second, in Britain, it can be locational from the village of Sanderstead in the county of Surrey. This place was first recorded as "Sonderstede" in the famous Anglo-Saxon Chronicles of the year 871, meaning the house on the sandy land. Third, from the pre-7th century word "sand", plus the Germanic suffix "-er", and as such describing a person who worked with or supplied sand, used for building or agricultural purposes. The various spellings of the surname include Sander, Saunder, and Sandar, and include Saunders, Sanders, and Sandars as the patronymic forms.

Webb—From the Old English "web" meaning 'to weave'. Originally "webbe" applied to a male weaver and "webster" applied to a female weaver.

Wilson—It is a patronymic form of the male given name Will, itself a diminutive of William. Introduced into England by William, Duke of Normandy, and known to history as "The Conqueror". The Norman form and that borne by the Conqueror, was "Willelm", a spelling adopted from the Frankish Empire of the 8th century. The name is a compound which originally consisted of the elements "wil", meaning desire, and "helm", a helmet which offered protection.

Appendix B — Selected Bibliography

Blake, Tom (transcriber) (2001). Carroll County, Mississippi Largest Slaveholders from 1860 Slave Census Schedules and Surname Matches for African Americans on 1870 Census, Retrieved from http://freepages.genealogy.rootsweb.ancestry.com/~ajac/mscarroll.htm

Central Georgia Genealogical Society, Inc. (1983). *First Hundred and Ten Years of Houston County, Georgia (1822-1932)*, Chelsea, Michigan: Bookcrafters, Inc.

Evans, Raymond (1979). The Graysville Melungeons (A Tri-racial People in Lower East Tennessee), appeared in Tennessee Anthropologist, (Vol: IV, #1, 1979), Retrieved from http://freepages.genealogy.rootsweb.ancestry.com/~appalachian/melungeons/THE_GRAYSVILLE_MELUNGEONS.txt

Farmer, Margaret Pace (1973). *One Hundred Fifty Year in Pike County Alabama 1821-1971*. Montgomery, Alabama: Brown Printing Company.

Heinegg, Paul. Free African Americans of Virginia, North Carolina, South Carolina, Maryland, and Delaware. Retrieved from http://www.freeafricanamericans.com/

Hemphill, Marie M. (1980). *Fevers, Floods, and Faith: A History of Sunflower County, Mississippi, 1844-1976*. Indianola, Mississippi: Sunflower County Historical Society.

Jones, Jacqueline (1985). *Labor of Love, Labor of Sorrow Black Women, Work, and the Family from Slavery to the Present.* New York, New York: Basic Books, Inc.

Keegan, John (2009). *The American Civil War A Military History,* New York, New York: Alfred A. Knopf.

Winschel, Terrence J. (2009). Chickasaw Bayou Sherman's Winter of Despair. *Blue & Gray,* Vol. XXVI, #3, 6-24, 44-50, 52.

Winschel, Terrence J. (2009). The General's Tour The Battle of Chickasaw Bayou. *Blue & Gray,* Vol. XXVI, #3, 53-65.

Appendix C—Will & Probate of James Abbington Everett

The writing in this will has faded greatly over time. To make it more easily read, digital photos were taken of the frail, faint pages and then enhanced to darken the old script. This is a transcription of the will. There were a few places where the script was exceedingly difficult to decipher. In those places, there are either underscores to indicate illegible letters or an attempt and then another possible reading enclosed in brackets. This will was written a long time ago and contains the use of capitalization, grammar, punctuation, and vocabulary in vogue at the time. The transcription is faithful to the original document and no updates to modern conventions of use have been made. There are page numbers to indicate the pagination in the original document because the last section of the will includes corrections based on page numbers.

The probate lasted for 21 years and was written by a number of different clerks of the court. Some of the records were easier to decipher than others. The probate transcription is not absolutely complete because there are a few pages missing. These missing pages contain the last few sentences of a few of the court minutes. I have annotated where this occurs. The following gives a good picture of what happened over the 21 years following James's death.

The Will of James Abbington Everett
Houston County, Georgia
Will Book 'A' Pages: 220 – 228

Page 220

In the name of God Almighty, I, James A. Everett of the said state and county being of advanced age and knowing that I must shortly depart this life deem it right and proper that I should make a disposition of the property with which a kind Providence has blessed me I therefore make this my last will and testament hereby revoking all former wills made by me.

Item first – I desire and direct that my Body be buried in a decent and Christian like manner suitable to my circumstances and condition. My soul I trust shall return to rest with God who gave it as I hope for Salvation through the blessed Lord and Savior Jesus Christ whose religion I have professed and as I humbly trust enjoyed for several {this sentence is not complete in the original document}

Item Second – I desire that all my just debts be paid without delay by my Executors herein after named as I am unwilling my creditors should be delayed of their rights as there is no necessity for withholding immediate payment.

Item Third – To my Beloved wife, Mary Beaufort I give the sum of Fifteen Thousand dollars which amount my Executors are required to lay out in the purchase of Negroes for her subject to the following conditions. Viz -- The negroes purchased in pursuance of this clause of my will not be liable to sale or subject to debt contracts by herself or any future husband. If she should contract any marriage hereafter and have children by such marriage the property purchased in accordance with this clause of my will to be

Page 221
the property of herself and the children of such marriage provided the children of such marriage service her. But in the event of her death without contracting any future marriage or in the event of her marrying again and dying leaving no living children by said marriage then the said negroes to revert back to and become a part of my estate and I do appoint my friend Adolphus D. Kendrick Trustee for the property herein bequeathed to my wife Mary Beaufort.

Item Fourth – I give and bequeath to the children of my deceased brother Charles Everett the sum of Five Thousand dollars to be equally divided between them.

Item Fifth – I give to the children of my deceased sister Nancy Furlow five thousand dollars to be equally divided between them the two last mentioned legacies to be paid as soon after my death as may be.

Item Sixth – I give and bequeath to the three Daughters (whose names I do not know) of my deceased sister Patsy Bynum the sum of one thousand dollars each and I require my Executors to invest said sum in Negroes for the said legatees the negroes so purchased not to be subject to sale or liable for debt contracted by said legatees or any present or future husband of said legatees but remain their own to descend to their children or these failing to their legal heirs. And I do hereby

Page 222
appoint their brother Sugars Bynum {Researcher's note: When the legacy was paid on 26 October 1849 this legatee is identified as "James S. Bynum". This is James Sugars Bynum (b. 1812 d. 1881) son of Patsy Everett and Sugars Bynum} trustee for the property herein bequeathed to my said heirs.

Item Seventh – I give and bequeath to my nephew Sugars Bynum son of my deceased sister Patsy Bynum the sum of Five Thousand dollars which sum my executors are required to lay out in negroes for him.

Item Eighth – I give and bequeath to my nephew George C. Everett the sum of Five Thousand five hundred dollars.

Item Ninth – I give to my nephew Turner C. Everett the sum of Three Thousand dollars in addition to the sum of Two Thousand dollars which I have heretofore given him.

Item Tenth – I give to the Revd Ruben H. Luckey the sum of One Thousand dollars.

Item Eleventh – To my nephews James M. Everett and Charles H. Everett I give the sum of one thousand dollars each.

Item Twelfth – To my sister-in-law Elizabeth Greene I give the sum of Four Thousand dollars to be expended by my executors in the purchase of negroes for her said negroes not to be subject to sale by herself or liable to any debts contracted by

Page 223
herself or husband if she should marry but said negroes to belong to herself and children these falling to her other lawful heirs and I hereby appoint Turner C. Everett Trustee for the property herein bequeathed to the said Elizabeth Greene.

Item Thirteenth – I give and bequeath to my Brothers-in-law William and Peter B. Greene the sum of Four Thousand dollars each the amounts to be invested by my Executors for them in negroes.

Item Fourteenth – To my brother-in-law Myles L. Greene I give the sum of Two Thousand dollars making with what I have already given him the sum of Four Thousand dollars.

Item Fifteenth – To my mother-in-law Mrs. Sarah E. Kaigler I give the sum of Two Thousand dollars and my gold spectacles also the use for life of the following negroes to wit Early Caroline Burrell Tatnall and Jerry after her death said negroes to revert back to and become a part of my estate hereinafter bequeathed.

Item Sixteenth – I give and bequeath the sum of two thousand dollars for the benefit of the mission established by the Methodist Episcopal church South in the Creek nation said sum to be paid to the Revd Bishops James O. Andrew and Joshua So___ and to be by them applied to the use above specified said sum to be paid in four annual installments unless it

Page 224
should be the opinion of the said Bishops that the money could be more advantageously used if paid in two annual installments in the latter event my executors are authorized to pay accordingly the first payment to be made within one year after my demise.

Item Seventeenth – I give and bequeath my old Friend the Revd James Dunwoody the sum of Five hundred dollars to be expended by my Executors in the purchase of a negro man or boy for him.

Item Eighteenth – I give my old Friend the Revd John Tulwood the sum of Five hundred dollars to be expended by my executor in the purchase of a negro man or boy for him.

Item Nineteenth – I give to Charity Hasell [possibly Harell] and Sarah Hasell [possibly Harell] the sum of One hundred dollars each.

Item Twentyeth – I give to Mrs. Mary Mathis widow of Isham Mathis deceased the sum of Twenty four dollars annually during her natural life.

Item Twenty First – I give to the foreign missionary society of the Methodist Episcopal Church South the sum of one hundred and fifty dollars annually until the last of my heirs becomes of age or marries at which time my estate will be finally wound up.

Item Twenty Second – I give to the Domestick [sic] Missionary Society of the Methodist Episcopal Church South the sum of one hundred and fifty dollars annually until my estate is finally wound up.

Item Twenty-third – To my sons James A. and Henry P. I give my Hogscrawl plantation and land attached thereto to be equally divided between them when my estate is finally wound up. Nevertheless said plantation shall remain in the hands of my Executors as part of my estate and be cultivated accordingly until a final division and my said sons shall not receive any rent or property themselves exclusively while it remains a part of my undivided estate as aforesaid.

Item Twenty-fourth – I give and bequeath all my estate both real and personal except what is heretofore or hereinafter bequeathed (subject to the provision in the latter clause of this item) to my five children two sons and three daughters Viz James A., Henry Peter, Sarah E., Ann E. and Theodocia to be equally divided between them in the following manner to wit. When either of my Daughters shall marry or my sons come of age my property both real and personal shall be valued by men legally appointed for the purpose and divided into five lots and the heir so marrying or coming of age shall draw one fifth part of its then value and the division so made shall be final as to the party then receiving his or her share so far as related to any change in the value of property which may occur thereafter and so far as relates to any addition or diminution which may be made to or lost by said estate after the said heir shall have received his or her inheritance. Provided that if either of my children shall die before receiving his or her portion of my estate all my remaining children or their heirs whether they have or have not received their inheritance shall share equally in the estate of the deceased child. Provided nevertheless that if I shall have any lawful heirs born after the making of this will the said child or children so born shall be entitled to equal share or shares of my estate with my five children named above in this item of this my last will and testament and the division shall be made not with reference to the children named above, but to the number of my actual lawful heirs. And in dividing my estate according to this mode prescribed in this item of my will the negroes shall be set off in families and not otherwise unless absolutely necessary.

Item Twenty fifth – And I further will and desire that all negro property which shall fall to my daughters in virtue of this my last will to wit – Sarah E. An [sic] E. and Theodocia shall not be subject to sale or liable for any debt contracted by themselves or their husbands if they should marry but shall belong to my said Daughters and their children and in the event of their not marrying or marrying and not having children living at the time of their death the said negro property shall revert to their lawful heirs and so hereby appoint Turner C Everett Trustee for all negro property bequeathed by me in this my last will to my said Daughters Sarah E. Ann E. and Theodocia and in the event of my having other heirs born after making this will the same being a daughter or daughters I will and devise that all Negro property which shall fall to them under this my last will shall be upon the same terms as is prescribed above in the devise to my other Daughters and the said Turner C Everett hereby appointed Trustee for the property so bequeathed in the event the contingency herein provided for should occur.

Item Twenty sixth – I request my executors hereinafter named carry on my plantations and add to them or establish new ones as they may have means and find it for the interest of my estate to do so and they are hereby empowered to purchase lands and negroes for that purpose. And I request my executors to give so much of their personal attention to the affairs of my estate which I now solemnly place in their hands trusting and believing that my children who are helpless and dependent on them will be secured in the possession of their just rights and my other bequests faithfully performed according to my intentions which I trust are plainly set forth in this my last will and I hereby declare the foregoing eight pages to contain my last will and testament and do appoint my friends Turner C Everett Myles L Greene and Adolphus D. Kendrick my executors. The following measures and interlineations were made before signing. ___ on page first Item Third bottom line the word contract interlined In item third page second line eighth from top the word marriage interlined On page fourth item sixteenth the fourth line from bottom erased – On page fifth item twenty fifth in the second line from the bottom the word my interlined.

James A. Everett Signed this 8th day of May 1848 in presence of Hardy Hunter W. H. Hollinshead Allen Wiggins {to the right of these three names is a bracket and then a word – perhaps Test}

Georgia
Houston County
Before us James E. Duncan, John Killen and Edward A. Harvey Justices of the Inferior Court of said county in open court personally came A. D. Kendrick, Turner C. Everett and Myles L. Greene Executors of the last will and testament of James A. Everett late of said county deceased and produced before us the last will and testament of said James A. Everett deceased and the witnesses of said will to wit Hardy Hunter W. H. Hollinshead which witnesses being duly sworn depose and say that they saw James A. Everett the testator sign seal declare and publish the instrument now prescribed as his last will and testament freely voluntarily and of his own accord and without any compulsion or influence whatsoever that at the time of the execution of said will said testator was...{continues on another page which I do not have}

Records of Probate of the Will

Minute Book 'B'
Pages 191, 193, 224, 239. 240, 250, 251, 254, 255, 260, 264, 266 & 271

Pg 191
July 1848

The last will and Testament of James A. Everett having been proven in open Court by Allen Wiggins William H. Hollenshead and Hardy Hunter subscribing witnesses to the same and the codicil to Said will having also been proven by Allen Wiggins William J. Anderson and Judson Kendrick subscribing witnesses to Said codicil It is ordered that the Said will and codicil be admitted to record and that the clerk of this court __ issued to Adolphus D. Kendrick and Turner C. Everett two of the executors in Said will names Letters Testamentary they having been duly indefite{?} to discharge the trusts confided to them

It is further ordered that William Thompson John J. Hampton Hardy Hunter Allen Wiggins and Matthew Darby (or Danby) ___and they are hereby appointed appraisers to appraise the estate of the Said James A. Everett Dec.

Pg 193
Whereas Miles L. Green one of the executors of James A. Everett Deceased is came in Court and ready to be qualified.

Therefore ordered by the Court that upon the Said Miles L. Green qualifying in Terms of the Law Letters Testamentary be issued to him by the Clerk of this Court.
William I. Green a minor is now in court and is desirous of having Miles L. Green appointed his Guardian of his person and property. It is therefore orders by the Court that Said Miles L. Green be and he is hereby appointed Guardian of the person and property of Said William I. Green upon his Giving Bond in the Sum of Eight Thousand Dollars with Turner C. Everett as his Guaratyes {sic} and taking the usual oath

Pg 224

It appearing to the Court that the executors of James A. Everett late of Houston County deceased have given Notice according to Law of their intention to make application at this term of the Court for Leave to Sell Certain Town Lots in Fort Valley belonging to the estate of the Said James A. Everett deceased Therefore it is ordered by the Court that the Said Executors of the Said James A. Everett have Leave to Sell Said Town Lots upon advertising the Same in Terms of Law

Pg 239
May Term 1850

The petition of Cary S Cox respectfully showeth that James A. Everett in his lifetime was the owner of the following lots of land to wit numbered Eight Ten Twenty four and Seventy two all situate lying and being in the Twenty fifth District of originally Lee now Macon County and Containing Eight Hundred and Ten acres more or less and your petitioner further showeth that Said Everett in his lifetime bargained {sic} and sold Said Lots to your petitioner for which your petitioner paid him all the purchase money except the Sum of eight hundred Dollars which was the last payment and when Said Sum of eight hundred Dollars became due and payable your petitioner was unable to make the payment thereof and applied to one Allen Walker to borry {sic} the sum of Eight Hundred Dollars for the purpose of making Said last payment for said lands and agreed with Said Walker to give him a loan on the same for security for the money so to be loaned and your petitioner further showeth that on the seventeenth day of March 1848 your petitioner paid Said Everett the balance of the purchase money for Said land and Said Everett by his agent then and there transferd{sic} the deed of the Sheriff of Stewart county to Said land to Said Allen Walker your petitioner further showeth that when Said Allen Walker agreed to loan your petitioner Said Sum of money and take a loan on Said lands as security therefor {sic} he said Walker agreed with said Walker your petitioner that when Said Sum of eight Hundred Dollars was paid to him Said Walker that Said Everett Should convey Said lands to your petitioner and your petitioner further showeth that Said Sum of eight hundred Dollars has been fully paid back to the estate of Said Walker and his representatives has no interest in Said lands therefore your petitioner prays an order may be passed by this Honorable Court requiring Turner C. Everett Executor of Said James A. Everett to execute the agreement of Said James A. Everett so made as aforesaid in his lifetime and convey to your petitioner by deed the land aforesaid and your petitioner will ever pray your petitioner further showeth that the following is a copy of the agreement of Said James A. Everett above mentioned

    T. B. Smith Atty for petitioner

Pg 240
Georgia
Stewart County

Know all men by these presence that James A. Everett of Houston County Georgia for and in consideration of the Sum of Eight hundred Dollars in hand paid me by Allen Walker of Talbot County Georgia through agency deliver relinquish and convey to Said Allen Walker all my right and title to the within described lands of __ Lots Numbers Eight Ten Twenty four and Seventy two containing Eight Hundred and ten acres more or less lying and being in the 25th District of originally Lee now Stewart County to have and to hold as his own right and property forever in fee simple the right and title of which is granted by the written deed of Daniel Mathison late Sheriff of Stewart County Georgia which deed is hereby conveyed and relinquished to Said A. Walker thirtyth day of March A.D. 1848
Signed Sealed and declared in presence of
Benjamin Simpson
H. A. Shipp

James A. Everett
T. C. Everett agent

Upon hearing the foregoing petition it is ordered that notice be given of this application according to the statute in Such cases made and provided and that the Said Executor will be directed at the March Term of this Court after the Said notice appeared to make titles according to Said bond or agreement unless Cause is shown to the Contrary

Georgia
Talbot County

Before me Henry Jones a Justice of the Inferior Court of Said County personally came Cary S. Cox who is executor of Allen Walker Deceased and being duly sworn says that Said Allen Walker in his lifetime by agency paid James A. Everett the Sum of eight Hundred Dollars it being part of the purchase money and last payment due for the land mentioned in the deed of Daniel Masstion {sic} Sheriff of Stewart Count to Said Everett and by Said Everett assigned to Said Allen Walker on the back of Said deed with the understanding and agreement that when the Sum of eight Hundred Dollars as aforesaid was paid back to him Said Allen Walker he would convey these lands to deponent {Note: legal term meaning one who gives written testimony under oath} who had bought them from Said Everett and paid all but the last payment aforesaid and deponent further says he has fully paid to the estate of Said Allen Walker Said sum of eight Hundred Dollars and all that is due to the estate of Said Allen Walker for said lands and that the estate of deponents testator has no interest or right in those lands whatever
Sworne to and subscribed before me this 2nd day of May 1850
Henry Jones J. J.C.   C. S. Cox

Pg 250

It appearing to the Court that by the Petition of William J. Anderson that James A. Everett Deceased did in his lifetime execute to Said William J. Anderson his bond Conditioned to execute Titles in fee simple to Said William J. Anderson for a Certain Town lot in which the Said William J. Anderson resides in Fort Valley in Houston County and it further appearing that Said William J. Anderson had paid the full purchase money

Pg 251

For Said lot and William J. Anderson having petitioned this Court to direct A. D. Kendrick Turner C Everett and Myles L Green Executors of Said Everett to execute to him Titles to Said lot in conformity to Said bond It is therefore ordered that notice be given at three or more public places in Said County and in the Georgia Telegraph of Such application that all persons concerned may file objections in the Clerks office why Said Executors as aforesaid should not execute titles to Said lot of land in conformity with Said bond.

Pg 254

It appearing to the Court by the petition of George Law that James A. Everett late of Said County now deceased in his lifetime to wit on the 17th day of September 1847 signed sealed and delivered to the Said George Law his bond or written obligation in the penal sum of Twenty eight hundred dollars conditioned to make to the Said George upon his paying the sum of fourteen hundred Dollars as provided in the Condition annexed to Said bond warranty titles to one lot and a fraction of Land containing two hundred and thirty acres more or less lying on the west side of Flint River in the County of Macon known as the Wartins place and containing as appears from Said petition of Lot No 149 and thirty acres more or less of Lot No 137 being that portion of Said Lot named Lot which lies on the north side of Toliver Creek all in the first District of originally Muscogee now the County of Macon in Said state and it also appearing

Pg 255

that the Said George Law had paid the full amount of the purchase money and that Said James A. Everett deceased in Said County of Houston without having performed the conditions of said bond or provided therefor {sic} by will and that Turner C. Everett Adolphus D. Kendrick and Miles L. Green all of Said County have been and are duly qualified as executors of the Last Will and Testament of the Said James A. Everett deceased It is therefore on motioned ordered that notice of this application be Given be a publication of a copy of this order according to Law and statute in such cases made and provided and that the Said executors aforesaid will be directed at the new Term of this Court after Said notice shall have been given to make titles agreeably to Said obligation unless cause is shown to the contrary

Pg 260

It appearing to this Court from the Petition of Asa Jolly that James A Everett late of Said County now deceased in his lifetime to wit on the 27th day of September 1845 made and Delivered to Said Asa Jolly his bond for titled under Seal Conditioned to make Good and Sufficient titles to Said Asa Jolly for lots of Land No 168 and No 169 in the first District of Macon County in Said state and that the Said Asa James A. Everett has departed this life without having performed his Said Agreement (a copy of which is annexed to Said petition) and without having provided therefor {sic} by Will and it also appearing that Adolphus D. Kendrick Turner C Everett and Miles L. Green of Said County are Executors of the Last Will and Testament of the Sid James A. Everett It is therefore on motion of John M. Giles Attorney for Said petitioner ordered by the Court that notice of this application be given according to the statute in Such cases made and provided and that the executors aforesaid will be directed at the next court to be held next after the Said notice has been Given to make titles agreeably to Said bond unless cause be shown to the contrary

Pg 264

A. D. Kendrick administrator as aforesaid be and he is hereby required and directed to make and execute and deliver unto David O. Smith petitioner as aforesaid Good and Sufficient titles to lot of Land No Two hundred and forty eight in the ninth District of Houston County

Also on page 264 further down the page

George Law having petitioned this Court praying an order to be Granted directing an order Adolphus D. Kendrick Turner C Everett and Miles L Green Executors of the Last Will and Testament of James A. Everett late of Said County Deceased to make titles to the Said George Law under a Bond for titles Conditioned to execute a Good and Sufficient titles on warrantee deed to and for a lot and a fraction lot of Land Containing two hundred and thirty acres more or less lying on the west side of Flint River and it appearing that the lots mentioned in Said land consist of Lot Number one hundred and thirty Seven being that portion of the last mentioned lot lying on the north side of Tole over {Note: this is probably Toliver} Creek all in the first District of originally the County of Muscogee now Macon County and it also appearing that notice has been Given of Said Application in Conformity to Law and no objection having been made it is therefore ordered Considered and adjudged that the Said Executors make and execute a Good and Sufficient warrantee deed to Said Lots in Conformity with the Conditions expressed in Said Bond for titles and it is further ordered and adjudged that the Said executors pay the Cost of these proceedings amounting to the Sum of {Note: there is no figure written here on the original} Dollars out of the assets of their Testator in their hand

Pg 266

Asa Jolly having petitioned this Court at the May Term thereof in the year 1851 Setting forth that James A. Everett of Said County deceased in his lifetime to wit on the 27th day of September 1845 made and delivered to Said Asa Jolly his bond for titles under Seal Conditioned to make Good and Sufficient titles to the Said Asa Jolly for Lots of Land No 168 and 169 in the first District of Macon County in Said state and that the Said Everett has departed this life without having performed Said agreement a Copy of which was annexed to Said petition and without having provided therefor {sic} by will and Setting forth that A. D. Kendrick Turner C Everett and Miles L Green of Said County of Houston are Executors of the Last Will and Testament of Said James A Everett decd and this Court having as the Said Term passed an order that notice of Said application be Given according to Law and that the Said Executors aforesaid would be directed at the Term of this Court to be held next after Said notice was Given to make titles agreeably to Said Bond unless cause be shown to the Contrary and now at this term of the Court it appearing that Said notice has been Given according to Law and no Cause being shown it is ordered and directed that the Said Executors make titles to Said Lots of Land according to the provisions of Said Bond and that they pay the Sum of $27.50 for the Cost of this proceeding out of the Assets of the Said Testator in their hands to be administered

Pg 271

Whereas the Court of Ordinary at a previous Term having Granted an order upon the petition of William J. Anderson directing A. D. Kendrick Turner C Everett and Miles L Green Executors of James A Everett deceased to make execute and deliver to William J. Anderson Good and Sufficient titles to that Lot of Land where William J. Anderson now resides in the village of Fort Valley and the Said order having been published in Terms of Law and no objection having been filed It is ordered by the Court that A. D. Kendrick Turner C Everett and Miles L Green be and they and such directed and required to make and deliver to William J Anderson Good and Sufficient titles in fee simple to that Town Lot in Fort Valley whereon Said William J Anderson now resides and it is further ordered the Said Executors pay the Sum of $26.75 Dollars Cost accrued in this case

It appearing to the Court that application has been made to this court for leave to Sell the following land belonging to the estate of James A. Everett Deceased South half of Lot No 150 South half of Lot 139 Lot No 170 and lot No 151 except six acres in the southwest Corner of Said Lot all lying in the 7th District of Dooly County and containing 707 acres Lots No 24 and 5 except 2 acres west half of lot no 6 and fifteen acres of Lot no 192 and Lot No 161 all lying in the 9th and upon{?} 14th District of Houston County and Known as the Mill Place and Lots No 141, 142, 148 and north half of Lot no 147 all lying in the Henderson District of Houston County and Known as the Jones Place East half of Lot No 55 and lot no __ Known joining (?) No 55 all lying in the 18th{? or possibly 13th} District of formerly Houston now Macon County Known as the Horse Head place and Lots No 197, 194, 195 and east half of 197 all lying in the 28th District of formerly Lee now Sumpter County and Lot no 193 lying in the 13th District of Sumpter County formerly Lee and an improved Lot in Fort Valley No 21 in Blo__ containing 1 acre more or less now occupied by William J Anderson and it further appearing to the Court that Said application has been published in Terms of the Law and no objection having been filed It is ordered by the Court that

A. D. Kendrick Turner C Everett and Miles L Green Executors of James A Everett late of Houston County Deceased have leave to Sell all the Said Land afore mentioned belonging to the estate of Said Dec^d after advertising the Same

Minute Book 'C'
Pages 166, 183, 314, 433 & 564

Pg 166
Court of Ordinary January Term 1855

Appearing to this Court, this Sarah E. Everett a daughter & legatee under the last will and testament of James A. Everett deceased has intermarried with James P. Flewellen upon the taking place of which marriage by a provision the said will of the said James A. Everett, his estate is to be valued & divided into six equal parts or shares between his six children. It is therefore ordered thus William Harris – Dr. Wm. H. Hollandshead. William J. Anderson. Dr. Wm. I. Thomas, & James T. Tooke be they or as three of them are hereby appointed to value & divide the Estate of the said James A. Everett in to six equal part or shares according to the directions & provisions of the said James A. Everett's will between his six children one of which was born after the making of said will. The said James P. Flewellen being present in court & assenting & agreeing to this order & raising any & all notice of our application for the same.

Pg 183

Court of Ordinary in Chambers April Term 1855
Georgia Houston County

It appearing to the Court that Myles L. Green Executor of the last Will & Testament of James A. Everett deceased has applied for leave to sell all the lands belonging to said Estate that are disconnected with and form no part of the plantation of said deceased, and it appearing to the Court that the said Myles L. Green has given due & legal notice of his intention to get an order of this court to sell such lands so as aforesaid not adjoining or joining forth any of the plantations of said deceased and it also appearing that said sale is necessary for a division of said lands among the legatees of said deceased…{continues to another page I do not have}

Pg 314
November Term 1857

Whereas at the June Term of this Court 1857, upon the petition of Davis N. Austin praying the Court to direct Myles L. Green Adolphus D. Kendrick and Turner C. Everett the executors of James A. Everett late of said county deceased to make titles to a certain tract or parcel of land situate & lying in the village of Fort Valley whereas said petitioner had built two houses for workshops said lot or parcel of land to be fifty feet in front and to extend to the land line between the said Everett and one Mathew Dorsey all in the Ninth District of said County of Houston, according to the Conditions and obligations of a certain obligation or undertaking in writing executed by the said James A. Everett in his lifetime whereby he obligated himself to make a {seems to be a missing word here} and for said premises to said Davis N. Austin whenever the said petitioner should pay up a certain note then held by said Everett against said petitioner for Two Hundred four 33/100 dollars together with the interest thereon. This Court granted an order requiring notice of such application to be made in terms of the law at least three months that all persons concerned should appear and show cause if any they had by the October Term of said Court then next why said executors should not make titles in conformity with said bond and said notice having been published in accordance with said order and the consideration of said cause having been regularly continued to this present term of the Court & no objection appearing and it further appearing that the amount of the purchase money and consideration for which the said contract was made has been fully paid and performed and it further appearing that Turner C. Everett one of said executors has moved beyond the jurisdictional limits of this state leaving the entire charge and management of said Estate of J. A. Everett in the hand of his said CoExecutors {sic}. It is therefore ordered by the Court that said Miles…{continues to a page I do not have}

Pg 433
June Term 1859
Georgia
Houston County
To the Hon this Court of Ordinary for said County.
The Petition of Myles L. Green who is the Executor of James A. Everett Dec^d Respectfully showeth that during the year 1858 he was at great trouble & lost a great deal of time from his own business in attending & Superintending the

plantations belonging to his said Testators Estate and also in attending to the Negroes in their sickness and looking after their safety and comfort. Whereby your petitioner claims extra Commissions for said services. Without such services his said trust would have greatly suffered pecuniarily, and the regular commissions not being sufficient to renumerate your petitioner for said Extra Services during the said year 1858. He therefore prays this Hon. Court to allow him the Sum of six hundred dollars for his extra services to renumerate him for the same during said year 1858. Your Petitioner will ever pray &c (this is the abbreviation of *et cetera* meaning 'and so forth'), M.L. Green

Upon hearing the fore going petition it is considered ordered & judged that the Sum of six hundred dollars be and the same is hereby allowed to Myles L. Green the executor of James A. Everett des[d] for his extra commission for his Services to Est. of said Des[d] for 1858.
   John S. Jobson O.H.C.

Pg 564
December Term 1860
Georgia
Houston County
To the Ordinary of Said County
The petition of Myles L. Green Executor of the last will & Testament of James A. Everettt late of said County deceased showeth that Ann E. Everett one of the daughters of said testator has intermarried with Benjamin W. Sandford that

under the will of said testator the said Benjamin W. Sandford and his wife Ann E. are entitled to have the share or portion of the property of testator both real & personal belonging to said Ann E. set apart according to the provisions of said will. Your petitioner having given notice to the said Benjamin W. Sandford & his wife Ann E. Sandford formerly Ann E. Everett that he would apply at this Term for the appointment of distributors to set apart said share of said Estate prays that the same may be now appointed.

   Jno McGiles Petitioners Attorney

Georgia
Houston County
To Benjamin W. Sandford and his wife Ann E. Sandford formerly Ann E. Everett Take notice that at the December Term of the Court Ordinary of said County I will apply to said Court for the appointment of Commissioners to distribute & set apart your share of the Estate of said testator under the provisions of the Will. This Sixth day of November 1860.

    Myles L. Green, Ex^r of James A. Everett Dec^d

We & each of us acknowledge service of the above notice & waive all further service, this November 6th 1860
   Benjamin W. Sandford
   Ann E. Sandford

Minute Book 'D'
Pages: 97, 153, 154, 253, 254, 273, 295, 296, 297, 330, 355, 356, 372, 396, 463, 464, & 521

Pg 97

Georgia
Houston County

To the Court of Ordinary of said County. The petition of Miles L. Greene Executor of the last will & testament of James A. Everett late of said County Dec^d respectfully showeth that at the December Term of said Court in the year Eighteen hundred & Sixty Distributors or Commissioners were appointed by the Court to appraise the estate real & personal of said James A. Everett & ascertain & set apart the share of Benjamin W. Sandford & Anne E. Sandford his wife formerly Ann E. Everett daughter of testator and that said Commissioners or distributors on the 15th day of January 1861 proceeded to perform said duty except as to the real estate which by consent of the Executor & said Benjamin W. Sandford was left out of said apportionment & division except lots of land NE2075 N÷178 in the Ninth District of said County which was set apart to this said Sandford & his wife at the value or price of five thousand & sixty two dollars & fifty cents & which said Sandford agreed to receive - all of which will more fully appear by the return of said Commissioners or distributors now of file & of record in this Court. Your petitioner further showeth that the period has now arrived when it is desirable & proper that the remainder of the share or portion of said Sandford & his Wife in the real estate of the said testator should according to the provisions of the Will of testator be apportioned & set apart to them. – Your petitioner therefore prays the Court to appoint five discreet & proper persons to complete the apportionment & division formerly made so far as to ascertain & set apart to the said Sandford & his Wife the balance of the real estate to which they are entitled.

 Jno McGiles Atty for Petitioner

Court of Ordinary January 26th 1860
Upon hearing & considering the above petition it is ordered that William H. Hollinshead, William J. Anderson, William R. Brown, Osborne H. Miller & Thomas D. King be & they are hereby appointed commissioners or distributors to appraise the real estate of the said James A. Everett deceased in which the said Benjamin W. Sandford & his wife, Ann E. are entitled to a share & ascertain & set apart the share to which they are entitled under the testator's will & not heretofore received by them.
And it is further ordered that said Commissioners be duly sworn to make a…

Pg 153
Georgia
Houston County
The petitioner Myles L. Green the Executor of James A. Everett deceased showeth that James A. Everett one of the minor children & legatees of said deceased has arrived at the age of 21 years and that under the provisions of the last will and Testament of said deceased he is now entitled to his ¼ share of his said Father's Estate wherefore your petitioner prays that commissioners be appointed to appraise the Estate of said deceased and to divide with four equal shares or lots and to set the same apart by lot or otherwise to the said James Everett on fourth share of the Estate aforesaid & your petitioner will ever prayth.

John S. Johnson Pet Atty

Pg 154

Houston Court of Ordinary in ___tion November 21st 1863. Upon hearing & considering the foregoing petition it is ordered that John F. Troutsman {sic}, Wm C. Anderson W. H. Hollinshead, Wm R. Brown Wm A. Wiggins be and they are hereby appointed to apportion the Estate of the deceased and to set apart and assign to James A. Everett ___ and legatee of said deceased his one fourth share of Estate of said deceased and that they report this action under said appointment to this Court.

 W. T. Swift OHC

Pg 253

Georgia

Houston County

To the Court of Ordinary of said County.

The petition of Myles L. Greene Executor of the last will & testament of James A. Everett late of said County deceased respectfully showeth that in consequence of the emancipation of the Negro slaves formerly belonging to said estate it is impracticable to keep up & carry on the farms belonging to said estate under this change & supervision of Overseers as heretofore done – that the freedmen on said farms account be controlled or induced to work faithfully or continually & it will be difficult with their labor to harvest the crops made this year Besides the estate is losing from the deportations of the Negroes on the stock. Your petitioner believes that it will be better for the estate that the personal property belonging to said Estate be sold and the land rented out for the next year at

least He therefore prays that an order may be passed granting him leave to sell the personal property of said estate upon giving the notice required by law. And your petitioner &c
    John M Giles. Atty for Petitionery

Upon hearing the above & foregoing petition it is ordered by the Court that the said Myles L. Green Executor of the last will & Testament of James A. Everett late of said County deceased have leave to sell the personal property of said estate upon giving the notice required by last that is to say by giving notice thereof in two or more public places in said County at least ten days before the time of sales.
    W. T. Swift O.H.C.

Pg 273
Georgia
Houston County
To the Court of Ordinary of said County.
The petition of Myles L. Greene Executor of the last will & testament of James A. Everett late of said County deceased respectfully showeth that Robert A. Holland has intermarried with Theodocia H. Everett one of the Daughters & legatees of said testator that under the will of said testator this said Robert A. Holland is in right of his said wife entitled to one third part of the laws of said testator now remaining undivided. – Your petitioner therefore prays that five discreet & proper persons may be appointed by the Court to appraise & distribute the real estate of said testator now undivided so far as to ascertain & set apart the share of the said Robert A. Holland in right of his wife Theodocia H. according to the

provisions of the will of testator. – And your petitioner will ever pray &c

 John M. Giles Atty for Petitioner

Wherefore it is considered and ordered by the Court that John F Troutman, William Hollinshead, William J. Anderson, William R. Brown, and Henry Love be & they are hereby appointed to appraise & distribute the real estate of James A. Everett late of said County deceased now remaining undivided so far as to ascertain & set apart the share of Robert A. Holland in right of his wife Theodocia H. under the provision of said testators will.

 W. T. Swift O.H.C.

Pg 295
Georgia
Houston County
February Term 1866
To the Ordinary of said County
The petition of the undersigned Adolphus D. Kendrick, now of the County of Sumter in said State but formerly of the County of Houston first aforesaid respectfully showeth that James A. Everett late of said County, departed this life many years ago leaving a very large estate worth at the time some three hundred thousand dollars, that at the time of his death he left a last will and testament and in which he appointed your petitioner, Miles L. Green and Turner C. Everett the Executors of his said last Will and Testament which said last will and testament soon after the death of said testator was duly proven and admitted to record in the Court of Ordinary of said County of Houston in the month of July 1848 when

your petitioner and said Turner C. Everett were duly qualified as Executors of said will and in the month of September of the same year Miles L. Green the other Executor named and appointed in said will also qualified to execute said will, to whom as well as your petitioner and the said Turner C. Everett letters of testimony issued. And your petitioner further showeth that soon after his said qualification as such Executor to said will he moved to the County of Sumter where he has ever since resided and still resides and has had nothing to do with the execution of said will or the management of the estate of said deceased. Your petitioner further showeth that if the said Turner C. Everett did not at the time of taking out letters testamentary on said will reside in the state of Mississippi, he soon thereafter removed to said state and has there resided ever since, still resides

Pg 296
and intends to reside there. Your petitioner and the said Turner C. Everett leaving the execution of said will and the management of the estate of said deceased entirely to the discretion, prudence & skill of the said Miles L. Green, who still remained a citizen of said County of Houston – now neither of them since the appraisement of the estate of said deceased, had anything to do with the execution of said will or the management of said estate. Your petitioner further showeth that the said Miles L. Green has recently departed this life intestate leaving said will still not fully executed and the real estate of said deceased not settled up. Your petitioner is well satisfied also that the said Turner C. Everett never can or will come back to Georgia to execute said will and settle up said estate even if he as a citizen of another state had a right

to do so. Your petitioner further showeth that he himself has become advanced in life, is in feeble health and utterly unable and incapable of executing said will and settling up said estate. That he would do great injustice to himself, to the estate of said deceased and the legatees if he were to attempt to do so in his advanced state of life and feeble health and that he never shall or will attempt it and absolutely and respectfully resigns said trust. Your petitioner further showeth that it is the interest of said estate and the legatees under the will as he is apprised that the affairs of said estate should receive the earliest possible attention by some one competent to do it, some one near it and willing to do it and which it is impossible for your petitioner or the said Turner C. Everett to do. Your petitioner therefore prays that your honor may at once pass an order revoking & rescinding the letters testamentary so granted to him and to the said Turner C. Everett for the causes and on the grounds aforesaid, and appoint some suitable and proper person or persons Admr or Admrs with will annexed on the estate of said deceased and you petitioner would respectfully suggest Dr. William I. Green and James A. Everett who are willing to take said trust, the first the brother-in-law and the other the son of said deceased as highly competent men for the execution of that trust. Both citizens of said County and both honest, trustworthy, honorable and responsible men and well acquainted with the condition and interest of said estate and of the legatees and whose appointment your petitioner is well apprized would be satisfactory to all concerned or interested. Your petitioner has felt it due to this court, due to himself and due to the estate and legatees of said deceased to give the information herein contained and ask for the causes herein set forth a revocation of the said letters testamentary so granted to him and the said Turner C. Everett not at all asking to be relieved from any responsibility heretofore incurred by him or said Turner C. Everett for any of their actions or doings as Executors of the estate of said James A. Everett deceased but that said estate and legatees may be benefitted thereby and your petitioner will ever pray &c.

  Eli Warren Atty for Adolphus D. Kendrick

The foregoing petition of Adolphus D. Kendrick Executor of the last will and testament of James A. Everett late of this County deceased, is read and considered and being well convinced of the truth of the facts therein stated and set forth and the said Adolphus D. Kendrick and Turner C. Everett the only surviving qualified Executors of the last will and testament of James A. Everett late of this County deceased, both refusing any longer to act as said Executors. The first because of old age, infirmity, and physical disability refuses longer to act as such Executor and the other because of his having moved from the state of Georgia to the state of Mississippi so far from where the estate of said deceased is situs (the place where something is held to be in legal proceedings) as to make it impossible for him to discharge the duties of Executor of the will of said deceased and both of said Executors absolutely resigning their trust and refusing to act any longer as said Executors. It is therefore ordered that the letters testamentary heretofore

Pg 297
granted by the Court of Ordinary of this County to the said Adolphus D. Kendrick and Turner C. Everett as the Executors

of the last will and testament of the said James A. Everett be and they are hereby revoked, repealed and set aside without prejudice to the creditors of the estate of said deceased or the legatees under the will for anything they did or omitted to do while they had their letters testamentary. And whereas the said Adolphus D. Kendrick and Turner C. Everett have recommended to this court William I. Green the brother-in-law of said deceased and James A. Everett Jr. the son and older son of said deceased as suitable and proper persons to be appointed Administrators on the said estate of said deceased with the will of said deceased annexed and no objection being made to them but on the contrary being fully satisfied that their appointment as such is entirely satisfactory to the legatees under the will of said deceased. And the said William I. Green and James A. Everett Jr. being willing to take upon themselves the Administration of the estate of said deceased with the will annexed and both of them having taken the oath and given bond as in such cases required, it is ordered that the said William I. Green and the said James A. Everett Jr., both citizens of this County be and they are hereby appointed Administrators de bonis non (Latin for 'of goods not administered') with the will annexed of the said James A. Everett late of the County deceased. And that the estate of said deceased having long since been appraised and the appraisement filed away in this Court, the appointment of appraisers of said estate is now dispensed with.

Court of Ordinary Houston County
February Term 1866   W. T. Swift O.H.C.

August Term 1866
Georgia

Houston County
To the Ordinary of said County
The petition of Wm. I. Greene and James A. Everett de bonis non with the will annexed of James A. Everett late of said county deceased represent to your honor that there are certain lands belonging to said deceased in the county of Pulaski of this state and in and adjoining the towns of Hawkinsville and Hartford in said county, which is to the interest of said estate to have sold for the distribution of the proceeds of the sale thereof among the legatees of said deceased. Your petitioner therefore prays your honor to grant and pass an order allowing your petitioners to sell said lands and your petitioners will ever pray &c.
    Warren & Warren – Petitioners Atty.

Pg 355
October Term 1866
Georgia
Houston County
Court of Ordinary
Wm. I. Green and James A. Everett Admrs. with the will annexed of James A. Everett late of Houston County dec^d having petitioned this court for leave to sell some of the real estate of said deceased for the purpose of a division thereof among the legatees thereto – and it appearing that such a sale is necessary for such division – and they having given due and legal notice of their intention to apply for such leave – it is therefore ordered that the said Wm I. Green and James A. Everett Admrs. as aforesaid have leave to sell the following lands belonging to the estate of the said James A. Everett deceased. To wit – One acre in the town of Hawkinsville in

Pulaski County and one half acre lot in the same town – letter O. Fractional lot No 896 in the 21st dist of originally Wilkinson now Pulaski County containing 88 acres more so up – Town lots No 18 and 11. Letter C. 15 and 16. Letter D. 15 and 15. Letter H - triangular square on letter T in the Town of Hawkinsville in said County of Pulaski – Fractional lots No 225 and 226 – and which sale is for division as aforesaid

Pg 356
And is to take place at the Court House in the County of Pulaski after giving forty days legal and published notice of the time and place of sale.
    W. T. Swift O.H.C.

January Term 1867
Georgia Houston County
To the Hon. the Ordinary of said County
The petition of Wm. I. Green and James A. Everett Jnr. Adms. with the will annexed of James A. Everett Snr. Late of said County deceased respectfully showeth that the said James A. Everett deceased owned & possessed at the time of his death about six hundred (600) acres of land mostly woodland situated in the state of Alabama & that the said deceased also owned & possessed at the time of his death a large quantity of land say some five thousand (5000) acres in the state of Mississippi also mostly woodland. Your petitioners further showeth that all its legatees of the said deceased being six in number & of age except two who are yet minors. That it seems to be impossible to divide advantageously to the legatees of said deceased the said lands in Alabama and Mississippi & the said legatees are both those who have

arrived at the age of 21 years & then who have not arrived at that age, are decisons that said land should be at once or as favorable opportunities may offer, sold for a division of them & the proceeds of the sale of them between the legatees of said deceased. Your petitioner therefore prays that your Honor may pass an order allowing us or either one of us to sell at private sale as Administrators with the will annexed of said deceased all the lands owned by the said James A. Everett deceased at the time of his death situated & being in the states of Alabama & Mississippi & divide the proceeds of the sale of the same among the legatees of said deceased as the lands should be divided if not sold, & your Petitioners will ever pray &c.

Wm. I. Green & James A. Everett Jnr. Admrs. with the will annexed of James A. Everett Snr. By Warren & Warren Their Attorneys at Law

The foregoing petition of Wm. I. Green & James A. Everett Jnr. Administrators with the will annexed of James A. Everett Snr. Deceased is __ & consider it hereby ordered that the said Wm. I. Green & James A. Everett Jnr. Administrators with the will annexed of James A. Everett Snr late of this County deceased have leave to sell at private sale all the lands of James A. Everett Snr. Deceased situated & being in the states of Alabama & Mississippi & which belonged to the said deceased at the time of his death & to divide the proceeds of the sale of the said lands as the lands themselves ... (continues to another page which I do not have)

Pg 396
June Term 1867

Georgia
Houston County
To the Ordinary of said Court
The petition of Henry P. Everett respectfully showeth that he is a son of James A. Everett late of said County deceased that he is a legatee under the last will and testament of said deceased that he has arrived at the age of twenty one years and is desirous of having partitioned and set apart to him his share of the land to which he is entitled under said last will and testament of said deceased in the plantation of the said deceased known as the Home Place. And your petitioner is in duty bound &c. June 18, 1867.
  Warren & Warren Petitioners Atty.
Court of the Ordinary Houston County June 18, 1867
The foregoing petition is considered and it is ordered that William R. Brown, William… (continues to another page I do not have)

Pg 463
July Term 1868
July 17 1868
Georgia
Houston County
To the Ordinary of said County
The petition of William I. Green & James A. Everett Jr. Administrators with the will annexed of James A. Everett Sr. deceased showeth that they have nearly or quite settled with all the Heirs & Legatees of said deceased as far as the property of the deceased in this State is concerned – except with John F. Everett a son of said deceased who is yet

Pg 464

a minor & without a guardian but who will be 21 years of age June 1869 (June of next year) and that most of the property of said Estate now in our hands consisting chiefly of lands choses in action & money due to said estate belongs to the said John F. Everett a minor Legatee of said deceased – that there is some 3000 acres of the lands & much of it in a fine state of cultivation and notes to the amount of some five thousand dollars.

Your petitioners pray your honor to pass an order allowing & authorizing them as administrators as aforesaid will the effects of said Estate & of the said John F. Everett to place or cause to be placed on the said lands a good suitable dwelling & necessary & convenient outhouses and to purchase as for & supply him the said John F. Everett with the necessary of horses & mules cattle & hogs & supplies of meat & corn & suitable farming utensils & implements to carry on & work a farm on his the said John F. Everett lands for the next year & until he shall arrive at the age of 21 years as your petitioners believe it to be to the best interest of the said John F. Everett thus to apply & appropriate & use the property ___ in our hands as administrators as aforesaid that belongs to the said minor July 21 1868.

  Warren & Warren
  Attys for Petitioners

Court of Ordinary Houston County in Chambers July 31 1868 The foregoing petition of William I. Green & James A. Everett Jr. administrators with the Will annexed of James A. Everett Sr. deceased read Considered & allowed and it is therefore

ordered that the said Wm. I. Green & James A. Everett Jr. Administrators as aforesaid be and they are hereby authorized and allowed with the money in their hands as such to place or cause to be placed on the lands of said deceased that belong to John F. Everett a minor heir & Legatee of James A. Everett Sr. deceased a good suitable dwelling house & necessary convenient outhouses kitchens negro houses Cribbs Smokehouses Gin house &c & to purchase for & supply him the said John F. Everett with the necessary stock of horses & mules cattle & hogs corn & meat & necessary supplies & suitable farming utensils & implements to enable him to work & carry on a farm on his the said John F. Everetts land for & during the year 1868 & until he shall arrive at the age of 21 years & that the said administrators return their proceedings in the premises in their nearest annual return to this Court.
 W. T. Swift O.H.C.

Pg 521
June Term 1869
Georgia
Houston County
To the Ordinary of said Court
The petition of Wm. I. Green and J.A. Everett Admrs de bonis non as with the will annexed of James A. Everett deceased showeth this they have fully discharged the duties assigned them as such Admrs. that nothing more needs to be done, and that the estate of the deceased has been fully administered under the will of deceased, the lands in Ala. and Miss. could not be sold without an order from Court allowing it. Such order was applied for and obtained, but owing to the low

price of lands & the difficulty of finding a purchaser at fair prices, it was deemed best not to sell. The land accordingly was retained by the Admrs. and have been turned over in kind to the heirs and devises ___ to them. Your petitioner therefore pray that letters dismissory may be granted them in conformity to law. And your petitioner will ever pray &c

    Warren & Grise Petrs Atty's

Appendix D—Maps

The following sketch maps provide location information for this family history. Enough information is provided to assist in locating these places on more detailed maps than given here. Any known locations of specific family interest (like towns, cemeteries, and homesteads) are noted. In some cases, notes explain additional information about these locations.

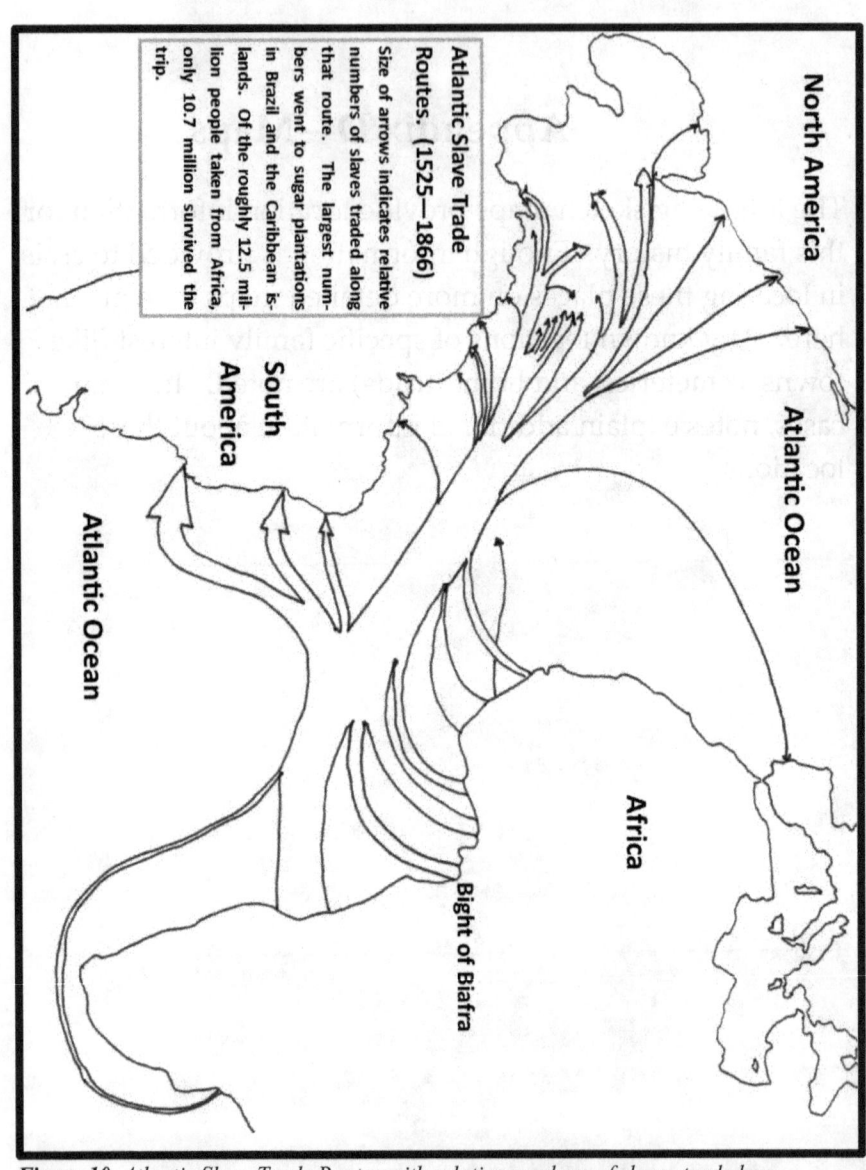

Figure 10 Atlantic Slave Trade Routes with relative numbers of slaves traded on particular route depicted by the size of the arrows. The Bight of Biafra is the probable starting point for the African side of the family based on DNA evidence.

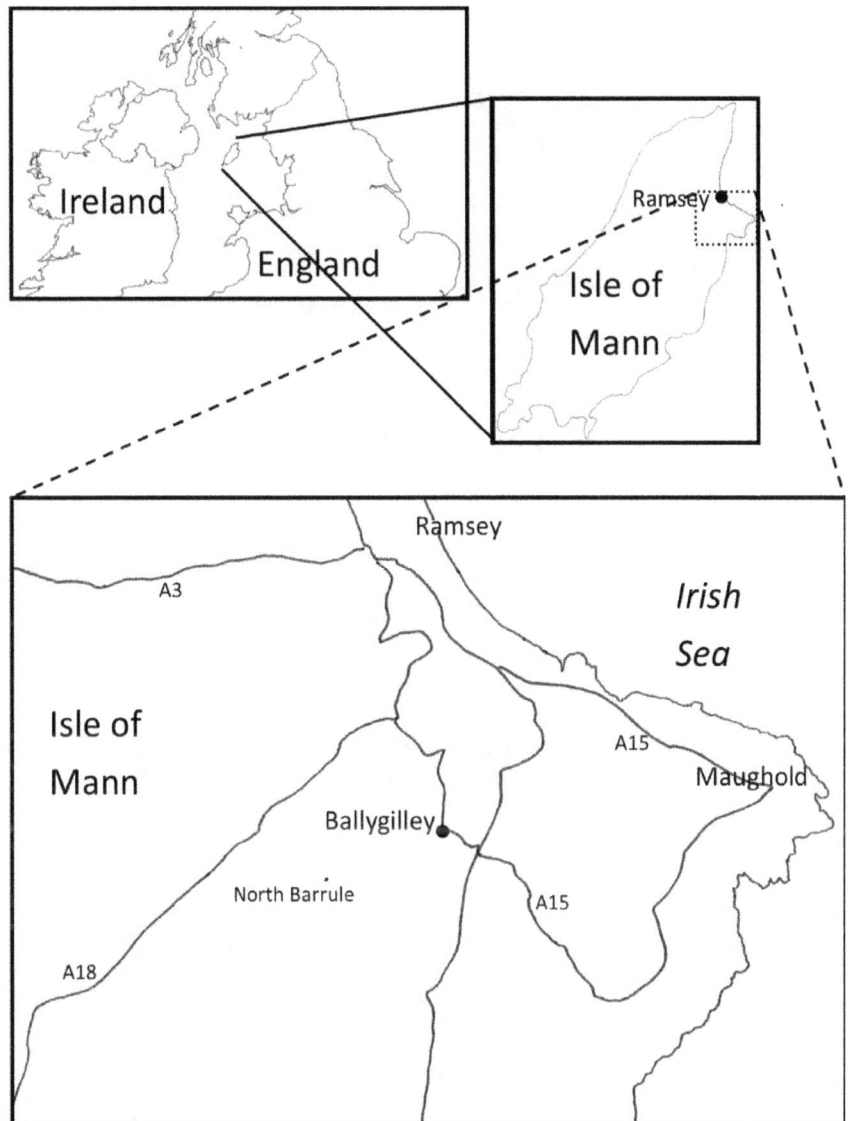

Figure 11 Location of Ballygilley, Isle of Mann the birthplace of Robert Looney (b. 1692) from whom the Looney side of the family descends.

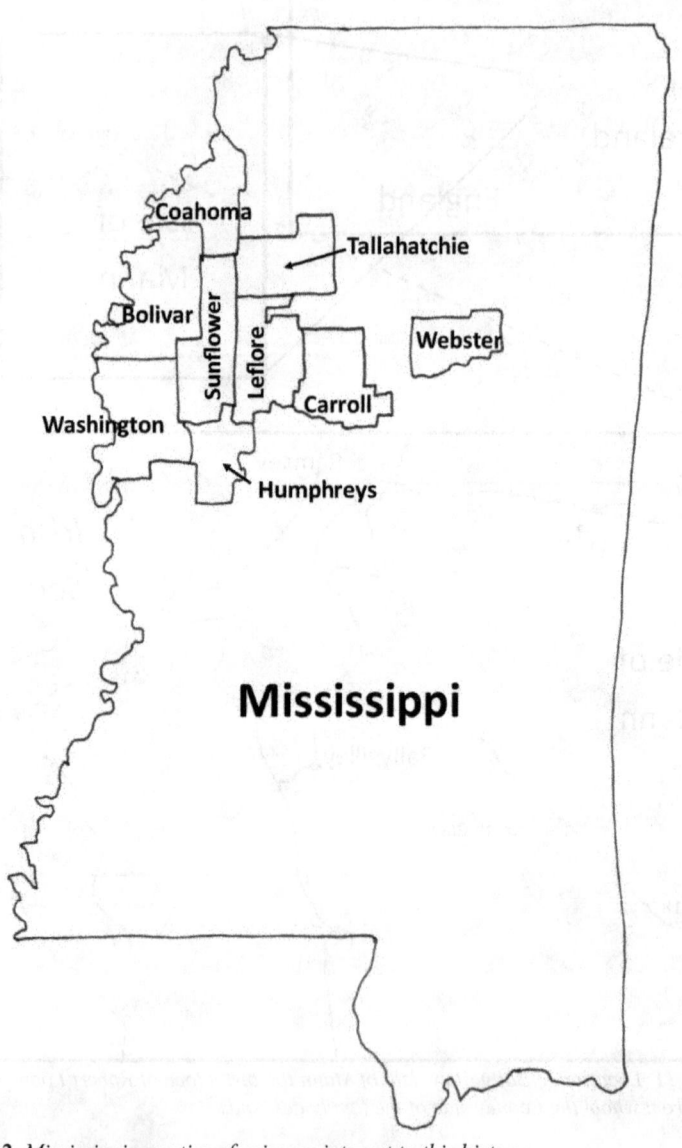

Figure 12 Mississippi counties of primary interest to this history.

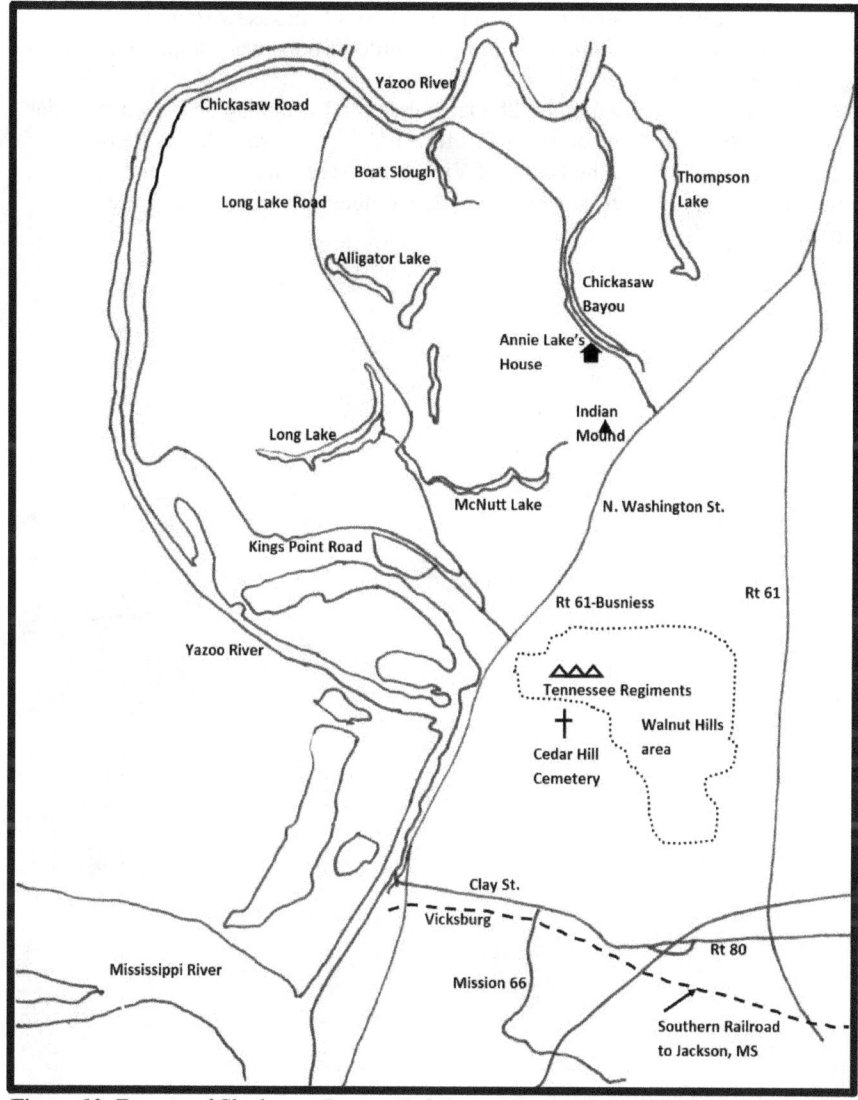

Figure 13 *Terrain of Chickasaw Bayou, Vicksburg, Mississippi with the location of the Tennessee Regiments.*

Notes:
1. Col. Vaughn's unit arrived via the Southern Railroad during the afternoon and evening of the 27th of December 1862 and marched into positions in the Walnut Hills overlooking Chickasaw Bayou.

2. General Sherman's planned attack was across Chickasaw Bayou near Annie Lake's House toward Indian Mound. The union troops were stopped by Confederate resistance.

3. William C. Looney died on 28 December 1862. He may be buried at Cedar Hill Cemetery where most of the Confederate soldiers from the Battle of Chickasaw Bayou and the Battle of Vicksburg were buried. He is not in a marked grave, but there are thousands of Confederate graves which are unmarked in this cemetery.

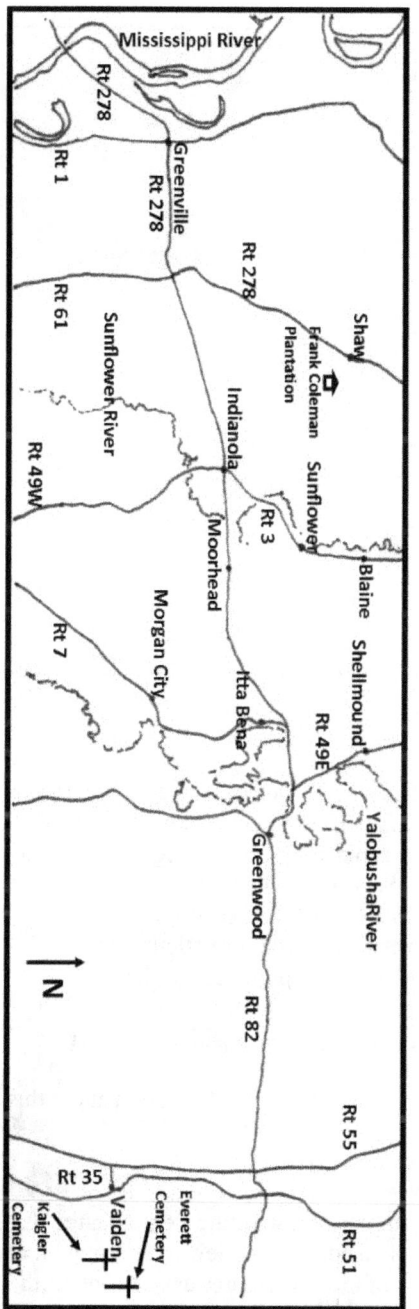

Figure 14 Sites of interest along Route 82 in Mississippi with regard to this history.

Notes:
1. Turn this map sideways for best viewing. The map covers roughly 82 miles from the Mississippi River to the far right area depicting the vicinity of Vaiden. Several of the roads change designations after crossing another road and changes are marked.
2. Farms in Mississippi are commonly called plantations.
3. The town of Webb is located on Rt. 49E north of Shellmound.
4. The Everett and Kaigler Cemeteries are most probably on land that was part of their respective plantations so the locations of these cemeteries tell us where Nellie Everett and her relatives lived prior to Emancipation.
5. The Everett Cemetery is located at GPS Coordinates: Latitude: 33.36330, Longitude: -89.68420.
6. The Kaigler Cemetery is located at GPS Coordinates: Latitude: 33.33727, Longitude: -89.69388.

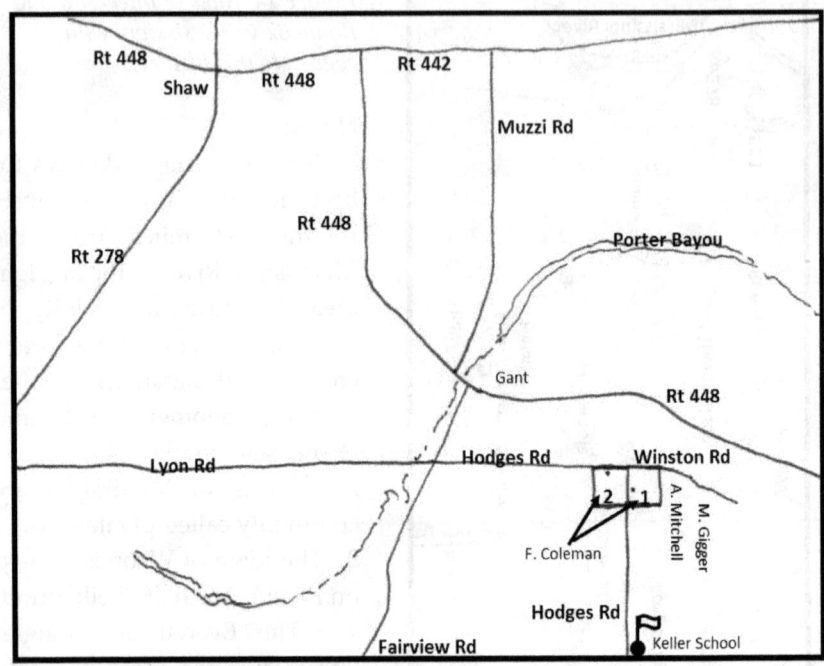

Figure 15 Location of Frank C. Coleman's Plantation south-east of Shaw, Mississippi.

Notes:
1. Parcel #1 was purchased 14 Nov 1896; sold 12 Oct 1936. Legal description: Northwest quarter of northwest quarter of Section 27, Township 20N, R5W.
2. Parcel #2 was purchased 10 Nov 1903; sold 1 Apr 1918. Legal description: Northeast quarter of northeast quarter of Section 28, Township 20N, R5W. Latitude: 33.5579573 Longitude: -90.7108488. Elevation: 128 feet.
3. This map combines present day information with information from the 1927 Ownership Map of Sunflower County, Mississippi prepared by Horace S. Stansel and an old topographic map.
4. In addition to noting the F. Coleman Plantation, the positions of other properties owned by people mentioned in this history are noted.
5. The Keller School no longer exists and no additional information about this school has surfaced thus far.
6. The plantation is 6.7 miles from Shaw using Rt. 448.
7. Hodges Road makes a 90° turn between the two properties.
8. The small dots on the parcels designate where a structure existed in the past. The Coleman family lived at parcel #1. The house had a few trees around it and a couple of outbuildings behind it. None of these structures exist today. Both parcels are completely given over to cropland.

Figure 16 Alabama counties of primary interest to this history.

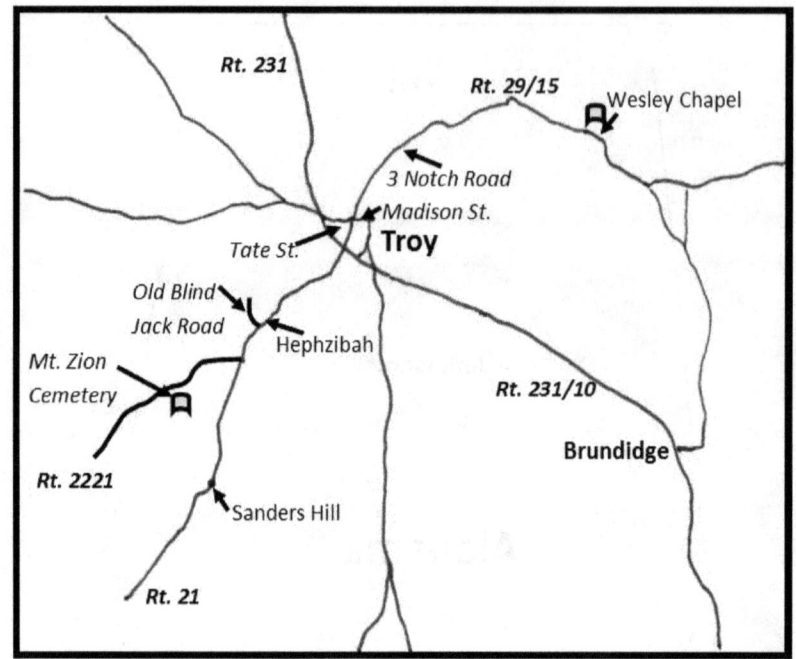

Figure 17 Enlargement of Pike County, Alabama depicting locations of particular interest.

Notes:

1. Troy is the county seat of Pike County. Some members of our family lived here over a great number of years. The Rhode Coleman family moved into the area in the 1850's. This family and some of their children lived in town during some periods of time and at farms in the surrounding area at others. At one point they lived closer to Brundidge.
2. Rhode Coleman, Jr. is buried in the Wesley Chapel graveyard.
3. A possible slaveholder for the Reuben Sanders family (James Nathaniel Sanders) built a house on Blind Jack Road. If James Nathaniel Sanders was the slaveholder, then Reuben and family lived there until Emancipation. They certainly were living next to James Nathaniel on 1 July 1870.
4. Mary J. Coleman Siler is buried in Mt. Zion Cemetery.

Figure 18 Georgia counties of primary interest to this history.

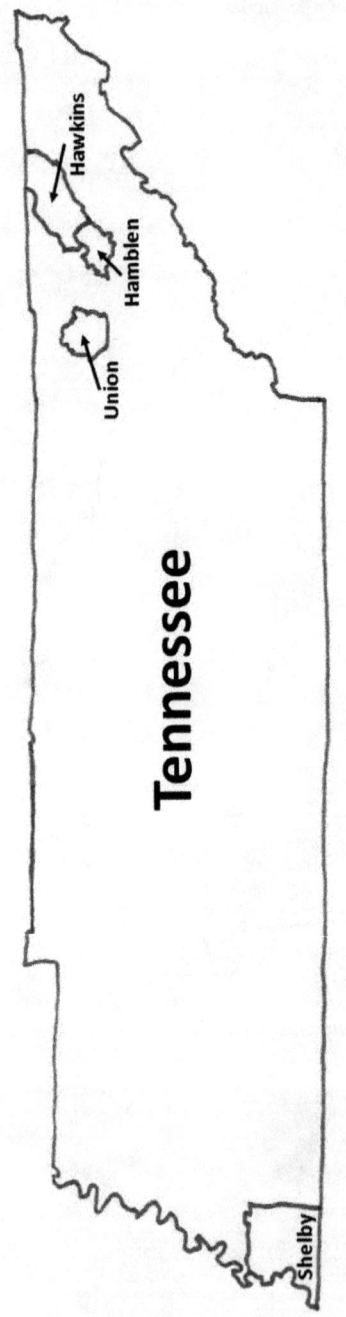

Figure 19 Tennessee counties of primary interest to this history.

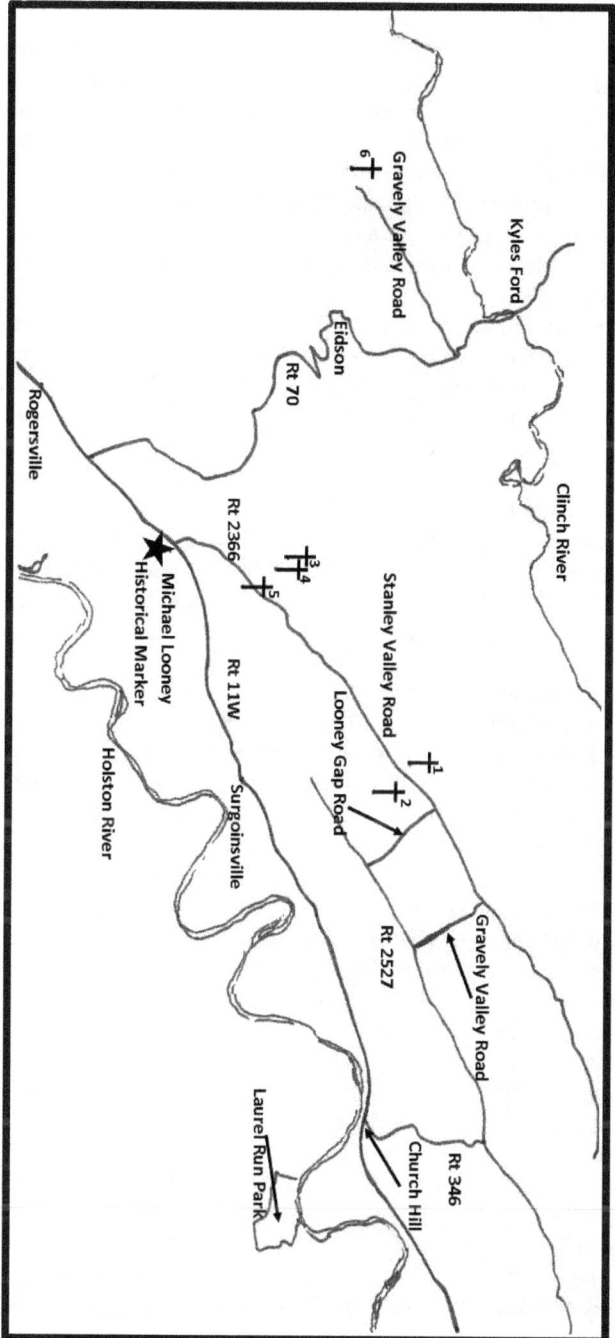

Figure 20 Looney sites of interest in Hawkins County, Tennessee.

Notes on Looney Sites of Interest:
1. Michael Looney Cemetery located at Lat: 36.53326 Long: -82.86351. This cemetery began about 1783, when Peter Looney (b. 1783 d. 1786), the three-year-old son of Michael Looney (b. 1758 d. 1839) and Temperance (Cross) Looney (b. 1752), died and was buried there. The cemetery is located on the old Michael Looney home place. In addition to family members, a number of Looney slaves were buried at this site. A Looney descendant, Cecile Jennings Chmelik, who at one time owned the property, estimates there were between 40 to 50 such graves marked with rocks, only of few of which had any inscription. The property was sold outside the family in 1995.
2. Looney-Mauk Cemetery located at Lat: 36.52042 Long: -82.85146. On the south side of Pine Street near Cold Springs Road, south west of Looney Gap Road, this cemetery is located on land reportedly once owned by William "Gravely Bill" Looney, a grandson of Michael Looney. The documented burials include Gravelly Bill's two sons (Samuel Looney (b. 7 Jul 1837 d. 7 Jul 1909) and William Pickney Looney (b. 11 Mar 1843 d. 4 Oct 1920)) and a daughter, Lousannah Looney (b. 17 Jun 1833 d. 3 Nov 1902).
3. Absalom Starnes Cemetery located at Lat: 36.49532 Long: -82.95099. The cemetery is located on a hill about 1/8 mile south of the old Absalom Starnes Looney homeplace in Hickory Cove. Absalom Starnes Looney (b. 30 Jan 1832 d. 6 Jul 1901) was a son of Absalom David Looney who was one of Michael Looney's sons.
4. Looney-Pearson Cemetery located at Lat: 36.48970 Long: -82.94190. Located on the second homeplace of Absalom David Looney (b. 5 Mar 1790 d. 12 Dec 1862), son of Michael, about ½ mile north east of his original home. It was established not later than 1862, the date of Absalom's death. He and his wife (Sarah Jane "Sallie" Starnes (b. 30 Jan 1799 d. 8 Feb 1874)), a son (John Blair Looney (b. 14 Aug 1828 d. 10 Dec 1906)), a daughter (Sarah Jane Looney Pearson (b. 25 Mar 1835 d. 11 Mar 1911)), and other family are buried in this plot that is about 100 yards east of the house at the foot of the garden. Absalom David Looney willed this farm to his son, Orville Bradley Looney (b. 11 Oct 1837 d. 19 Sep 1863), and in the event of his death without issue, to his daughters Margaret Catherine Looney (b. 5 Mar 1830 d. 17 Dec 1872), Sarah Jane Sallie "Sadie" Looney, and Susan Shanks Looney (b. 10 May 1840 d. 10 Sep 1905). Unmarried, Orville died at the Battle of Chicamauga. Sarah (Sadie) and her husband, Pryor Lee Pearson, bought out her sisters and made their home on the farm. As the years passed the cemetery became known as the "Pearson Cemetery".
5. Looney Cemetery located at Lat: 36.47854 Long: -82.93591. The cemetery is on the south side of Stanley Valley Road north of Meadowview Road and includes members of the Joseph Payne Looney (son of John Payne Looney who was one Michael Looney's sons) line.
6. Looney-Shields (now Bray) Cemetery located at Lat: 36.51530 Long: -83.09890. The Looney-Shields Cemetery is on the Israel Looney homeplace in

Black Sheep Hollow on the south side of Sweet Creek Road, north west of Rogersville between Hickory Cove and Stanley Valley. Joseph Israel Looney, (son of Absalom David) and his wife, Willie Ann Shields, and several members of the Shield's family are buried here. Their daughter, Mrs. Florence (Looney) Bray married Fidello Bray. The farm was inherited by grandson, Phipps Bray. At some point in time during the Bray ownership of the property, the cemetery name changed to the Bray Cemetery.

7. The Michael Looney Historical Marker 1B49 is located north of Rogersville near the intersection of Route 11W and Route 2366 (Stanley Valley Road).

8. There are two Gravely Valley Roads in Hawkins County; both are marked on the map. William "Gravely Bill" Looney lived on one of them, probably the one near Looneys Gap Road as he and William Carroll Looney and their families were reported to be quite close with the children treating both places as "home".

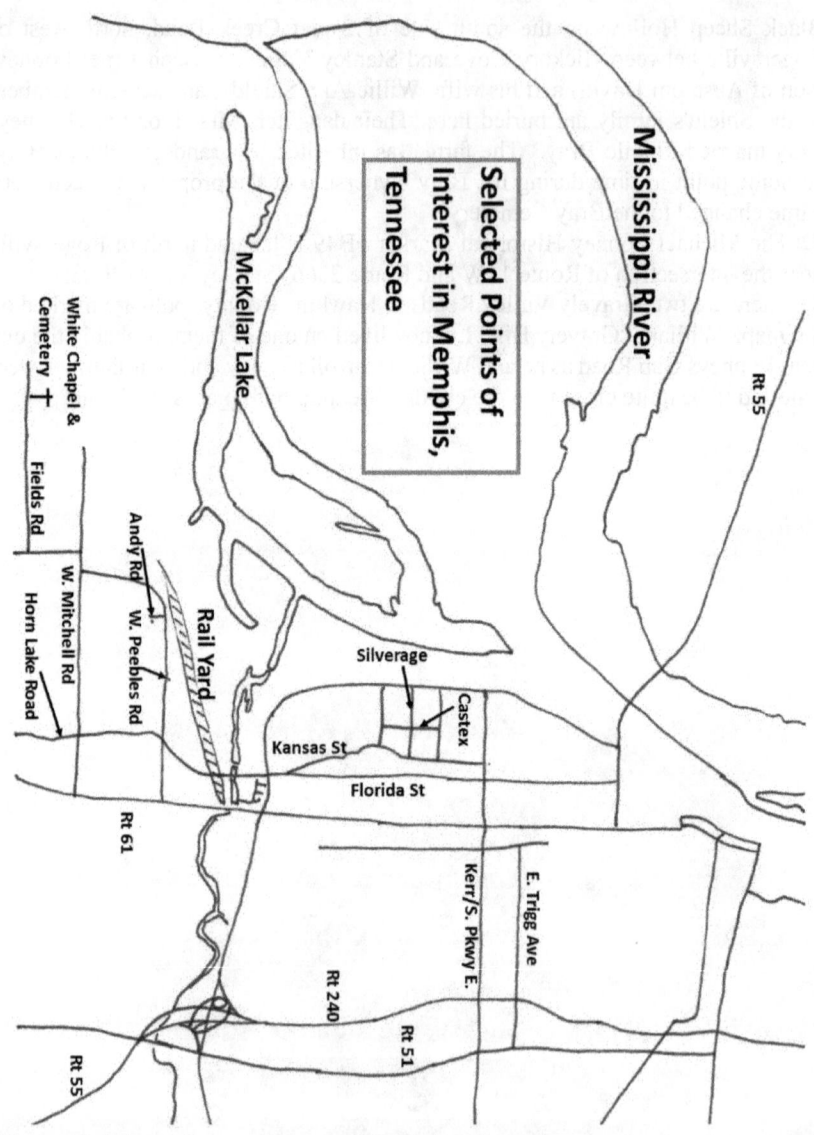

Figure 21 *Selected Points of Interest in Memphis, Tennessee*

Notes:
1. James K. Looney and family lived on the west side of Horn Lake Road in the late 1800's and first few years of 1900.
2. Delia (Hart) Keglar lived at the intersection of Kerr and Kansas at one point.

3. Solomon and Lucy (Looney) Phillips lived on Silverage at the intersection with Castex until 1922. Solomon had a barbershop on Florida Street in 1922.
4. In 1920, Arthur and Minnie (Lott) Reed lived on the north side of Silverage 10 west of Kansas.
5. Katherine Looney is buried at White Chapel on Fields Road. She lived on Andy Road.
6. Burrell Looney (b. 1889) lived at 400 W. Peebles Road at the time of his death.

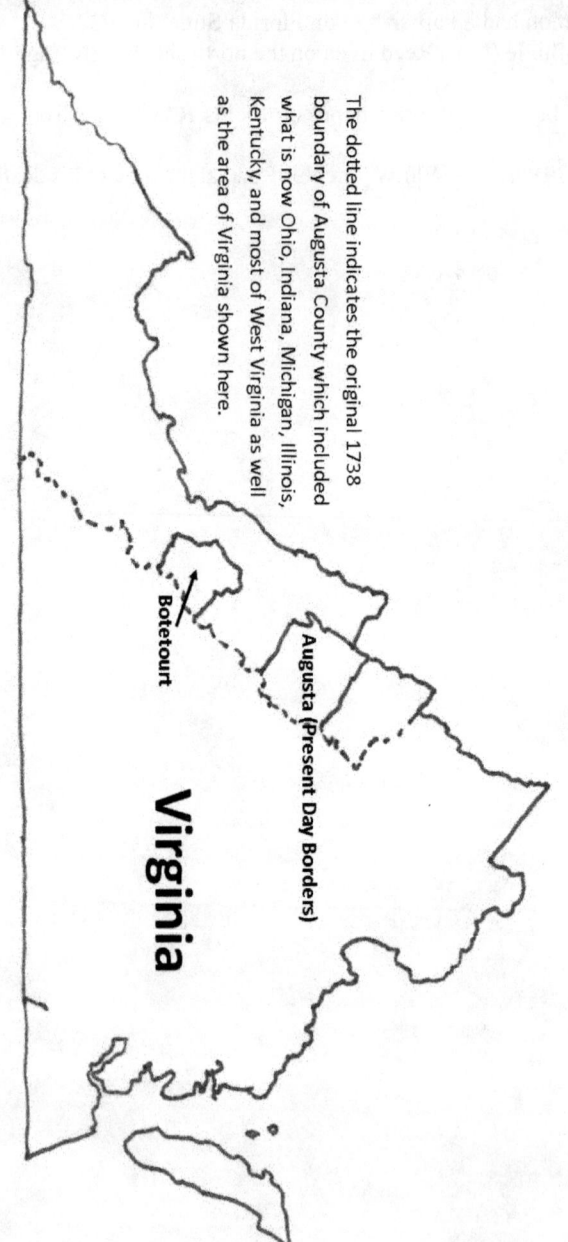

Figure 22 Virginia counties of interest to this history.

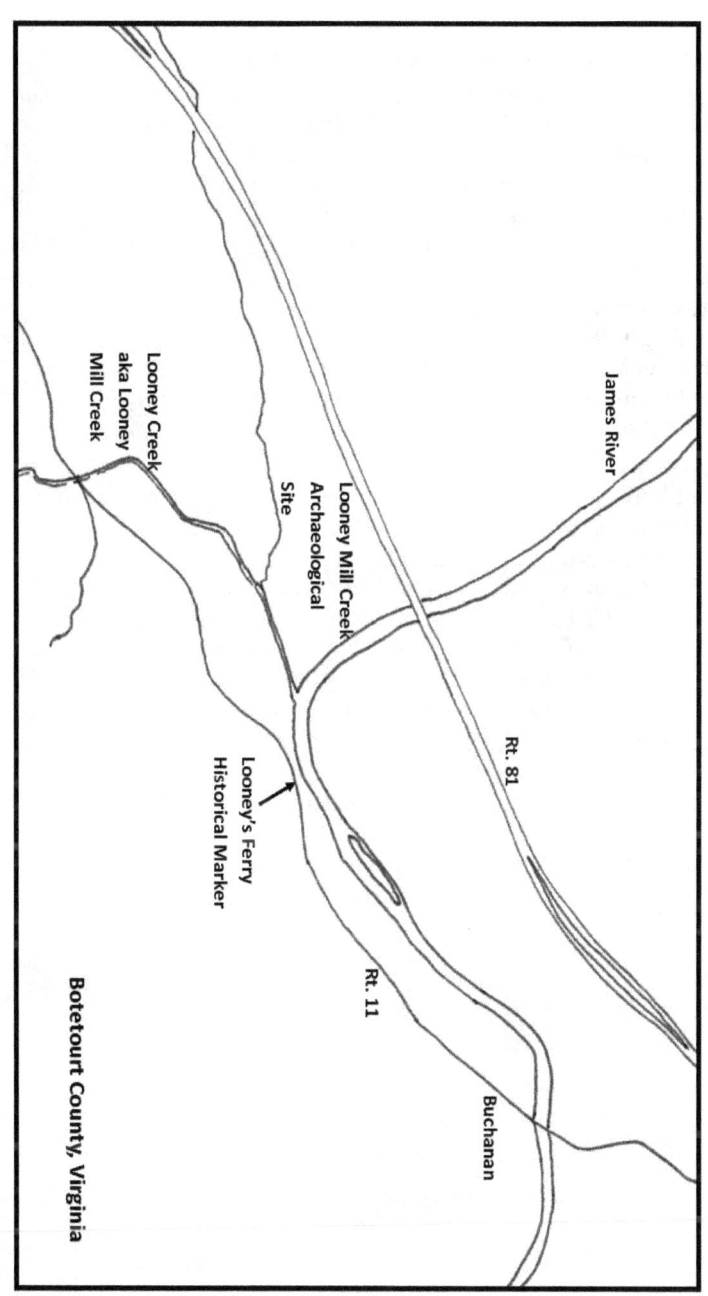

Figure 23 Robert Looney Homestead at Looney Creek, Botetourt County, Virginia.

Notes:
1. Virginia Historical Marker A91 Looney's Ferry. *"Looney's Ferry, established in 1742, was the first crossing over James River in this region. On the other side of the river was Cherry Tree bottom, home of Colonel John Buchanon, and above the mouth of this creek stood Fort Fauquier, 1758-1763."* Marker placed in 1934 at 18288 Main Street (Route 11) Buchanan, VA 24066. Marker is on the right when traveling south about 0.2 miles south of the intersection of Main Street and James River Terrace. GPS Location: 37.518387, -79.697603.
2. The Robert Looney ferry was part of what became known as the "Great Philadelphia Wagon Road" leading from Philadelphia, Pennsylvania through the Shennadoah River Valley to Augusta, Georgia. Refering to the Robert Looney Ferry, Emily McMullan Williams who studied the McMullan family history wrote *"The ferry license for this crossing was granted by the Orange Court at the time the road was blazed to wagon width."*
3. The Robert Looney homestead originally consisted of 250 acres with an additional 400 acres added later.
4. Looney's Creek was originally named Looney's Mill Creek and "Looney" is frequently spelled "Luney" or "Lunie" in older documents.
5. The Looney Mill Creek Site was added to the U.S. National Register of Historic Places on 3 August 1978 (Reference Number 78003007). It is privately owned and consists of 1.5 acres of land.
6. Robert Looney's Fort (1755-1759) was built on the north side of Looney Creek, west of town and south of the James River. In 1756 this fort was visited by Colonel George Washington. The site was excavated in 1968.
7. Fort Fauquier (1758-1763) was a Virginia colonial militia fort that replaced Looney's Fort.
8. The elevation of the homestead site is about 700 ft. above sea level.
9. Buchanan is roughly 50 miles by road from Lynchburg, Virginia.

Appendix E — Mortality Information

Figure 24 Average life span based on birth year. Note the large increase between 1930 and 1950 largely based on the discovery and widespread use of antibiotics and immunizations.

Birth Year	1850	1890	1910	1930	1950	1970	1990
White men	38	42	50	59	66	68	73
White women	40	44	54	63	72	75	79
All other men	N/A	N/A	34	48	59	61	67
All other women	N/A	N/A	35	50	63	69	75

Figure 25 Causes of Death compared for 1850, 1900, and 2013. Infectious diseases are bolded.

1850	1900	2013
Tuberculosis	**Pneumonia or influenza**	Heart Disease
Dysentary/diarrhea	**Tuberculosis**	Cancer
Cholera	**Gastrointestinal infection**	Noninfectious respiratory diseases
Malaria	Heart Disease	Accidents
Typhoid Fever	Cerebrovascular disease (such as stroke)	Cerebrovascular disease
Pneumonia	Nephropathies (kidney disease)	Alzheimer's
Diphtheria	Accidents	Diabetes
Scarlet Fever	Cancer	**Pneumonia or influenza**
Meningitis	Senility	Nephropathies
Whooping Cough	**Diphtheria**	Suicide

The largest drops in mortality risk occurred in children from birth to age 14. As an example, between 1935 and 2010 the largest decrease occurred in children ages 1 to 4 which fell by 94%. Changes in medical care (with antibiotics and immunizations leading the way) and availability, improved sanitation and nutrition, and vector control have greatly contributed to the marked increase in lifespans.

Index

To clarify entries where different people had the same name there are notations to indicate which person is referenced. Sometimes a birth year is given. In other instances a relationship is cited. The list includes names of family members, historical figures, experts in areas of interest, and community members who shaped our family's history. Women are indexed by their maiden surnames. Some women who would have been known or mentioned among the family only by a married name have a reference index entry directing readers to the maiden surname listing. There are a couple of males who changed their surnames and a similar procedure has been followed.

Abbington
   Elizabeth 87, 102
Anderson
   William C. 263
   William J. 250, 255, 256, 262, 265
Andrew
   James O. 239
Ardis
   Fred 39
Ashley
   Monroe, Jr. 168
   Virda Thelma. *See* Virda Thelma Phillips (b. 1943)
Austin
   David N. 98, 257, 258
Baker
   Annie Bell 181, 184
   Phebee 184
Baldwin
   T. B. 122
Banks
   Elizabeth (b. 1665) 23
   Elizabeth wife of Thomas 23
   Thomas 23
Barnes
   Frederick "Jack" 219
   Gertha Lee "Beauty" 219
   J. B. 219
   Jessie 219, 222
   Julia Lee "Bae" 219, 220
   L. C. 219
   L. V. 219
   Lemmie 219
   Lenora 222
   Martha 222
   Mary 222
   Matilda 222
   Nathaniel "Nate" (b. 1930).. 219, 220
   Nathaniel "Ned" (b. 1908) ... 219, 221, 222, 224
   Ned (b. 1877) 221, 222, 223

Ruth Mae (b. 1907)... See Ruth Mae Hunter
Ruth Mae (b. 1934)......146, 206, 207, 208, 211, 219, 220
Baruchman
   Bessie...................................111
Battle
   Ernestine Phillips..................... ii
Beatty
   Henrietta..................75, 117, 118
Beavers
   Herman Lee..........................201
Bedford
   Ophelia..........................197, 198
Bivings
   Karl Stanley..................200, 201
Blackmon
   Clarence...............................147
Blair
   Carnelia................................198
   Manella................................197
Booker
   Cilla.......................................132
   Daniel...................................132
   Egusta Mae "Gussie"....133, 134
   George A. 135, 137
   Gilbert..................................132
   Handy...........................132, 133
   Jane......................................137
   John (b. 1875).......132, 135, 137
   John (b. 1896)......................133
   John (b. 1907)......................132
   Joseph...................................137
   Lillie Bell.....127, 129, 132, 133, 134, 137, 139
   Mary.....................................137
   Minnie..........*See* Minnie Gordon
   Tom.......................................132
Bowman
   Viola....................................127
Bray

Fidello.....................................291
Phipps.....................................291
Briggs
   Bettie....................................205
   Isaac......................146, 204, 205
   James....................................205
   Julia......................................204
   Lee..205
   Mary.....................................205
   Tom......................................204
Brock
   Allen.....................................222
Brown
   Jack..38
   William R......262, 263, 265, 273
Burks
   Jesse James................i, 151, 160
Bynum
   James Sugars........................238
   Sugars.............................88, 238
Cadenhead
   Elizabeth Naomi.....................58
Caldwell
   Tom......................................134
Canada
   Bertha..................................112
Carroll
   Charles.................................131
Chmelik
   Cecile Jennings....................290
Cobb
   Deborah...............................174
Coleman
   Alph.......................................38
   Anna......................................36
   Annie.....................................41
   Arter "Art".......................36, 40
   Charles..................................41
   Dixie......................................41
   Dora........151, 160, *See* Savanna Coleman

Elbert 140
Ella 45
Emily 45
Fannie 38
Frank C. 35, 38, 44, 51, 142, 148, 150, 151, 161, 216, 284
Georgia A. 38
Harriet .... *See* Harriet Williams
Henry 140
James 41
James C. 37
Joe 36
John 35
Julia (b. 1854) 35
Julia (b. 1894) 46
Lafayette 38
Lizzie 36, 40
Martha 34, 35, 36
Mary (b.1906) 41
Mary J. 36, 39, 41, 43, 286
Milton 34, 35, 38
Pernella 151, 158, 159
Pernella Emma 46
Rhode (b. 1833) ... 34, 35, 38, 39, 40, 41, 43, 44, 286
Rhode (b. 1870) .. 36, 38, 40, 286
Rhode (b. 1896) 46, 52
Robert 35, 38
Sarah (b. 1886) 46
Sarah (b. 1915) ..... 151, 158, *See* Sarah Webb
Savanna 160
Sina 38
Tobe 37
Walter (b. 1890) 46
Walter (b. 1908) 41
Willie 45, 111, 142, 150, 151, 158, 216
Collins
   J. J. 39
   Valentine 24
Coppelpower
   Katherine 105

Coss
   Randall 122
Cox
   Cary S. 249
   Minnie 52
   Wayne Wellington 52
Crawford
   Jonathon Alex 68
   William Harris 90
Criss
   Emma Virginia 36, 50
Cross
   David C. 196
   Temperance (b. 1752) 290
Crowder
   R. D. 174
Crowley
   H. W. 130
Dalton
   Perry W. 39, 54
Davis
   Fannie 186
   Henry 186
   Joseph E. 97
Downing
   Thomas 23
Duncan
   James E. 244
Dunwoody
   James 94, 240
Dye
   Sandra Webb ii
Edwards
   Cornelius E. 169
English
   Sampson 92
Everett
   Allen 71, 107
   Ann Elizabeth 93, 98, 100, 241, 242, 260, 261, 262

Bearl/Burrell 71, 74, 95, 104, 107, 108
Burrell 239
Caroline 95, 239
Charles (b. 1780) 88, 237
Charles H. 88, 91, 238
Charlotte 74, 76, 108
Early 95, 239
Evaline 74, 107
George C. 89, 102, 103, 238
Henry (b. 1760) 87, 102
Henry Peter 93, 97, 98, 101, 241, 273
James Abbington (b. 1788) 87, 89, 90, 91, 92, 94, 95, 96, 98, 100, 101, 102, 103, 105, 106, 108, 236, 243, 244, 245, 246, 248, 249, 250, 251, 252, 253, 254, 255, 256, 257, 258, 259, 260, 261, 262, 263, 264, 265, 268, 269, 270, 271, 272, 273, 274, 275, 276
James Abbington (b. 1840) .93, 97, 98, 99, 100, 101, 241, 262, 263, 267, 269, 270, 271, 272, 274, 275, 276
James M. 88, 238
Jerry 95, 239
John Fletcher .. 93, 97, 101, 274, 275
Nancy 88, 237
Nellie 71, 74, 76, 77, 103, 108
Patsy 88, 237, 238
Sarah Eliza 92, 98, 100, 241, 242, 256
Tatnall 95, 239
Theodocia H. 93, 100, 241, 242, 264, 265
Turner C. (b. 1781) ... 88, 89, 102
Turner C. (b. 1821) 87, 88, 89, 94, 95, 97, 100, 102, 103, 104, 105, 238, 239, 242, 243, 244, 250, 251, 252, 253, 254, 255, 256, 257, 258, 266, 267, 268, 269
Fleeton
    Bessie 190
    Robert 190
Flewellen
    James Persons 92, 98, 256, 257
Ford
    Harold, Jr. 77
    Harold, Sr. 77
    Lee Ann .... *See* Lee Ann Webb
Fox
    Howard 172
    Margaret .... *See* Margaret Reed
Franklin
    Benjamin 197
Funderburk
    C. M. 146, 199
    Celess ii
    Joyce S. 199, 201
Furlow
    Robert 88
Futrell
    Frank 167
Gaden
    Angeline 135, 136
    Charity 137
    Francis 136
    Rubin 136
Gammon
    Samuel Rhea 68
Gant
    Inell Wanetta 46
Garrett
    G. E. 219
Gater
    Dr. Herbert, Jr. 169
Gates
    Henry Louis, Jr. 22

Gigger
  Adlena "Lena" 148, 150
  Alonzo 149
  Bessie 150
  Charlotte (b. 1834) 149
  Charlotte (b. 1877) 150
  Delia 151
  Henry (b. 1835) 149
  Henry (b. 1868) 149
  Major G. 148, 150, 151, 160
  Mary (b. 1865) 149
  Mary (b. 1871) 149
  Nicholas 149
Gilbert
  Annie 124
  Caleb 123
  David 121, 123, 124, 129
  Fannie 121, 123, 124
  Fred 122, 124, 125, 127, 128, 129, 133, 138, 139
  John 122, 124, 131
  Julius Caesar 124
  Maud 122
  Ollie Mae 128, 131, 134, 139
  Pearlie ... 120, 127, 130, 134, 139
  Susan 123
  William 122
Giles
  John M. 264, 265
Glenn
  Pamela 170
Glover
  Horace 168
Gordon
  Alford 131, 132
  Lillie 131, 132
  Minnie.. 128, 131, 132, 133, 135, 138, 140
Grammar
  Mollie 150
Grant
  Ulysses S., General 68

Green
  Harriet 36, 40
  Lewis 40
Greene
  Elizabeth F. 94, 102, 238
  John 93
  Mary Beaufort ... 92, 93, 97, 102, 236, 237
  Miles LaFayette. 94, 95, 97, 98, 99, 100, 239, 243, 244, 245, 246, 250, 251, 252, 253, 254, 255, 256, 257, 259, 260, 261, 262, 263, 264, 266
  Peter Buford (b. 1795) 90, 91, 92, 93, 102
  Peter Buford (b. 1836) 94, 106, 239
  William Ingram... 94, 100, 101, 239, 246, 267, 269, 270, 271, 272, 274, 275, 276
Greer
  Angela "Sophie" Battle ii
Griffin
  Samuel 139, 140
Grissom
  Callie 196
  Fred Douglas 196, 197, 198
  Fred, Jr. 198
  J. L. 198
  Lavern 198
  Lawrence Gene . 192, 194, 197, 198
  Martin 195
  Osie 196
  Thomas 196
  Verneda 196
  Zelma 196
Hall
  Celia 36
Hare

Mary 150
Harold
   Ben 200
Harper
   Araminta 218
   Caroline 217
   Darcus 217
   John 217
   Joseph 217
   Martha 217
   Matilda 215, 218
   Nancy A. 217
   Randall R. "Ran" .. 216, 217, 218
   Rena M. 218
   Rosa M. 218
   Wesley 215
   Willie 215
Harris
   Frank 183
   Thomas W. 91
   William 256
Hart
   Chena 109
   Delia 79, 80, 109, 110, 111, 155, 292
   Peter 109
   Thomas 109
Harvey
   Edward A. 244
Hasell
   Charity 240
   Sarah 240
Haynesworth
   Allene 169
Heinegg
   Paul 22
Hemphill
   Walter 222
Henderson
   Fletcher 55

Fletcher Hamilton, Sr. 55
Herron
   Romiestein 118
Hill
   Jeptha "Jep" 39, 54
   Senator Joshua 121
Holland
   Robert Afton. 93, 100, 264, 265
Hollinshead
   John W. 101
   William H. . 243, 244, 256, 262, 263, 265
Houstoun
   John 90
Howard
   Liza 191
   Nettie 191
Howe
   Thomas 36
Humphreys
   Benjamin Grubbs 223
Hunter
   Annie Mae 216, 221
   Candacy 214
   Hardy 243, 244
   James "Jimbank" 213, 214
   Millie (b. 1846) 213, 215
   Millie (b. 1878) 214
   Otis 215, 221
   Richard 214, 215
   Ruby 215
   Ruth Mae ... 215, 218, 221, 222, 224
   Sally 216
   Sam 215
   Sherman 215, 221
Ingram
   Sarah W. 93, 102, 105, 106, 108, 239
Jackson

Allen 149
Almus 149
Anthony 149
Chalmus 149
Edmund 147, 150
Ida 142, 149, 151, 158, 160
Isaola 149
Joy 149
Lavel 149
M. J., Rev. 150
Ollie 122, 123, 124, 129
Silas 148
Thomas "Tommy" 149
Tololo 149
Jeffries
 Louis, Jr. 118
Jobson
 John S. 259
Johnson
 James 66
 John S. 263
 Larry W. ii
 Rachel Payne George 66
Johnston
 John P. 59
Jolly
 Asa 252, 254
Jones
 Elizabeth 171
 Ethel 190
 Nettie B .....*See* Nettie B. Phillips
 W. C. 167
Kaigler
 Andrew 105
 Artimissa 106
 Augustus 106
 Charlotte .... 107, *See* Charlotte Everett
 Cowles Mead 105
 Henry 87, 111
 Henry b. 1804 92, 103, 104, 105, 106, 107

Lucy 108
Michael 105
Nellie .... *See* Nellie Everett
Rebecca 107, 108
Sarah. 104, *See* Sarah W. Ingram
Stephen 108
Susan 108
Walton 108
Winfield 106
Keglar
 Delia .... *See* Delia Hart
Kendrick
 Adolphus D. .. 95, 100, 237, 243, 244, 245, 250, 251, 252, 253, 254, 255, 257, 265, 268, 269
Killen
 John 244
King
 Anna 193
 Ida 143
 Lewis 193
 Lewis, Jr. 194
 Lorena 188, 194
 Mary 194
 Minnie 194
 Oscar 194
 Thomas D. 262
Knox
 Henry 64
Law
 George 250, 251, 253
Lewis
 Bertram B., Sr. 166
 Elbert 128
Llewillyn
 Elizabeth 20, 62
Logan
 Annette .... *See* Annette Phillips
 Grant 170
Long

A. H. 99
Looney
    Absalom David (b. 1790) 290, 291
    Absalom Starnes (b. 1832) ...290
    Andrew 81
    Annie ....*See* Lee Ann Webb
    Asa V. 19, 81, 86, 120
    Burrell (b. 1889) 75, 77, 79, 111, 113, 114, 118, 119, 293
    Burrell (b. 1916) 113
    Burrell, Jr. (b. 1933) 118
    Carl son of Robert E. .... ii, 140
    Cecil T. 19, 80, 81, 120
    Christopher C. H. 82, 86
    Dorothy 119
    Eddie 113
    Eleanor 80
    Elmyria L. 119
    Elnora 84
    Fannie 67
    Florence (b. 1861) 291
    Freddie Lee 119
    Henry 73, 75, 77
    J. Walter................................113
    James Knox 1, 19, 22, 28, 62, 64, 65, 69, 71, 74, 76, 79, 80, 82, 84, 86, 108, 111, 151, 155, 161, 172, 292
    James, Jr. 76, 79, 80, 172
    John Blair (b. 1828) 290
    John Payne (b. 1799) 290
    Joseph Israel (b. 1833) 291
    Katherine .75, 77, 111, 112, 118, 119, 293
    Lee Ann ....*See* Lee Ann Webb
    Lousannah (b. 1833) 290
    Lucille "Dear" 118
    Lucy ....i, 1, 8, 22, 42, 76, 79, 80, 84, 111, 117, 120, 137, 143, 145, 151, 153, 158, 161, 182, 183, 204, 206, 293
    Margaret Catherine (b. 5 Mar 1830) 290
    Martin (b. 1895) 76, 79, 80, 117, 172
    Martin (b. 1931) 118
    Mary..................................65, 67
    Meta 67
    Michael (b. 1758) 290, 291
    Michael Jackson 68
    Montgomery 67
    Nancy 67
    Nellie .... *See* Nellie Everett
    Nellie Grace 118
    Orlanders 118
    Orville Bradley (b. 1837) 290
    Peter (b. 1783) 290
    Robert (b. 1692) . 20, 62, 68, 296
    Robert (b. 1914) 113
    Robert Emmett .. 19, 81, 86, 111, 120, 140
    Roseanna "Rosie" 119
    Samuel 65
    Samuel (b. 1837) 290
    Sarah Jane Sallie "Sadie" (b. 1835) 290
    Sarena 73
    Susan Shanks (b. 1840) 290
    Tomanna ....*See* Tomanna Mack
    Wiley 67
    William "Gravely Bill" (b. 1805) 290, 291
    William C. (b. 1838) 68, 69, 282
    William Carroll (b. 1822) 65, 66, 291
    William Pickney (b. 1843) ...290
    Willie Bell 19, 81, 86
Looney-Johnson
    Cheryl ii
Lott
    Austin 185
    Becky 186
    Boyne 186
    Cressey 185

Dennis 185
Fannie 187
Henry 186
Jacob 184
Johnie 186
Louisa 185
Magie 186
Maria 186
Martha 186
Minnie ... 181, 182, 183, 186, 293
Rafe 184, 185
Reuben 185, 186, 187
Seargant 186
Thomas 186

Love
   Henry 265

Luckey
   Ruben H. 238

Mack
   James 109
   James F./T. 109, 110
   Susan 109, 110
   Tomanna 77, 79, 80, 83, 109, 110

Mahone
   Inell .... *See* Inell Phillips
   Thomas Carver 168

Mathews
   William A. 97

Mathis
   Isham 240
   Mary 240

Maynor
   Charles 35

McGiles
   Jonathan 260, 262

McKinney
   Annie Belle 76

McMillan
   Findley 36

Meacham
   E. E. 111

Megget
   William McD. 199

Meyer
   Delia 150, 160

Miller
   Elizabeth 68
   John 68
   Osborne H. 262
   Reuben 122

Minton
   Minnie Ann 172

Mitchell
   Benjamin 142, 151, 158
   Lula 147
   Robert Lee 158

Modlin
   Wayne ii

Montjoy
   William Hemingway 128

Mullen
   H. P. 181

Muzzi
   Vincent 52

Norman
   Lucinda 112, 117
   Rich 112

O'Neal
   Ted 198

Ossman
   Sandra A. 146, 211

Parker
   Bearl/Burrell 108
   Cansey 83
   Caroline 108
   James H. 82
   Jeremiah J. 83
   Robert 82

Parks
   Isam 38
   James 121

Joe 36, 39, 43
Pasteur
  Louis 42
Peacock
  M. L. 150
Pearson
  Pryor Lee 290
Perry
  Annie Lee 204
  Arthur L. 203
  Bertha Mae 203
  Charlene 200, 201
  Charlie (b. 1906) . 202, 203, 204
  Charlie, Jr. 203
  Clara 202, 203
  David Lee 203
  Dorothy 203
  Elberta I. 203
  F. (no middle initial) 202
  Frank 203
  Fred 203
  Ida 202
  Inez 203
  James H. 202, 203
  Jimmie 203
  Josy Bee 203
  Mary (b. 1852) 202
  Mary F. (b. 1918) 203
  Michael 201
  Myrtle Lee 203, 204
  Red 203
  S. Nathaniel 202
  Thomas J. 203
  Tilena 202
  Vergie 203
  Walter 202
  Willie Lee 146, 199, 203, 204
Perryman

  Etta 121
  Joseph 121
  Peter 121, 123
Phillips
  Alvin "Spanky" 170
  Annette 170
  David ii
  Harry Gordon 137, 152, 155,
    156, 161, 166, 181, 182, 183,
    188, 207
  Inell 168
  John "Johnny" Edward, Sr. ... 168
  John, Jr. ii
  Laura 170
  Lawrence Allen 169
  Lucy .... *See* Lucy Looney
  Mary 23
  Nettie B. 167
  Solomon "Sol" 22, 71, 76, 80,
    143, 145, 152, 154, 156, 161,
    182, 293
  Thomas 23
  Virda Thelma (b. 1916)137, 152,
    171, 181, 182, 183, 224
  Virda Thelma (b. 1943) 162, 167
  William 23
  Willie B. 167
Pilkington
  William Q. 168
Porter
  Robert 136
Powell
  John H. 92
Puckett
  L. A. 172
Pugh
  James H. 112
Pulliam
  Samuel 147
Purnell
  Carroll 72
Randle

Alex 146, 199
Elof 199
Isaac C. 199, 204
Louiase 199
Malisey 199
Marie 199
Walter ii

Randolph
John 55

Razor
Vivian 169

Reddock
Eliza 58
Fannie 58
Franklin 58
Isaac 58
John Thomas 58
Martha 58
Naomah 58

Reed
Alpia 178
Ann 177
Arthur .. 172, 178, 180, 182, 183, 293
Belle 178
Ben D. 184
Benford 178
Caroline 178
Catherine 181, 182
Delilah 177, 180
Eckford 177
George W., Jr. 175
George W., Sr. 174
Inell 152, 162, 166, 181, 183
Jackie ii
John "Jake"(b. 1911) 181, 183
John (b. 1877) 178
Lee Ann .... *See* Lee Ann Webb
Luthus or Luthur 178
Margaret 172
Minnie .... *See* Minnie Lott

Noah (b. 1848) 173, 174, 177, 180, 181
Noah (b. 1896) 179, 182
Seaborn 177
Seaborn H. 177
Seborne .... *See* Sebren Reed (b. 1894)
Sebren (b. 1894) 178
Sebren (b. 1912) .. 152, 171, 181, 183
Sebren (b. 1937) 173
Sebren brother of Noah (b. 1848) 174, 175, 177
Senior 181, 183
Walter 178
William (b. 1874) 178
William (b. 1882) 178

Riley
Allen 158
Allen J. 159
Bertha T. 159
Ethel 159
Payton L. 142, 158, 159
Tennie 158

Rimson
William 173

Roberts
H. M. 118

Rodgers
Flutie "Lizzie" 36, 50

Rouser
Jack 170

Sanders
Alexander 58
Amanda 58
Amas/Amos 57
Austin 55, 56
Dick 53
Elizabeth Naomi Cadenhead .. 56
Emily 45, 53, 58
Fannie 53
Flora 35, 45, 53, 54, 142

Fox 54, 55
Guss 54, 55
Henry 53, 54
Isaac M. 57
James Isaac "Isaac" 56, 57, 58
James Nathaniel ... 44, 54, 56, 58, 59, 286
Joel 58
John 58
John R. 58
Joseph "Joe" 53, 54, 58
Lila 55
Mack 53, 54, 58
Manerva 55, 56
Martin 58
Mary 56, 58
Naomah daughter of Martin 58
Reuben 39, 45, 53, 54, 55, 56, 58, 286
Sarah 58
Susan 53, 54
Thomas S. 57
Warren 53, 54
William 53, 54
William Bryan 44

Saunders
   Maxine Perry ii

Sellers
   Marianne 109, 110

Shabazz
   Emmanuel ...... *See* Emmanuel A. Webb

Shaner
   Annie Mae .... *See* Annie Mae Shavers
   Edward .... *See* Edward Shavers
   Florence .... *See* Florence Shavers

Shavers
   Annie Mae 75, 113
   Edward "Ed" 113
   Florence 113

Shepherd

Anita 212
Hezekiah Hosea 212

Sherman
   William Tecumseh, General .. 68, 121, 282

Shields
   Willie Ann 291

Shipman
   W. S. 50

Silas
   Lucinda 112

Siler
   Given 36

Simmons
   Augusta 128
   James Arthur 41
   Will 128

Sledge
   Amos 56
   Maria 55, 56
   Nancy Jane 56, 57, 58

Smiley
   Eddie, Sr. 189
   Lorraine . *See* Lorraine Josephine Webb

Smith
   F. H. 120, 140
   Flim, Sr. 167
   Martha Lee 134
   Willie B. .... *See* Willie B. Phillips

Smyth
   William 23

Starnes
   Sarah Jane "Sallie" (b. 1799) 290

Stephens
   William 148

Stevens
   Will 133

Stringer
   John 36, 43
   Leona 43

Rebecca.................................43
Sular.....................................43
Swift
  W. T.....263, 264, 265, 270, 271, 275
Switzer
  Will....................................222
Tanton
  Nathan..................................92
Taylor
  Annie ....*See* Tomanna Mack
  Danny Earl............................225
  Willis Norman.............147, 224
Terry
  Elick......................................40
Thomas
  Darrell.................................225
  Flossie...................................46
  William I.............................256
Thompson
  Florida................................150
Tooke
  Allen.....................................89
  James T...............................256
Troutman
  John F. 263, 265
Tulwood
  John....................................240
Upson
  Stephen.................................57
Vaughn
  John C., Colonel....................69
Walker
  Allen............................248, 249
  Ella..37
Warren
  Benjamin Warren ..93, 98, 260, 261, 262
  Eli (no middle initial)............268
  Ruby...................................112

Washington
  Henrietta Annamae...............218
Webb
  Anita.......................................ii
  Bernice........................146, 204
  Emmanuel A. "Spider" 189, 190, 208
  Flora 146, 183, 199, 201, 204
  George Austin William "Bill" ..i, 64, 143, 147, 154, 156, 187, 205, 208, 224, 225
  Joseph Garlin144, 146, 166, 183, 187, 188, 192, 194, 200, 205, 206, 208
  Joseph, Jr. 189
  Laverne Gail...........................ii
  Lee Ann... 19, 29, 77, 79, 80, 83, 86, 110
  Leon....................................224
  Lorraine Josephine"Cute eyes" 188, 189
  Lucy (b. 1892) *See* Lucy Looney
  Lucy (daughter of Mack, Sr.) ..ii, 212
  Mack Henry, Jr......................i, 1
  Mack Henry, Sr.i, 143, 146, 188, 205, 206, 208, 211, 219
  Mary Eliza "Mickey" .. 120, 147, 224, 225
  Raymond.............................147
  Samuel................................195
  Samuel, Sr. 144
  Sarah....160, *See* Sarah Coleman
  Versa Lee............................189
  William S. 86, 110
  Willie (b. 1881)..i, 1, 8, 83, 138, 145, 147, 152, 161, 182, 183, 204, 206, *See* Willie Coleman
  Willie (b. 1923).......76, 146, 153
  Yvonne Denise.............211, 212
Webb-Broughton
  Sheryl.....................................ii

West
  Maria Louise 124
White
  J. W. 188
Wiggins
  William Allen 243, 263
Williams
  Clara 216
  Harriet 35, 39, 40, 41, 43, 44
  Hattie 76
  John 150
Wilson
  Artense 191
  Carry 191
  Clinton 192
  Ethel L. 192
  Eugene 193
  Gladys 192
  Ida 191
  Isaac 192
  James 191
  James, Jr. 191
  Liza Ann 191
  Lorena 191
  Louise 146, 188, 192, 194
  Mary "May" 192
  Square 188, 191, 194
  Square "Frog", Jr. 193
  Susie B. 192
  Theaola 192
  Wesley 193
  William C. 192
  Zack 191
Windham
  Ilene 172, 181
Winschel
  Terrence J. 69
Wood
  F. S. 44
Works
  Joe F. 76, 77, 111, 112
  William Henry 112, 117
Wright
  Richard R. 55

Meet the author

Celia Webb enjoys researching and writing in several topic areas; family history being one. She is an award-winning photographer, a book illustrator, and multimedia artist. She also writes extensively on developing language-related skills. Celia earned a degree in Business from Indiana University, Bloomington, Indiana and in Systems Engineering from the Naval Postgraduate School, Monterey, California. A renaissance woman, she is a co-inventor of a patented antenna design. Celia served 21 years as an officer in the U.S. Army. She now enjoys gardening and creating books with her husband, Mack.

She appreciates the family's involvement in this project and looks forward to meeting more family members as time goes on.

You can help!

Your contributions to this family history are welcome! Photographs, Funeral Programs, birth announcements, marriage announcements, and family stories are helpful in identifying more paths of research, verifying parts of the family history, completing lines of the family, and enriching the detail of this diverse and intriguing family. Please send only copies of original material – not the original.

Photographs should include the names of as many people as known, location, occasion if appropriate, and a date. An estimated date and location is helpful if the actual date and location are not known.

Please include your name, address, phone number, and family connection with your submission.

Send your submissions by e-mailing them to:
mainoffice@pilinutpress.com
Subject: Family History

*Thank you for choosing a
Pilinut Press book!*

About Pilinut Press

Pilinut Press, Inc. is an independent publishing company founded in 2006. Our quality books are available through on-line book vendors like Amazon.com and your local bookstore as a special order item.

In addition to our books, we support our readers and educators through our **Reference Desk** feature on the company website which offers free articles, lesson plans, printable teaching aids, bookmarks, interviews, and more. Check us out at

www.pilinutpress.com

« Other Titles by Pilinut Press »

Can You Keep a Secret?
ISBN: 978-0-9779576-4-4
Danny and the Detention Demons
ISBN: 978-0-9779576-2-0
Little Bianca
ISBN: 0-9779576-0-8
The Snickerdoodle Mystery
ISBN: 978-0-9779576-5-1
Webb's Wondrous Tales Book 1
ISBN: 0-9779576-1-6
Webb's Wondrous Tales Book 2
ISBN: 978-0-9779576-3-7

Seoul-Full Letters
ISBN: 978-0-9779576-6-8
Feed Your Family of Four for $4 a Day
ISBN: 978-0-9779576-8-2
Small Gym Big Workouts
ISBN: 978-0-9779576-9-9
Publish Today!
ISBN: 978-0-9779576-7-5

www.ingramcontent.com/pod-product-compliance
Lightning Source LLC
Chambersburg PA
CBHW071237160426
43196CB00009B/1099